DUQUESNE STUDIES

Philosophical Series

7

THE SOUL IN METAPHYSICAL

AND

EMPIRICAL PSYCHOLOGY

DUQUESNE STUDIES

Philosophical Series

7

THE SOUL IN METAPHYSICAL

AND

EMPIRICAL PSYCHOLOGY

DUQUESNE STUDIES

Philosophical Series

7

THE SOUL IN METAPHYSICAL
AND
EMPIRICAL PSYCHOLOGY

by

STEPHAN STRASSER, Ph.D.

DUQUESNE UNIVERSITY
Pittsburgh 19, Pa.
EDITIONS E. NAUWELAERTS, LOUVAIN, BELGIUM
1957

DUQUESNE STUDIES
Philosophical Series

Andrew G. van Melsen, D.Sc., D.Ed., and Henry J. Koren, C.S.Sp., S.T.D., Editors.

Volume One—Andrew G. van Melsen, From Atomos to Atom, 1952. Pp. XII and 240. Price: paper $3.50, cloth $4.25.

Volume Two—Andrew G. van Melsen, The Philosophy of Nature, 2nd ed. 1954. Pp. XII and 263. Price: cloth $4.50 (*paper* out of print).

Volume Three—P. Henry van Laer, Philosophico-Scientific Problems, 1953. Pp. X and 168. Price: paper $2.50, cloth $3.25.

Volume Four—Cajetan's The Analogy of Names and The Concept of Being, by Edward A. Bushinski and Henry J. Koren, 1953. Pp. X and 93. Price: paper $1.50, cloth $2.25.

Volume Five—Louis de Raeymaeker and Other Professors of the University of Louvain, Truth and Freedom, 2nd impr., 1955. Pp. VII and 132. Price: cloth $3.00 (*paper* out of print).

Volume Six—P. Henry van Laer, The Philosophy of Science. Part One: Science in General, 1956. Pp. XVII and 164. Price: paper $3.00, cloth $3.75.

Volume Seven—Stephan Strasser, The Soul in Metaphysical and Empirical Psychology, 1957. Pp. X and 275. Price: paper $4.25, cloth $5.00.

Twenty percent discount on standing or continuation orders.

Outside the U. S. A., orders may be placed through the following dealers:

Argentina, Sapientia, 24-65 y 66, La Plata; *Belgium,* Editions Nauwelaerts, Louvain; *Brazil,* Herder, C. P. 7509, Sao Paulo; *Denmark,* Nordiske Videnskabsboghandel, Romersgade 27, Copenhagen; *France,* Béatrice-Nauwelaerts, 10 rue de l'Abbaye, Paris; *Germany,* Orient Buchhandlung, Antwerpenerstrasse 612, Köln; *Great Britain,* Blackwell, Broad Street, Oxford; *India,* The Book Centre, Ranade Rd., Dadar, Bombay; *Italy,* The Catholic Book Agency, 5 via del Vaccaro, Roma; *Japan,* Japan Publications Trading Co., Central P. O. Box 722, Tokio; *Mexico,* American Bookstore, Apdo 72 bis, Mexico; *Netherlands,* Coebergh, Haarlem; Meulenhoff, Amsterdam; Brill, Leyden; etc.; *Philippines,* The Bookmark, Regina Bldg., Manila; *Spain,* Anaquel, Conde de Penalver 36, Madrid; *Sweden,* Lundeqvista Bokhandeln, Uppsala; *Switzerland,* Librairie Dousse, Fribourg; Daeneker, Bederstrasse 51, Zürich.

TABLE OF CONTENTS

PREFACE

From the time of Socrates' challenge "Know thyself," man has never ceased to occupy an important position in the human quest for knowledge. Perhaps, however, he has never been so much the focal point of philosophical and scientific interest as in our times. Numerous new branches of special philosophies of man, such as the philosophies of culture, history, language and society, have sprung up to investigate problems of man hitherto almost neglected. Successful attempts have been made to construct empirical sciences of man, and these attempts have led to the many modern branches of experimental or empirical psychology. Alongside these, there still flourishes the strictly philosophical investigation of man's nature or philosophical psychology.

Both empirical and philosophical psychology, as their very names indicate, are supposed to be concerned with man's psyche or soul. There are serious reasons, however, to doubt whether one is justified in identifying the object studied empirically with the soul studied in philosophy. In the present study Dr. Strasser convincingly proves that such an identification is unwarranted.

As history shows, philosophy somehow is never quite the same after the appearance of a truly great philosopher, witness, e.g. Aristotle, Aquinas, Descartes, or Kant. One of the greatest of our time undoubtedly was Edmund Husserl, to whom philosophy and the sciences dealing with man owe the use of the phenomenological method. The use of this method can render pretious services within the scope of perennial philosophy, as is demonstrated by the work of many ontologically orientated thinkers. We may quote here, among others, Louis de Raeymaeker and his PHILOSOPHY OF BEING. The present work of Dr. Strasser represents, in part, a bold and vigorous use of the phenomenological method leading to the great positions of the traditional philosophy of man. How stimulating and successful this attempt has been may be gaged to some extent from the fact that, since its first appearance in 1950, this study has been published in Dutch, French, and German. Dr. Strasser's recent appointment as Visiting Professor of philosophical psychology at Duquesne University offered us an opportunity to introduce his thought to the English-speaking world, in which far too little attention has been given to the phenomenological approach.

A few remarks may be added here regarding the English text. The translation is based on the recent German edition (SEELE UND BESEELTES, Vienna, 1955), prepared by the author himself, although occasionally the Dutch and French editions[1] have been consulted. Because to the best of my knowledge many of the technical terms used by the author have no accepted equivalent in English, it has been

---

[1] *Het Zielsbegrip in de metaphysische en empirische psychologie,* Louvain-Nymegen, 1950; *Le problème de l'ame,* Louvain-Paris, 1953.

necessary to coin new terms or to use existing terms in a new meaning. While frequently this meaning is explained in the text itself
or immediately clear from the context, there are also instances where
a clarification would be desirable. For this reason, with the consent
and the aid of the author, I have added a glossary of terms at the end
of the book. Only the division into Studies and the immediate sub-
division of the Studies into sections preceded by arabic numerals
occur in the other editions. To facilitate reading I have subdivided
longer sections, giving them suitable subtitles. For the same reason
throughout the text titles in italics precede each more or less complete
passage. Indexes of names and subject matter have been added at
the end of the book. The author has profited of the occasion to make
a few corrections and additions.

I would like to draw special attention to the use of the term 'to
besoul' and its derivative 'besouling.' Although the English terms
'to animate' and 'animation' are more commonly used, I have systematically abstained from using them, because they are likely to be
immediately associated with as yet unproved explanations of the
body-soul problem and thus would prejudice the author's careful
phenomenological approach of the Aristotelian-Thomistic position.

There remains only the pleasant duty of expressing my thanks
to all those who have contributed to the preparation of this edition:
in the first place, the author himself, who has read and approved
the English text; Fr. John F. Kanda, C.S.Sp., and others who have
helped by corrections and suggestions; and last but not least, the man-
agement and staff of The Ad Press, who with unfailing patience and
skill have again produced a superb addition to DUQUESNE STUDIES.

DUQUESNE UNIVERSITY   HENRY J. KOREN, C.S.Sp.

This edition contains two new sections, in addition to numerous
smaller changes. The first (pp. 126 ff.) serves to clarify the connection between the philosophical analyses of nature and classic
hylomorphism. The second (pp. 229 ff.) investigates the philosophical
presuppositions of the psychology of behavior. This investigation
seems important to me now that this work is going to appear in the
land that was the very cradle of the science of behavior.

I wish to use this opportunity to express my thanks to Fr. Henry
J. Koren, C.S.Sp., who with so much skill has fulfilled the role of
translator.

DUQUESNE UNIVERSITY, Pittsburgh, Pa.
UNIVERSITY "CAROLUS MAGNUS,"
Nymegen, Holland

                                        STEPHAN STRASSER

INTRODUCTION

Object and Method of This Study

These studies are the fruit of many years of philosophical research, investigations and meditations. Yet, now that they are going to be published, they cannot be said to constitute a finished and adequate whole. Many questions have been neglected; others have been intentionally avoided; others, again, have been treated in a short and sketchy way. For this reason this book can give rise to a variety of misunderstandings. To prevent possible misinterpretations, we want at once to indicate clearly what the object is of our studies. It is to pursue the investigation of a problem of the theory of science and to arrive at its solution upon a *philosophical basis* by the use of the *phenomenological method*.

Undoubtedly, it will be manifest to most readers, without any further explanations, that a problem of the theory of science or epistemology can be clarified only within the framework of a philosophy of science. It is simply a matter of fact that the comparative determination of ultimate and fundamental concepts is something pertaining to philosophy. For the determination of these concepts must show what the reality in question *is,* how it is related to other realities, and how its mode of being deviates from other related modes of being. Briefly, a genuine determination of its essence is bound to throw light upon the question to which realm of the universe of beings the being belongs whose nature is to be uncovered. These very words express our conviction that the order and clarification of the fundamental concepts used in the positive sciences are to be expected only from a philosophy which indicates *what is,* i.e. from a metaphysics of being. Moreover, in the present case, one of the concepts to be compared is a metaphysical concept. Therefore, it follows immediately that also the point of comparison must be a metaphysical concept, and even one which is more fundamental than the terms whose relationships are to be considered.

What causes perhaps more surprise is that we hope to solve a problem of the theory of science phenomenologically. Concerning this point, a few words of explanation will not be amiss. They are all the more necessary because for the modern reader the term "phenomenology" evokes the most diverse associations and connec-

1

tions of ideas.   Whoever calls himself a "phenomenologist" is by the very fact exposed to a great variety of prejudices.   This is understandable inasmuch as the term "phenomenology" has become quite fashionable, and the modern educated man thinks he ought to use it.   However, the roots of possible misunderstandings go deeper. Even distinguished thinkers do not always attach the same meaning to the notion of phenomenology.   As a matter of fact, the term has quite a different sound when used by Edmund Husserl, Max Scheler, and Martin Heidegger, to name only these three.   Since the appearance of the French existentialists the confusion has become even greater.

Meanings of the Term "Phenomenology"

To indicate, compare and classify the various meanings given to the term "Phenomenology" among philosophers would be enough material for a special scientific work.   Nevertheless, we think that among the innumerable more or less divergent conceptions three *totally* different views may be distinguished.   In the subsequent pages we shall designate these views by the brief expressions "phenomenology as a science," "phenomenology as metaphysics," and "phenomenology as an ontological method."   Let us try to give very brief characterizations of these three fundamentally different views concerning the nature of phenomenology.

Phenomenology as a Science.   According to the first view, phenomenology is the science of immanent phenomena.   In this case the phenomenological reduction is the method which makes it possible to exclude from the sphere of immanent phenomena any affirmation of transcendent realities.   Only the *cogitata qua cogitata,* the thought as thought, constitute the object of phenomenological research.   These *cogitata* are in the most immediate way accessible to the phenomenologist because, unlike the realities of the world, they do not present themselves in different perspectives.   However, it is not the actual contents of consciousness and the actually lived events which are to be studied, but their essence, their *"eidos."* Phenomenology as a science is the twin sister of the purely intentional psychology of consciousness, but it moves on the eidetic level and therefore is the very foundation of the latter.

Phenomenology as Metaphysics.   An entirely different view is presented by phenomenology as metaphysics.   Only a very special method, the transcendental phenomenological reduction, gives access to this metaphysics. By adopting the reductive attitude one learns immediately to distinguish between the transcendental ego and the psychological "I." The transcendental ego is, first or all, the only apodictic datum which is left to us when we systematically abstain from making a judgment about the whole world, including in this world also the psychological order. This ego represents, moreover, the reality whose being, ontologically speaking, precedes that of the world. But as a transcendental "I" I am not a *solus ipse,* a solitary "I," for I and other egos constitute a transcendental intersubjectivity. Insofar as "we," as a transcendental community, constitute or co-constitute in our intentional acts the "world," we take part in the transcendental life of a creative "world foundation." Evidently, this metaphysical phenomenology shows an affinity with objective idealism.

Phenomenology as an Ontological Method. Phenomenology plays a totally different role when it is considered as a method in the framework of a metaphysics of being. Here it serves above all to find the correct starting point. The metaphysicist encounters very great difficulties in trying to describe being in such a way that it applies to both being as a subject and being as an object. He is faced with the necessity of transcending both these categories, and it is only the phenomenological method which makes it possible to satisfy this requirement. The phenomenologist places himself "inside" the existential movement of the ego, i.e. inside the ego's being-related-with and being-receptive-of a universe of persons, living beings and things. In this authentically phenomenological attitude the world no longer appears to us as a whole of objective data, but as an "intentional configuration"[1] which is born and becomes meaningful in the course of an existential movement of orientation. With the dialectics of this "history of intentions"[2] corresponds a hierarchy of evidences, which the phenomenologist always takes into account in his progress from the more original, the more concrete, to the derived, the abstract. As a result, that which is held to be "evident" and "obvious" reveals itself as the product of most complex intentional activities. The most original evidences are based upon "experience,"

---

[1]German *Sinngebilde*. A meaningful picture of reality which results from the intentional turning towards . . . of an ego (Tr.).

[2]German *Sinngeschichte*. The process of gradually constructing a meaning-full "intentional configuration" (Tr.).

i.e. pre-predicative familiarity with being and certain modes of being. This condition allows the phenomenologist to study the material-*a-priori* of various ontological regions. Thus his judgments concerning the material-*a-priori* are susceptible of being proved, in the sense that it is impossible to deny the contents without at the same time in *actu exercito,* actually, contradicting oneself as an existent ego. For this reason phenomenology is fruitful as a scientific method, in the broader sense of the term, wherever it is a matter of raising questions concerning being and the existent by starting from the existent ego and its experiences. But, as is implied in this, the phenomenological description, analysis and explanation cannot represent the whole contents of ontology. After showing and analyzing what appears to be, the ontologist must meditate upon the conditions which must be fulfilled to make possible the very appearance of what appears. However, the description of intentional configurations and their origin is not a mere playing with examples. The examples can be omitted if need be. The transition from what is given in itself to what in principle can no longer be intuited is not wholly justified and convincing unless in the process the philosopher is able to appeal to the most concrete experience of being. In this sense the phenomenological method constitutes an indispensable tool for the ontologist.[3]

---

[3]Compare the foregoing with the following remarks of Edmund Husserl, which notwithstanding their length we want to reproduce fully: "The systematic description of the world as a world of pure experience. I who proceed to make the description follow the method which consists first of all in rendering explicit in a pure experience the most universal structures of the world of my experience and then in reducing them to my 'original experience,' to the world, in the proper sense, of my perception. What is the meaning of this method? All my knowledge of the world presupposes the world which is given by experience; it presupposes also a first realization of experience in my views of the world, i.e. my views concerning worldly objects, connections of objects and perhaps the world in general, from the viewpoint of the actual objective substrata. I distinguish statements, and more generally views concerning objects, from these objects themselves as 'objects about which'; and a pertinent experience will first have to show me these objects before I will be able to make, in accordance with their proper nature, the corresponding acts of thought in such a way that they are not vague assumptions but insights gained from the things themselves. Hence I leave aside (*epoche*) acquired knowledge or science and consider only experience and the world of experience. This is a first thought, which leads to the further question, Why do I need a universal consideration of experience, since thought in general is turned towards particular objects and particular realms of objects? I am guided here by the idea of a universal science. I can say: a first and most easily attainable "knowing" is the progressive becoming acquainted through experience and description; I endeavor to obtain an experience of the world as general as possible and begin with a clear exposition of the universal descriptive structures which have to provide the framework for all possible particular descriptions. I do not yet know what can be achieved beyond the descriptive level. Such a general knowing must always

Sense of the Term "Phenomenology" in this Study

The preceding remarks indicate the character of three views of phenomenology which are different in principle. Of course, the inadequacy of this elementary characterization does not escape us. Nevertheless, the brief sketch suffices to define the position which we ourselves have adopted and will take in the following investigation. Let us briefly circumscribe this position. We reject phenomenology as a science, because this so-called science finds its starting point in a number of unjustified presuppositions, one of which—though by no means the most important one—will be criticized later (Cf. pp. 81 ff.). We are likewise unable to adhere to phenomenology conceived as a transcendental idealism, because this metaphysics leads to untenable consequences (Cf. pp. 54 ff. and 68 ff.). We consider phenomenology as a method of the metaphysics of being. It is in this sense that we want to use it in the subsequent philosophical investigations. This procedure is, we think, wholly justified. The problems which hold our interest here are closely connected with the phenomena pertaining to the relationship of the ego to the world and that of the ego to itself. It is to our "experience," in the sense indicated above, that we owe everything we know about the being-alive, the being-besouled, the being-I, and the being-a-spirit of an ego. Thus we have good reasons for hoping that by taking our guidance from the phenomenological analysis of these primordial experiences we will find the right approach to our problems and succeed in justifying a reference to structures of reality which themselves are no longer phenomenologically given.

Scope of this Investigation

Our procedure has its roots in an ontologically orientated metaphysics. On the one hand, it will constitute the continuation and completion of such a metaphysics, while on the other hand it will

---

be a general theoretical thought which is not simply a general description of experience. But no matter what be the nature of such a possible theoretical thought, it will always refer to objects or general domains of objects whose reality must be previously rendered certain. This, however, can be done only because of the possibility of a relevant experience which renders such a thought secure. Hence in every case there is presupposed a relevant and precise description which in its own way is certain because of its method." MS *Wintervorlesung 1926-27,* Husserl Archives, no. F I 33, pp. 104a and b of the original copy. As can be seen from this, although the third viewpoint may not claim to be Husserl's official teaching, nevertheless it is in agreement with certain tendencies of his mind in its restless quest and search.

bring, we think, the proof of many of its fundamental truths. Nevertheless, we do not consider it our task to develop and critically justify *all* concepts and *all* categories which will be used. In our research we presuppose knowledge of the general principles of fundamental ontology. Such a presupposition is not against our phenomenological attitude. For we are convinced that these ontological categories and concepts are capable of phenomenological derivation and even that in more than one recent work they have already been given a large amount of such a phenomenological development. We are thinking here especially of Louis de Raeymaeker's PHILOSOPHY OF BEING.[4] To this work we must refer those who desire to study the phenomenological foundations of certain general metaphysical concepts. Our own responsibility begins where the passage is made from universal insights to the metaphysical problems that are special to psychology. In this domain we want, insofar as it is possible, to allow philosophical thought to grow from concrete essential analyses.

Finally, we must explicitly draw attention to the fact that the limits of our problems are indicated by the very title of this work. This means, among other things, that we cannot do more than prepare, within the framework of our studies, the solution of questions which the psychology of behavior has to face. Neither is it our intention to give a formal definition of the object of psychology and to trace the limits which separate the domain of psychology from those of physiology and biology. Nevertheless, we hope to be able to give a new impetus also in this direction. It may be mentioned here that it is our intention to make the last-named questions the object of a special study.[5]

---

[4]Herder, St. Louis, 1954. First Dutch edition, Antwerp-Nymegen, 1944; 2nd Dutch ed., 1947; first French ed., Louvain, 1946, 2nd ed., 1947. A 3rd French ed. is in preparation.

[5]A brief explanation of the problems of behavior and their fundamental importance will be given in the Appendix, pp. 229 ff.

PART ONE

CRITICAL CONSIDERATIONS

FIRST STUDY

THE PHILOSOPHER AND THE EMPIRICAL
NOTION OF THE "SOUL"

1. *Introduction to the Problem*

The problem to be investigated here, which we must first learn to see as a problem, lies in the relationship between two branches of learning, namely, philosophical psychology and empirical psychology, both of which claim to describe in a scientifically correct way the mode of being of the psychical. The relation between these two sciences depends of course upon what their proponents mean by the concept "soul." For this reason the question may be formulated very simply as follows: When a metaphysicist and an empirical psychologist use the term "soul," do they attach the same meaning to it? Is the same *sound* for both the symbol of the same *thing?* Is it either in whole or at least in part the same reality, whose more accurate determination they pursue in their research?

This question imposes itself as a matter of principle upon every philosopher who tries to fathom the nature of the psychical. It arises with a special urgency within the framework of traditional philosophy. For in this philosophy the following method is often used: the data of empirical psychology are collected and systematically arranged in order to use these very same data as the foundation of a description of man's way of being in terms of metaphysics. Note that we say "these very same data." It is, indeed, of capital importance for a proponent of the perennial philosophy to know whether or not the "soul" which moves him to attribute a definite place to man in the universe of being is the same soul as the one which is examined by empirical psychology.

A Neo-Thomist Position. Many neo-Thomists do not see the slightest difficulty in this point. Those of them who raise the question give a very simple answer. In their opinion, empirical psychology is the science of empirical facts, their laws and interconnections, insofar as these connections can be established by observation and scientific experience; speculative psychology, on the other hand, considers these same facts, but has, of course, as its special task to penetrate into the

9

ultimate causes, foundations and principles of these data.[1] Alexander Willwoll expresses this idea in the following way:

> What the experience of life and that of science of psychical life teach us "the philosophy of the soul" attempts to reduce to its ultimate "metaphysical causes," which lie beyond the immediate experience of the sciences concerned with nature and mind, [i.e.] to the essential structures and fundamental laws of all created being.[2]

This viewpoint may be found expressed in a very similar form by Christian Wolff, who assigned to rational psychology the task of giving a philosophical account of the ontological reality and possibility of whatever is observed by the empirical psychologist in the domain of the psychical.[3] According to these authors, the metaphysicist and the empirical scientist investigate, materially speaking, the same object, namely, the soul as it reveals itself in the various psychical phenomena. They differ, however, in their scientific way of treating their object. The philosophical psychologist makes use of speculative methods, while the empirical scientist relies upon empirical and experimental methods. Because of this formal difference in their way of considering the same object, the two have their own respective fields, and the results which they reach complement each other most harmoniously.

Critique of This View. The problem is not as simple as it seems to be according to these philosophers. Let us ask a philosophical and an experimental psychologist to make complete abstraction of everything which in the course of their life they have heard, learned, or read concerning the concept of the soul in the context of religion, philosophy, psychology, or biology. Let us ask them to put aside this category and to act as if they do not know what a soul is and invite them to describe in all liberty and as accurately as possible the X

---

[1]"Nowadays psychology has begun to be divided into 1) an empirical science which gathers and arranges facts, infers laws from them by means of induction, and thus endeavors systematically, especially by means of experiments, to increase our knowledge of psychical life; and 2) a speculative science which deduces from these facts conclusions, especially concerning the nature of the faculties and the soul itself." J. Fröbes, *Psychologia sensitiva,* Valkenburg, 1911, p. 3. Cf. also of the same author *Psychologia speculativa,* Freiburg i. Br., 1926, vol. 1, p. 1.

[2]*Seele und Geist. Ein Aufbau der Psychologie,* Freiburg i. Br., 1938, p. 12.

[3]"In rational psychology an account is given of that which is in the soul or can be in it.... Accordingly, because it is understood by means of reasoning why something is rather than not...; through the teachings offered in rational psychology that which is taught in empirical psychology is more fully understood." *Psychologia rationalis,* 2nd ed. Frankfurt and Leipzig, 1740, par. 7, p. 6.

which is the object of their scientific statements. If they agree to our request, we will to our surprise witness something like the following dialog.

Philosopher: The object of my study is one and absolutely simple.

Experimentalist: There cannot be any question of simplicity with respect to my X. What I study is so manifold that I am not capable of separating, identifying and describing all the various shades of its manifestations which fuse into one another. As far as the unity of these phenomena is concerned, if I stick to the facts, I can at most observe a certain continuity.

Philosopher: Not at all! What I am talking about is precisely a subsistent unity.

Experimentalist: I would prefer to avoid the term "to subsist," for it is not certain that the object of my research continues to be present in conditions such as profound sleep and unconsciousness.

Philosopher: But is not this X by its very nature above time, incorruptible and immortal?

Experimentalist: What is given to me immediately is a series of phenomena which are extremely subtle, fleeting and labile. I am hardly able to conceive anything for which the term "above time" is less appropriate.

Philosopher: This changing character of X can be explained by its freedom.

Experimentalist: Freedom is something about which I cannot say very much. What I observe obeys laws which, in part, can be formulated with mathematical exactness. Where such formulas are not possible, I try, with increasing success, to arrive at relationship of the type "If . . . then . . . ." In many cases knowledge of these relations allows me to foresee the subject's decisions.

Such a dialog can be carried on for a long time. However, the short specimen given above is sufficient to make us realize that the experimental and the philosophical psychologist often attribute contradictory properties to the reality which they call psychical. This extremely disturbing fact cannot be explained by an appeal to the difference of their viewpoint. Such a difference would have to show itself in judgments referring to formally different aspects of the same object, as exemplified in the two sentences "the object is round" and "the object is red." If, however, two judgments are contradictory, this means that opposite affirmations are made from one and the same point of view.

The matter may be clarified by means of comparisons taken from other sciences. The object of the research, for instance, of the agronomist and the botanist, viewed materially, is the same, but their way of viewing this object is different. The botanist will observe, for example that the potato belongs to the family of "solanaceae," while the agronomist will say that the use of potassic fertilizer is to be recommended for growing potatoes. Likewise, the philologist will give a closer determination of the idiom in which a literary masterpiece is written, while the historian of literature will define its artistic value. Never will it happen that the agronomist, *as agronomist,* affirms something which the botanist denies; nor will the philologist, when he remains within the limits of his specialty, pronounce a judgment which the historian of literature will reject from his point of view. Such a thing is in principle unthinkable.

We must exclude also the possibility that the empirical psychologist studies another "layer" or another "part" of the soul than the philosopher, for the X of the philosopher must be a simple and undifferentiated whole. But if this is so, we see ourselves obliged to raise *the question whether these two are speaking about the same thing.*

Another Difficulty. Moreover, the following also must be taken into consideration. The psychologist who spoke above in the dialog was, so to speak, the "psychologist of yesterday." By this we mean a psychologist who has accepted the idea that the facts of consciousness, in the widest sense of the term, are the proper object of psychological research. He starts from the fact that everyone is conscious of certain thoughts, feelings, affections, volitions, acts, etc. which constitute his psychical ego. As an introspective psychologist, he considers these contents of consciousness as the proper objects of his investigations; he endeavors to distinguish their types, analyze and classify them, and determine empirically the laws which they reveal.

Evidently, it is not possible to characterize the relationship between metaphysical and empirical psychology in the sense of Fröbes and Willwoll unless one accepts the conceptions of the introspective psychologist. But the "psychologist of today" does not want to have anything to do with consciousness, psychical facts, etc. His X is a living thing with four feet, or two hands and two feet, or often even four hands. What he studies is the typical behavior of this living X in various situations. By the term "psychologist of today" we designate in the first place the numerous and often outstanding men of research who, without being behaviorists in the proper sense, approve *in principle* McDougall's characterization of psychology as the science of human behavior. These psychologists study primarily the way in which man and higher animals behave, the way in which they show themselves sensitive to impressions, the way in which they adapt their attitudes and activity to these impressions, etc. Obviously, the facts which interest the psychologist of this tendency are not strictly "psychical" facts in the older sense of the term, for he makes the being as a living whole the object of his research. The depth psychologist too starts from a similar point of view insofar as he also admits "that consciousness cannot be the most general character of psychical processes, but only a particular function of them."[4] Thus a dialog between the philosophical and the experimental psychologist concerning the nature of the soul or the psychical has now become entirely impossible, because empirical psychologists recognize the authority of the modern conceptions.

Importance and Difficulty of Contact Between Philosopher and Psychologist. So the philosopher in general and the neo-Thomist in particular has the choice between two possibilities. He can definitely suspend all conversation with his modern fellow psychologist. He can consider him a narrow-minded and one-sided specialist who shows no interest at all in the problems of the mind. In this case, he will not even try to understand the position of the modern psychologist, being *a priori* convinced that such an effort is doomed to failure. In this way the philosopher cannot escape from losing all contact with the living stream of psychological research. Such an attitude would be most regrettable. We can see it only as a loss for the philosopher as well as the modern psychologist. For the benefit of both parties concerned, the dialog between the students of these two branches of research must not be broken off. But if a systematic exchange of views is to be established, the experimental and the metaphysical psychologist must first of all make a clean sweep of it and declare: The object of our research is not the same. Perhaps we will be able to adopt a viewpoint from which we can understand each other. But we will first have to search for this point of view, for it is not immedi-

---

[4] S. Freud, *Jenseits des Lustprinzips, Werke,* London, 1940, vol. XIII, p. 23.

ately given to us, i.e. not at the same time as the object of our investigations. In our own areas we do not speak of the same X.

The search for this new viewpoint will give rise to great difficulties. It will not do to resort to empty verbal formulas. The temptation is great to say, for instance, simply: Both the philosopher and the psychologist speak of man. Therefore, man is the common object of their research. The difference is only that the experimental psychologist considers man as a being "having a behavior," while the philosopher considers him as an existent being. Thus both investigate the same object, but from a different formal viewpoint. We call this an empty formula, for how do we know that these two aspects are formally different? Is a finite being necessarily also a being having a behavior? What is behavior from the metaphysical point of view? What is the relationship of behavior to existence? So we see that not much meaning can be attached to formulas like the one quoted above. That many philosophical as well as many psychological statements refer to man is only too obvious. But the important point is to grasp the nature of such affirmations, their inner direction, their implied finality, and this is possible only when certain fundamental metaphysical questions have been answered. It is the task of the philosopher to replace in this matter superficial pseudo-solutions with exact phenomenological analyses and the carefully considered essential determinations which flow from these analyses.

2. *Introspective Psychology and the Metaphysics of Being*

The road we want to follow is the long, painful and perilous road of radical philosophical speculation. It is the road of the "long and subtle inquiry" spoken of by St. Thomas.[1] At the beginning of this study it is not yet known what philosophical interpretation must be given to the fact that there is experimental psychological research. In our view, it is only in the course of a series of philosophical considerations that it will be possible to penetrate into the nature of this fact.

No Short Cut. The objection can be raised that perhaps another shorter route may be followed. Perhaps one can start with the presupposition that the object of experimental research is materially identical with that of philosophical psychology. Perhaps it would be possible simply to fuse the two branches of learning synthetically into a single science.

---

[1]*Summa theol.,* p. I, q. 87, a. 1 c.

However, as soon as an effort is made to do this, certain difficulties arise. Upon closer inspection the so-called experimental science of the soul shows itself to be quite different from a logical whole consisting exclusively of systematically ordered experimental data. It includes of necessity also a theory of the reality to be studied, a theory which always presupposes certain philosophical principles. These principles play a role in the approach to scientific problems or in the choice of methods, but especially in the integration of the scientific results into a global view of man. Just as the physicist somehow pictures "that which gives to the world its cohesion,"[2] just as every biologist has definite ideas regarding the nature of vital processes, so also every experimental psychologist professes certain ideas of man, human society, civilization, etc. Thus, for instance, to quote only from the past, the associationists and the psychological atomists openly adopted a mechanistic and deterministic point of view; the defenders of psychophysical parallelism formulated a series of extremely daring philosophical theses; the founder of experimental psychology, Wilhelm Wundt, was a militant antisubstantialist and the father of the so-called theory of actuality.

Introspective Psychology and Metaphysics. Among the numerous directions taken by empirical psychology there was one whose fundamental conceptions did not offer an immediate obstacle to an ontological interpretation. It is called the psychology of consciousness or introspective psychology. In a vague way this trend seemed even to be in accordance with certain traditional theses. The introspective psychologist put the accent upon the special character of the psychical in opposition to the physical. In his own way he described the inner aspects of man, his conscious life, his intentional activities, his self-awareness. He took into account the impossibility of applying the exact methods and quantitative concepts of physical science to the whole of psychical phenomena. But above all he considered the concept of the "psychical" as a fundamental category and held the admission of the existence of "souls" to be the most important working hypothesis in the domain of his research. "My soul is the real, in itself unknown, *condition* for the existence of my lived experiences[3] of consciousness," affirmed Theodor Lipps; hence

---

[2] J. W. Goethe, *Faust,* 1st Act.
[3] German *Erlebnis.* We will systematically translate this term by "lived experience" or "lived event." "Experience" or "event" alone do not sufficiently convey the idea that there is question here of an activity of mental life. The French edition significantly translates *"Erlebnis"* by *"vecu,"* the past participle of *"vivre,"* to live (translator's note).

we have the right to call the soul also "a substratum" or "support," although "only as a figure of speech."[4] "Psychology is the science of the soul," emphasizes likewise Oswald Külpe,[5] and he develops this thesis as follows:

> Leaving aside all metaphysics of the soul, one can understand by this term 'soul' nothing else than *the unknown substratum of psychical facts,* of subjective phenomena.[6]

August Messer expresses himself somewhat more carefully, but he too affirms:

> However, it is possible also to distinguish the ego from the body itself; the latter belongs of course to the ego in an especially intimate way, but it does not constitute *the ego in the proper sense.* This ego is rather something psychical and spiritual. It is the soul, the mind itself. . . . Psychology of a metaphysical orientation, insofar as it was not tied to materialism, has always unhesitatingly identified the ego with a being that is an immaterial substance.[7]

So nothing seemed more simple than to complete the reserved and prudent affirmations of the introspective psychologists with a few metaphysical theses. It was not the task of experimental scientists to formulate philosophical statements. But their descriptions of the life of the soul contained nothing which could not be interpreted in the sense of a spiritualistic anthropology. There was even more—in formulating their psychological theory the introspective psychologists seemed to count on its completion in a metaphysical sense. They almost gave the impression of indicating the place where the philosopher had to intervene to broaden the results of experience into a complete anthropology, and considered themselves personally incompetent to formulate theorems in the domain reserved for philosophical speculation. Thus the last word of the introspective psychologist became the cue for the metaphysicist.

This situation gave rise to the great temptation to use the "short cut" mentioned at the beginning of this section. The matter seemed so simple. The philosopher had merely to describe in terms of spiritual reality that which was postulated by the most important of the hypo-

---

[4]*Leitfaden der Psychologie,* 3rd ed., Leipzig, 1909, p. 4.

[5]*Vorlesungen über Psychologie,* edited by K. Bühler, 2nd ed., Leipzig, 1922. p. 12.

[6]*Ibid.,* p. 25.

[7]*Psychologie,* 4th ed., Leipzig, 1928, p. 359.

theses of introspective psychology. What Theodor Lipps considered as the, in itself unknown, explanatory principle of the ego and its psychical life, the philosophical psychologist had to justify as a reality in the light of his speculative insights. In this way the relationship of the two branches of learning seemed to be determined in the sense indicated in the preceding section—namely, material identity of their object and a formal difference of their point of view.

Geyser's Synthesis. The most comprehensive, most mature and elaborate attempt to unify the empirical science and the philosophy of the soul upon the foundation of their identity of object is undoubtedly the one made by Joseph Geyser. His LEHRBUCH DER ALLGEMEINEN PSYCHOLOGIE[8] may be considered as the mature fruit of a broad and systematic investigation. For this reason a critical analysis of his concept of the soul is likely to be very enlightening for us. For, as Geyser himself emphasizes, the purpose of his work is

> a systematically arranged integrated description of man's psychical life by means of the organic fusion of all experimentally established facts with the principles and concepts that live in Aristotelian philosophy insofar as they reveal themselves as fruitful both in themselves and with respect to the explanation of phenomena.[9]

If it becomes evident that the principle of Geyser's synthesis is philosophically satisfactory, one has patently the right to identify the metaphysical concept of the soul with the psyche of the introspective psychologist. If, on the other hand, there are in Geyser's basic psychological ideas contradictions which flow from his concepts of the "soul," "psychical states," and "psychical becoming," then his identification must be rejected as unjustified.

3. Ontological Study of Geyser's Concept of the Soul

A. EXPOSÉ OF GEYSER'S THEORY OF THE SOUL

The Object of Psychological Inquiry. To the first and most important question concerning the object of psychological research Geyer answers with a distinction. The object immediately investigated by the psychologist is the activities and conditions of consciousness. But the ultimate goal of his research is the fundamental principle which gives unity to consciousness, i.e. the soul. This ultimate founda-

---

[8]2 vols., 3rd ed., Münster in W., 1920.
[9]*Op. cit.,* vol. I, p. IV.

tion, however, is not reached by means of experimental science, but by making the empirical data the object of a philosophical study which "in the course of our reflection leads us to the concept of the soul. Thus the soul is the second and most remote object of psychology, its final object."[1] It must be admitted that man is not able to grasp the soul empirically. However, this does not jeopardize the empiriological character of psychology, because in every empirical science there are factors and moments which one has to "supplement in thought."

> If, then, *complementary* and *interpretative* thought is a procedure which belongs to the scientific method itself of empirical psychology, it follows that the investigation of the soul also is not outside the scope of empirical psychology.[2]

Accordingly, Geyser holds that upon the basis of its experimental data psychology is justified in postulating the existence of the soul as an empirical hypothesis.

The Conscious Subject. Everything psychical is characterized by the fact that man is aware of it in a simple unreflected way. This property of the psychical is called "consciousness." Only the psychical has this mark of consciousness. True, Geyser does not deny in principle the possibility of unconscious psychical activities.

> Nevertheless, the greatest reserve must be shown with respect to the admission of such unconscious events. Many facts adduced in proof of it can be explained by means of the low stage of development reached by many conscious processes.[3]

At any rate, changes which take place in consciousness itself are "real processes and determinations of the soul itself."[4]

In contrast to the manifoldness of changing and unstable phenomena of consciousness stands the one and identical subject which perceives these phenomena.[5] Here we reach the turning point of Geyser's thought which is decisive for our problem.

> The question must be raised whether or not we are able to recognize also other relationships of this subject to the processes of

---

[1] *Op. cit.*, vol. I, pp. 3 and 20.
[2] *Op. cit.*, vol. I, p. 33.
[3] *Op. cit.*, vol. I, p. 120.
[4] *Op. cit.*, vol. I, p. 270.
[5] *Op. cit.*, vol. I, p. 280.

consciousness and even other properties that are inherent in its nature. This question must be answered in the affirmative. The principle of consciousness is related to that which occurs in consciousness not only as the perceiving subject but also as its producing cause and as the substratum in which consciousness exists.[6]

There has to be such a subject, because the states and changes of which we become conscious are of a transitory nature. They arise, continue, and cease in time.

[There must be something] in which and in connection with which these things arise and exist. If the contents of consciousness existed in themselves instead of inhering in a substratum, they would come to be from nothing at the moment of their origin.[7]

The brain cannot be this substratum, because events of consciousness, such as "colors, sounds, pleasure, unpleasantness, odor, etc." are in their very principle different from cerebral process.

Hence a satisfactory explanation is required why such effects can arise from cerebral processes. The only possible explanation is that in the production of these effects a role is played by a substratum whose nature differs specifically from that of the brain.[8]

This substratum is "the soul-substance," for

conscious processes do not exist independently as substances, but by their very nature are attached to a being in which they are rooted with respect to both their origin and their existence.[9]

Thus, metaphysically speaking, all psychical phenomena are accidents with respect to the autonomously existing soul. How, then, do contents of consciousness arise? How, for instance, does a simple perception take place? The answer is

The contents of sensation and their relationships are the common effect of both the soul (consciousness) and the external world acting upon our senses and determining our soul to produce the sensations.[10]

Of course, the objects of the external world "are" not in the soul. When the soul imagines a round blue object, the soul itself is neither

---

[6]*Ibid.*
[7]*Op. cit.,* vol. I, p. 281.
[8]*Ibid.*
[9]*Op. cit.,* vol. I, p. 282.
[10]*Op. cit.,* vol. I, p. 18.

round nor blue. If the question is asked how the soul can know this object,

> we reply that blue exists in the soul, but in the form of the perceived, by means of the *percipi;* and it is precisely through this special mode of being that the perceived blue differs essentially from the blue existing in bodily things.[11]

Briefly, sensations, perceptions, and representations refer to material realities, but they are also immaterially in the soul. It is precisely in this that lies the difference between outer and inner perceptions— the former has as its object spatially extended reality, while the reality which is the object of the latter is not extended in space. In this way Geyser proves the immateriality of the soul. The soul is an "unextended non-spatial reality."[12]

B. CRITIQUE OF GEYSER'S VIEW

Let us now subject the theory of this well-known philosophical psychologist to a double critical examination. First of all, we will have to determine whether or not his theory offers a satisfactory explanation of the nature and process of conscious events. Next, we will have to ask ourselves whether or not the synthesis he offers effectively takes into account the essential principles of a philosophy with an ontological orientation.

Does Geyser Satisfactorily Explain the Nature and Process of the Phenomena of Consciousness?

When we examine these questions, it becomes manifest that Geyser's interpretation of the phenomena of consciousness is not satisfactory. What is presented under the name of "psychical states" is much more complex than the simple relation expressed by "accidents inhering in a substantial substratum." Let us mention only two of the many difficulties arising in this matter.

First Difficulty. One and the same autonomously existing being is able to support an indefinite number of different and changing states, but it cannot have within itself opposite properties. Opposite qualities and conditions exclude one another. One and the same thing, for instance, can be red and round, but not at the same time blue and red. At most it can be blue here and red there—namely, if the object

---

[11]*Op. cit.,* vol. I, p. 117.
[12]*Op. cit.,* vol. I, p. 301.

has real parts[13] extended in space. But obviously this possibility is excluded in an unextended and non-spatial reality. Now it is easy to prove that what is usually designated as the "life of the soul" is unthinkable without such opposites. A simple example taken from the visible sector of our perceptive life may be adduced as evidence. Let us suppose that I see first a blue and then a red surface. Geyser interprets this psychical event as follows. My soul is an immaterial substance. The acts of seeing the blue and perceiving the red are two accidents which "are riveted" to the being of this substance. Accordingly, my experience of the change in color would be nothing but the transition of my soul from *one* state (that of seeing blue) to *another* (that of perceiving red). One state evidently excludes the other, for otherwise my experience of the change would not occur. Let us take another example. I see a blue object upon a red background. In this case my soul would be the substratum of two states which cannot simultaneously exist in it—namely, the state of perceiving the blue and that of seeing the red. The interpretation that my soul sees *here* blue and *there* red is immediately excluded, because different spatially dispersed "constituent parts" of my soul would have to correspond with such a diversity. But the soul is an "unextended and non-spatial reality," as Geyser himself emphasizes.

The importance of this analysis becomes evident when one considers that we obtain differentiated knowledge of our surroundings most of all by means of the perception of simultaneous contrasts. On the level of the more primitive senses this differentiation is less clearly present. For instance, only *one* sensation corresponds with the taste of bitter coffee and sweet sugar. Likewise, we are not at once capable of distinguishing different odors in smelling a perfume that consists of a mixture of volatile oils. The power to objectivize, which the higher senses possess, evidently reposes upon the simultaneous reception of contrary impressions, such as blue-red, bright-dark, deep-pale, loud-soft, high-deep, cold-warm, rough-smooth, etc.

Undoubtedly, Geyser himself was not ignorant of this difficulty. He thought that one could escape from it by emphasizing that the domain of consciousness is "not an aggregate of juxtaposed and separate contents" of consciousness.[14] But this is beside the point.

---

[13]In a footnote the author explains that he uses the term *"real"* with respect to that which is as a *res* (a physical thing), while he reserves the term *"wirklich"* for non-physical or metaphysical reality. This distinction cannot be maintained in the English text (Note of the translator).

[14]*Psychologie,* vol. I, p. 113.

What we want to know is why "notwithstanding their diversity . . . these contents nevertheless always [constitute] a unified whole."[15] Geyser's theory of the soul accounts neither for the diversity nor for the differentiated unity. Notwithstanding its apparent simplicity our example shows that the schema of introspective psychology is not able to explain the origin of our objective picture of the world. It does not make us understand how we as spiritual beings seize a world which contains things that are dispersed in time and space, qualitatively and quantitatively different, and subject to change.

Second Difficulty. The second difficulty likewise is a matter of principle. As has been remarked by numerous philosophers, phenomenologists and psychologists, in principle our relation to our own states of consciousness and conscious activities can be of a twofold nature. *Through* my perception, evaluation, desire, etc. I can live "with" the object-poles of the world. In this case the stream of my psychical acts carries me to the things, the valuable and desirable objects. But I can also direct my attention to my own sensations, the lived events and states of awareness. In that case the nature of my conscious life undergoes a change of a very special nature. My consciousness is no longer the medium through which I reach the objects of the world, but itself has become a kind of object before which I stand. Geyser tried to indicate this difference by distinguishing the "simple awareness of a content"—which is the general criterion of consciousness—from properly "cognitive knowing" or acts of reflective thought.

> If we designate as "knowing" only the grasping of the content of consciousness which has its root in these acts of thought, then undoubtedly only a part of the actually present contents of consciousness will be the object of our knowing in this sense.[16]

Let us examine these special acts of thought in the light of a concrete analysis. Suppose that I have cut my finger and now feel pain. Evidently, this feeling of pain is a content of consciousness,[17] and as such a "real event and determination of the soul itself."[18] But is it not rather remarkable that within certain limits this determination of my soul is *"at my disposal"?* I am able to observe it, compare it, judge it. I can, at least in principle, cease to pay attention to it and thus eliminate it from the world of my objects. That which I thus treat more

---

[15]*Ibid.*
[16]*Op. cit.*, vol. I, p. 109.
[17]*Op. cit.*, vol. I, p. 114.
[18]*Op. cit.*, vol. I, p. 270.

or less freely as an object is, of course, not my finger nor the wound, but the *feeling* of pain, the *psychical* fact. So to a certain extent I stand there *facing* a lived event, a "determination of my soul itself." For example, I try to banish this state from my consciousness till a burning impression again draws my attention to the feeling of pain. Accordingly, between this feeling and me there are relations of action and being-acted-upon. So we are led to the question, Is it possible that a thing which acts in such a way upon me be identical with "my soul"? Reversely, is it possible for something which is "at my disposal" almost like an object to be a state of my most intimate ego? Must such a support of action and being-acted-upon not be more than a mere accident? The same follows among other things from the fundamental Thomistic principle, *non est operari nisi entis in actu,* only a being-in-act can act.[19]

Analogous remarks can be made from an epistemological point of view. When I pay attention to my sensation of pain, I perform an intentional action. In doing so I am tending to "something else," which originally is not fully given to me, but with which I am able to become better acquainted through observation, comparison and judgment. As Joseph Maréchal remarks,

> Whatever be the contents of consciousness, as soon as it falls under my reflection, it reveals an opposition of object and subject, of ego and non-ego. When reflection reaches the subject, it reveals in it a new level of objectivity.[20]

I, the knowing subject, in my acts of knowing am ruled by an object, i.e. "something else." What is the meaning here of this "something else"? In any case it points to a reality which does not simply coincide with my own reality. How we have to describe correctly the mode of being of the psychical fact called "sensation of pain" we do not yet know. Provisionally we limit ourselves to the negative statement that the objects of internal experience may not at all be considered as accidental states of the "soul in the metaphysical sense of the term."

Does Geyser's Synthesis Do Justice to the Basic Principles of Aristotelian-Thomistic Metaphysics?

This brings us to the second part of our critique. May the psychology of Geyser be considered as a synthesis which does justice

---

[19]*Summa theol.*, p. I, q. 75, a. 2 c.

[20]*Le point de départ de la métaphysique,* cahier V, Louvain-Paris, 1926, p. 14.

to the fundamental principles of Aristotelian-Thomistic philosophy? We think that the answer will have to be in the negative. Geyser, it seems, shows little understanding of the metaphysical contents of certain basic ontological concepts. This applies in the first place to the transcendental relationship of substance and accidents. If it is true, as Geyser claims, that the human soul is the substantial support of all activities and states of consciousness, then many other of his assertions which are directly opposed to this affirmation become untenable. Let us begin with Geyser's definition of psychological research. According to his definition, psychical activities and conditions are immediate data of the psychologist, but we have to "add in thought" the soul as the substantial substratum of these accidents. Does this conception correspond with the metaphysical structure of reality as it reveals itself concretely? When we tend to an activity or property, do we not grasp at the same time and immediately also "something" which "exercises" this activity and "possesses" this property? "Immediately" here means of course that we do not need any kind of conceptual structures and hypothesis. We simply *experience* the phenomenon "red" as the being red of something, the phenomenon "flying" as the flying of a being, etc. When Geyser claims to have discovered the initially unknown substance (the psyche) by means of a scientific investigation of the accidents (the psychical states and activities), he has presumably something else in mind than the soul in the metaphysical sense.[21]

The same applies to Geyser's assertion that the substratum of conscious events "knows" these events. This view likewise cannot be reconciled with the fundamental principles of ontology. The idea of a substance which knows its accidents is untenable if only for this reason that thus the autonomous existence of a being is conceived as independent of its states. Such a view commits the well-known mistake of making autonomous beings out of metaphysical principles of being.

The assertion also that the soul is the producing cause of its own states[22] is open to criticism. Here too the substantial substratum is

---

[21]Louis de Raeymaeker brands as "false" the view that the existence of accidents can be considered to be an empirically verifiable fact, while on the other hand a strenous effort would be needed to prove that there must of necessity be a substance corresponding with these accidents. He compares this view with that of Descartes: "But if after this we wished to strip this same substance of all its attributes which make us know it, we would destroy all the knowledge we have of it." Cf. *The Philosophy of Being*, Herder, 1954, pp. 177 and 184.

[22]*Op. cit.*, vol. I, p. 18.

conceived as separate from the states inherent in it. Evidently, in this way violence is done to the fundamental principles of a metaphysics with ontological orientation.

These misconceptions are not incidental mistakes; rather they arise from the fact that the concept of soul in introspective psychology has hardly anything in common with the metaphyscial study of man. As far at the introspective psychologist is concerned, the soul is primarily a support of lived events which mirrors reality. For the philosopher of being the soul is the ontological principle which explains my existence as a corporeal being. A synthesis of two viewpoints which are so fundamentally different is altogether impossible. If one tries anyhow to "fuse them together," contradictory results are bound to make their appearance.

4. *Sensing as a Metaphysical Problem*

THE ARISTOTELIAN-THOMISTIC POSITION

Our problem assumes immediately a quite different aspect if the principles of the Aristotelian philosophy of man are kept in mind. Once we understand that it is solely as a spiritual-material unit that man exists, lives, perceives, behaves and acts, we are able to understand in principle also how he can take part in a cosmos which is qualitatively differentiated, quantitatively extended, and stretched out in space and time. But precisely in this decisive point Geyser thinks that he must deviate from traditional metaphysics. He objects to a union of body and soul which would lead to a "unique existence for both."[1] In his view the bond of body and soul is the "interdependence of their respective functions."[2] This solution, however, is not at all satisfactory, for it is evident that the human body would not have any function if it were not an animated body. It is precisely sensation and perception which belong to the functions that are exercised by the "body-soul unit" as such, as Willwoll expresses it. Undoubtedly, it would be superfluous to show in a detailed proof that this view agrees with that of Aristotle, who is very clear and unequivocal in this matter in his work *De anima.*[3] St. Thomas also explicitly states: "All activities which depend upon the animal level of animation proceed from the animated being as such"[4]; and: "The subject of the powers which are

---

[1]*Op. cit.,* vol. I, p. 364.
[2]*Op. cit.,* vol. I, p. 366.
[3]See e.g. 412b and 413a.
[4]*Summa theol.,* p. I, q. 75, a 3: "Omnis operatio sensitivae animae est conjuncti."

principles of such activities [i.e. sense activities] is the animate being as such and not the soul alone."[5]

Its Value for the Solution of Problems

Thus it is easy to become convinced that the "living principles of Aristotelian philosophy" show themselves effectively "fruitful for the explanation of the phenomena."

The First Difficulty. Regarding the first difficulty, which was concerned with the simultaneous perception of contrasting phenomena, it finds a very natural solution if we admit that the seeing of red and the seeing of blue are not states of the soul but states of the besouled being. Blue and red are contraries, and I, the perceiving subject, must allow myself to be determined by their contrasting character. The lived experience of this contrast, which starts in my besouled organs, somehow irradiates my whole ego. In this sense, and only in this sense, we may take over the modern psychological terminology and assert that perception is "psycho-physically neutral." As such, it gives us indeed a well-ordered picture of the cosmos. Contrast remains contrast. However, as a result of its progressive mental assimilation this opposition is rendered relative, combined and transcended. In the example given above this integration into a higher complex of interconnected senses may take place, for example, in the form of a simple statement such as: the object on the red background is blue. How the mind arrives at this synthesis we do not have to examine here. Provisionally we merely want to draw this methodological conclusion: wherever we encounter contrasts which are not, not yet, or no longer, fused into a meaningful unit we are in the sphere of sensing. Sensing evidently is the domain of manifoldness and diversity, of functional groups which act in harmony but also—within limits—in disharmony, of inner tensions and contrasts. In the sphere of the mind all these contrasts are bridged, united into a simple or complex synthesis, enclosed in the unity of a "giving of meaning." St. Thomas expresses this thought as follows:

> In the intellectual soul there cannot be any contrariety, for this soul receives everything according to its own mode of being. Whatever things are received in the soul are without contrariety, since even the notions of contraries are not contrary in the soul, but constitute a single knowledge of contraries.[6]

[5] *Op. cit.*, p. I, q. 77, a. 5 c.
[6] *Summa theol.*, p. I, q. 75, a. 6. Cf. also p. I-II, q. 85, a. 6 c.

The Second Difficulty. The second difficulty may be overcome in the same way. Obviously, again the soul is not the support of the sensation of pain. This sensation is not a state of the soul but of the besouled human being and starts in certain besouled organs. It is for this reason and only for this reason that we can internally detach ourselves from it. As a matter of fact, as we will show later, our ego does not coincide completely with this or that besouled part of the body. From this we may deduce a second methodological guiding principle. Whenever we have to do with something with which we do not constitute a perfect unit, something from which we are able to detach ourselves to a certain extent, something whose mode of being is like that of an object so that we are able to face it as a subject, we may not identify this "something" with our spiritual principle of life.

The Anthropological Problem of Sensing

The two methodological principles indicated above are valuable indeed, but should not be considered as more than "road signs," taken from the traditional philosophy of man. A few fundamental principles are borrowed from this philosophy, but as soon as we apply these principles, new difficulties arise which we have to overcome on our own. For instance, behind the concept of "sensing" a serious problem of the philosophy of man is hidden,[7] for the solution of which great prudence is required. Undoubtedly, the ancient view that the soul is a kind of mechanical recorder of any stimulations coming from the surface of surrounding objects and things has been generally abandoned. The descriptions of phenomenologists, such as Husserl, Scheler, Merleau-Ponty, etc., and the research of psychologists (gestaltists) and physiologists, such as Buytendijk, E. Straus, von Weizsäcker and his circle, has left practically nothing standing of this abstract structure. It will be sufficient to adduce here a single concrete case from the abundant literature in this field. We may take it from the famous work of Auguste Michotte, La perception de la causalité (Louvain-Paris, 1946).

Michotte's View of Perception. In his work Michotte describes several experiments in which two dark shapes move against a white background. The impression made by their movements upon the

---

[7]Note that our question is concerned with sensing and not with sensibility. To speak of the sensibility of man before we know what a sensory act is seems equally impossible as to determine the meaning of bluish before one has a clear idea of what blue is.

onlooker may be reduced to these words: "Shape A *takes* shape B *along,* and shape A *pushes* shape B *away.* Regarding this matter Michotte remarks:

> In the two cases of these two experiences the genesis of the movement is *directly lived.* There is no question of an inference or a "signification" added to an impression of movement; in other words, "what is given" is not a simple representation, a symbol of causality. Just as stroboscopic movement is not, psychologically speaking, the "symbol" of a movement but *is* a phenomenal movement, so also perceived causality.[8]

> In the repulse there is something which is intrinsically necessary. . . . Undoubtedly, we have here a manifestation of that strange "intuitive logic" which plays such a great role in the solution of "visual" problems.[9]

Gredt's Definition of Sensing. Let us confront this view of perception with the definition which Joseph Gredt gives of the concept of "sensing." According to Gredt,

> Sense perception is the kind of knowing whose object is the corporeal thing which is inseparably fused together (*concretum*) with its individual characteristics, the "concrete" individual thing.[10]

Spontaneously the question arises in us whether or not the "observed causality" and the "intuitively perceived necessity" of which Michotte, relying upon his experiments, speaks without the slightest hesitation, are individual things located in space and time? The question arouses a feeling of uncertainty in us. Clearly, we lack a definition of the concept of "sensing" which is more profound, better founded, and philosophically more warranted. The metaphysical determination of this concept is not easy. Perhaps our subsequent investigations will show that a special philosophical method is required. In any case, we do not have the right to continue the use of concepts and categories which have not been completely examined, are not wholly without ambiguity, and really justified. For this reason it seems more honest to confess in all humility that for the time being we do not yet know what is meant by "sensing" than to be satisfied with a pseudo-solution.

---

[8]*Op. cit.,* pp. 18 f.

[9]*Op. cit.,* p. 252. Cf. also M. Pradines, *Traité de Psychologie générale,* 2nd impr., Paris, 1946, vol. III, p. 139, who likewise speaks confidently of a "perceptive abstraction and generalization."

[10]*Die aristotelisch-thomistische Philosophie,* Freiburg i. Br., vol. I, p. 315.

CONCLUSION

An example of such a pseudo-solution has been given above. The "fusion" mentioned by Joseph Geyser, which consists in this that every fact, state and act called "psychical" by the introspective psychologist is without any further ado metaphysically interpreted as an accident of a subsistent soul offers no explanation even of the most elementary "egological" event. Our analyses give us the right to state that the discoveries of the introspective psychologist concerning the phenomena, functions and internal connections of human consciousness have no direct bearing upon the concept of soul which the metaphysicist has in mind. Both the introspective psychologist and the metaphysicist make use of the concepts of "soul," "psychical state," and "psychical activity," but they do not attach the same meaning to these terms. They do not understand each other, even when they think that they do. Their exchange of views is marked by ambiguity, and their apparent unity of thought is based upon a misunderstanding. It is not surprising that no fruitful collaboration has developed upon this shifting and treacherous soil.

SECOND STUDY

THE MODERN CONCEPT OF THE SPIRITUAL EGO

1. *The Origin of the Modern Concept of the Soul in Descartes and Locke*

If we search history for the source which gave rise to psychology's misunderstanding of itself, we will end up with the Father of modern philosophy, René Descartes. It was Descartes who as the founder of a new philosophy of man deliberately and radically broke with the views held by Christian Aristotelianism concerning soul and body, mind and matter, "understanding" and "sensing." The matter seems important enough to establish the point clearly.

The Aristotelian-Thomistic View. In Aristotelian-Thomistic philosophy the soul constituted a first perfection of a portion of the material cosmos which was disposed for the reception of life. Thus the soul was the first principle of life in *all* its forms, organic as well as spiritual life, instinctive drives as well as purposive willing, conscious as well as semiconscious and unconscious life. In this way it was possible to explain metaphysically the life of man in its various levels and manifold manifestations. The spiritual soul of man was conceived as the virtual principle of his animal and vegetative animation. Thus one could understand how a process which originated as the reaction of a sense organ to a stimulus could end in the synthesis of spiritual knowledge; one could understand how the energy of organic drives could be in the service of a spiritual "I will." In this conception the transition from the "psychico-physically neutral" to the explicitly spiritual was made possible by an immanent development. The question how this immanent process of development had to be conceived was answered epistemologically by the theory of species. Perhaps it is true that this theory was often explained in a crude and simplistic way, but at all events it was not ambiguous.

Descartes' "Cogito." This profound, well-conceived and balanced view of man's nature was destroyed by a single word of Descartes—his famous *Cogito*. The new method of philosophy which was announced under this title is too well known to need much comment. To Descartes human self-consciousness seemed to be not merely the most

30

perfect starting point of philosophical research, but the only one possible. I am able, he says, to doubt everything, with one exception—I
am absolutely certain of that which I grasp in my immanence.[1] "Sensing" can deceive, but not the thought of sensing. Only consciousness
and its clear and distinct contents cannot show themselves deceptive.
The support of this *cogito* is identified by Descartes with the *"mens
sive animus sive intellectus."* In this series of names expression is
given to the view that the soul is only mind and that there is no animation.

> And because we do not doubt that there are inanimate bodies
> which are able to move themselves as much or even more than
> our bodies, and which have as much or even more heat..., we
> must admit that all heat and all movement in us, insofar as they
> do not depend upon thought, belong only to the body.[2]

Concepts such as "vegetative soul" and "sensitive soul" are based
upon medieval superstitions. We, modern men, do not need any
longer such metaphysical hypotheses. Our physical sciences, our anatomy and physiology show how the body can exist and function independently; we do not need to take refuge in the untenable concept of
an act which gives reality and life to the body. My body is an independently existing physical system whose activity can be wholly explained by the laws of positive physical science. That was the idea of
Descartes when he said: my body is a machine.[3]

The Ambiguity Resulting From This Position. With the Cartesian
cogito the above-mentioned ambiguity arises immediately. To show
this it will be sufficient to make a careful analysis of a single proposition of Cartesian philosophy, namely, the famous *"cogito, ergo sum."*
The much-disputed question whether this statement must be considered as a conclusion or the expression of an immediately evident
intuition is irrelevant as far as we are here concerned. In any case,
its contents corresponds with objective knowledge.[4] According to

---

[1]Cf. *Les méditations métaphysiques, 2e med., Oeuvres de Descartes,* Adam-
Tannery ed., Paris, 1904, vol. IX, p. 23. Hereafter we shall quote this edition
as *Oeuvres.*
[2]*Les passions de l'ame, Oeuvres,* vol. XI, p. 329.
[3]"I have not admitted in it [the machine] any hypothetical organs or 'springs'
which are not of such a nature that similar ones can easily be admitted to exist
both in us and in various kinds of irrational animals. For as far as organs are
concerned which can easily be perceived by sight, the anatomists have already
observed them all." *Traité de l'homme, Oeuvres,* vol. XI, p. 200.
[4]Cf. the preface of *Méditations métaphysiques,* in which there is explicit
mention of "demonstrations." *Oeuvres,* vol. IX, pp. 4 f.

Descartes, this knowledge must even be the indestructible foundation for the lofty edifice of a total philosophy and a universal science.

Accordingly, I reflect, I think, meditate and discover myself as an existing ego. Thus I become the first object of scientific knowledge, an object whose existence is, objectively speaking, beyond doubt.[5] Hence it is I who am the model, the exemplar and prototype of the object which is integrally knowable.

> What shall I affirm, what shall I say, of this "ego" which seems to conceive this piece of wax with so much clarity and distinction? Do I not know myself, not only with greater truth and certainty, but even with greater distinction and clarity?[6]

For Descartes, the ideal science, the science which is purged of all its traditional prejudices, uncertain suspicions, and untenable hypotheses, must seize its objects with the same clarity and distinction with which I see my object-ego.[7]

At the same time, however, I am the subject *par excellence.* My *cogito* is the beginning of all wisdom, my self-consciousness is the source of all certain knowledge, my spiritual ego is the absolute starting point. Hence the question arises, Who exactly am I? The thinking ego or the ego whose existence I, in thinking, discover? Do I coincide with the knowing subject-ego or with the known object-ego? Am I the mind which meditates or the mind about which I meditate? Adapting ourselves to Descartes' style of thought, we could also ask, Whose being is considered to be absolutely beyond doubt? That of the subject-ego? But objective knowledge is not possible without an object. Is it then the existence of the object-ego that we must see as the apodictic datum? But if the object-ego does not coincide with the ego of the undoubtable starting point, in what consists, philosophically speaking, the absolute priority of knowledge of the object-ego with respect to other objects?

One should not try to answer this question quickly with the evasive reply that in this case there is identity of subject and object. The identity of two realities means that they have only one existence, that they are not two realities, and that no intelligent being has any

---

[5] ". . . so that after careful thought and diligent examination of all things, one must conclude and hold as established that the proposition, "I am, I exist," is true and necessarily true." *Méditations métaphysiques, Oeuvres,* vol. IX, p. 19.

[6] *Op. cit.,* pp. 25 f.

[7] "Therefore, it seems to me that I can already establish as a general rule that all things which we conceive very clearly and very distinctly are wholly true." *Op. cit.,* p. 27.

reason to assert in a true judgment that they are two. Of course, it would be another matter to say that the categories of subject and object are not irreducibly opposed and intrinsically refer to a higher unity in which their opposition is "overcome." There can be no question here of this answer. As we have seen above, Descartes' starting point is an objective judgment. He says, *"Cogito,* I think." From this follows necessarily the further question, What do I think? Descartes' answer is: Myself as existing object, myself as thinking substance, myself as *"res cogitans,"* a thinking thing.[8] But what Descartes calls a *res cogitans,* a thinking thing, is at the same time a *res cogitata,* a thought thing; for wherever there is a directed activity there must be also something to which this activity is directed. Wherever anyone "aims" at something there must be an object to be aimed at. Here we have the above-mentioned ambiguity. Descartes says *ego,* and attaches two meanings to this term. He says "a thinking thing" and means at the same time "a thought thing." He says "soul" and gives the term a double conceptual contents.

John Locke. It was John Locke who introduced this ambiguity into the realm of psychology. Contrary to Descartes, he asserts that all knowledge is due to our experience. Our experience has a two-fold character. It is either sensation, i.e. sense experience of the so-called outer world, and as such it supplies the necessary data for physical science; or it takes the form of reflection, i.e. of internal experience, and then the contents of consciousness, the ideas, are its objects. With great emphasis he affirms that contents of consciousness which do not directly originate in sensations but are derived from immanent data are just as capable of becoming objects of our contemplation as the impressions received from the outer world.

> The mind receiving the ideas . . . from without, when it turns its view inward upon itself, observes its own actions about those ideas it has, takes from thence other ideas, which are as capable to be the objects of its contemplation as any of those it received from foreign things.[9]

Concerning this text Fraser remarks: Locke "is apt to treat Intellect and Will as merely finite phenomena."[10] For Locke, *the* intellect and *the* will and a number of similar objects constitute the so-called inner

---

[8]"I am certain that I am a thing that thinks." *Op. cit.,* vol. IX, p. 27.
[9]*An Essay concerning Human Understanding,* edited by A. C. Fraser, Oxford, 1894, vol. I, p. 159.
[10]*Ibid.*

world and thus belong to the domain of research reserved for the psychologist.

In this way the above-decried ambiguity manifested itself for the first time clearly in the philosophy of the West. What in Descartes' philosophy was still situated within the limits of an entirely different perspective was developed by Locke in a way that can be indicated only as objectivistic.[11]

This objectivism remained predominant in later times. To cite only one representative of rational psychology, Christian Wolff regularly speaks in one breath of the experience of the self and that of the things of the world.[12] This one-sided conception leads among other things to the following strange consequences. As a conscious being, I am a complex of conscious facts, facts that are capable of becoming objects of an objective experience. But, on the other hand, as a conscious being, I am also the one for whom the data of consciousness are there as data, for they are accessible only to me, only to my reflection. Thus the consciousness which I am is at the same time that which I contemplate, investigate and judge. As a psychologist, I am psychically active, and the object of my psychical activity is my own active psyche. As an explorer of the soul, I would like to know my soul, but the part of me that tries to know my soul evidently is my-soul-not-knowing-my-soul.

For one hundred years the study of rational psychology was pursued upon the basis provided by Descartes and Locke. For one hundred years they were satisfied with the comfortable ambiguity. For one hundred years it was thought possible to harmonize philosophy and psychology upon Descartes' *"cogito"* and Locke's "reflection."

But then there arose a great thinker, an impeccable logician. He laid bare the ambiguity. He caused the collapse of the edifice constructed by the psychology of the Illumination. He showed that the harmony of philosophy and psychology as conceived by Locke is based upon a misunderstanding.

This thinker was Immanuel Kant.

[11]Concerning the sense of the concepts "subject," "object," "objective" and "objectivistic" we must explicitly refer to our explanations contained in the study *Objectiviteit and Objectivisme,* Nymegen-Utrecht, 1947.

[12]"At every moment we experience the being of ourselves and that of other things which are placed outside us as conscious. Nothing is necessary to be certain of this except attention to our perception." *Psychologia empirica,* 2nd ed., Frankfurt-Leipzig, 1738, par. 11, p. 9.

2. *Kant and the Origin of Modern Trialism*

Kant's Contribution to the Evolution of Modern Thought. When Kant branded the concept of the soul used in rational psychology as an idea which inevitably imposes itself but is fallacious, the divorce proceedings between philosophy and psychology had been formally begun. This issue marks a turning point in the course of the historical development of both sciences. The great thinkers before Kant did not show a purely non-professional interest in psychological problems. They had their own views concerning the nature of the soul, perception, affections, etc. They were philosophers as well as psychologists. Descartes, Malebranche, Spinoza, Locke, Berkeley and Hume must be considered as men devoted to psychological research. Leibniz still believed in the possibility of a psychology upon an *a priori* basis. But from the time of the appearance of the CRITIQUE OF PURE REASON a great change can be observed in this respect. The place of psychology in the system of sciences before 1781 differs from that assigned to it after the great philosopher of Königsberg made his appearance. When we ask ourselves today which definite result of Kant's ideas has determined the evolution of modern thought concerning the mind-ego, we may answer very briefly: the conviction that *that which gives our thought objective validity cannot be identical with any object of this thought.*

His Critique of Rational Psychology. As is known, Kant proves his thesis in the part of his CRITIQUE which is entitled *Concerning the Paralogisms of the Pure Reason.* Let us first explain this title. What is meant by the term "paralogism"? Kant himself provides the answer. A logical paralogism, he says, implies a formal error, but the cause of a transcendental paralogism, on the other hand, lies in the nature of man's thought. Therefore, such a paralogism becomes the occasion of a general and necessary error. With respect to the object of a transcendental paralogism, we foster an "unavoidable, though not insoluble, error."[1]

Rational psychology, i.e., as Kant notes ironically, the psychology whose whole domain consists in the short sentence "I think," rests on four such paralogisms. After proving that the four main theses of rational psychology are untenable, Kant draws the conclusion that *a priori* psychology is impossible and that psychology can be conceived only as an empirical science. It is a kind of physiology of the inner

---

[1]*Critique of Pure Reason,* translated by J. M. D. Meiklejohn, Revised Edition, New York, n. d., p. 213.

sense. As such, it does not rank as a philosophical discipline. Psychology is a physical science, and strictly speaking, it is not even more than a descriptive study of nature. For this reason its results have only a very limited scientific value.

> Even more than chemistry, empirical psychology is condemned to remain below the rank of physical science in the strict sense. . . . It can never become more than a highly systematic history of the inner sense.[2]

One-Sidedness of This Critique. It is manifest that Kant, obsessed by Newton's ideal of exact science, goes too far. His judgment also concerning metaphysical psychology is very one-sided. From the fact that the philosophical psychology of his time rests upon unexplained presuppositions Kant concludes that no philosophical psychology can be critically justified. Of course, this view is connected with his opinion concerning the nature of philosophy, an opinion which nowadays hardly anyone is still willing to share. However, it is not our intention to consider all these questions here. We deliberately abstract from everything which separates us from Kant—his blindness to ontological evidence; his formalism, which prevents him from recognizing the importance of the material *a priori;* his physical mechanism, which induces him, for instance, to use the concept of substance as almost synonymous with "immutable mass." We want to remain silent also with respect to his agnosticism, although his concept of "paralogism" represents a peculiar result of this attitude of thought.[3] All this is better left out of consideration here. The only thing we want to do here is to interpret one argument of Kant's CRITIQUE which seems to us to be perfectly correct. It is directed against the way in which rational psychology endeavors to give a foundation to its most important thesis—namely, that the soul is a substance. To prevent misunderstandings, we must point out once more that Kant's idea of substance has hardly anything in common with that of traditional philosophy. What the difference is between the two concepts of substance does not concern us here. Let us assume that the thesis of the rational psychologist is: The soul is

---

[2]*Metaphysische Anfangsgründe der Naturwissenschaft, Werke,* vol. IV, p. 373.

[3]According to Kant, as we have just seen, the human intellect is such that man in general and of necessity must form judgments which are irrational, so-called paralogisms. The question arises immediately how it happens that an illusion form which no man is able to escape nevertheless can be "overcome." If this illusion is so profoundly rooted in human nature, not even Kant himself will be an exception to the rule.

an intentional object. This assumption does not decrease the value of Kant's argument, but enlarges it because the extension of the concept "intentional object" is much wider than that of substance in the Kantian sense.

Convincing Force of His Critique. Taking these preliminary remarks as a starting point, one can show that Kant's critique of the method of rational psychology derives its convincing force from the following considerations.

1) In every act of consciousness, in every "I think," I am "present" as the subject in the sense that I am the "determining self." This self-consciousness, however, which accompanies every *cogito* is nothing else than the mode of thought itself and gives me no certainty regarding the nature of my thought. "All the modi of self-consciousness in thought," says Kant, "are hence not conceptions of objects."[4]

2) The statement that I am a substance can refer only to something determinable, i.e. an intentional object. Only that which is the object of an "intuition" can be grasped by me in concepts and classified in a categorical way. Accordingly, what I consider here as substance is my ego insofar as I am for myself a "this-thing-here," an object of inner experience, a "determinable self."

3) Thus I am not authorized to identify that which in every conscious act I experience as self-consciousness with an objectively present substance. It is only because of my being self-conscious that I know what a thinking thing is. "I cannot obtain the least representation of a thinking being by means of external experience, but solely through self-consciousness."[5] A substance, on the other hand, is always and of necessity given as the object of an intentional experience. Hence it is not possible to identify the subject-ego, the determining ego, with the object-ego of my inner intuition conceived as a substance. For "not the consciousness of the determining, but only that of the determinable self, that is, of my internal intuition . . . is the object."[6]

In this whole argumentation of Kant an indelible impression was made especially by the negative discovery of a fundamental distinction between, on the one hand, the being which "can be cogitated . . . as it may be given in intuition" and, on the other hand, the being "in so far as it regards itself as subject, relatively to thought and the

---

[4]*Critique of Pure Reason,* p. 217.
[5]*Op. cit.,* p. 216.
[6]*Op. cit.,* pp. 217 f.

unity of consciousness, . . . by which it is presented as object to thought."[7] What is given to us in inner experience evidently constitutes the object of empirical psychology, whether we want to call it "soul," "empirical ego," or "psychological ego." Its Kantian opposite is "pure synthesis," "pure apperception," "transcendental consciousness," briefly, that which can never become the object of an act of knowledge, because it is the very thing in which are locked in the conditions that make objective knowledge possible.

Consequences of Kant's Speculation. Kant's notion of "pure apperception" was conceived in such a formalistic and ambiguous way that for later generations it became, as could be expected, the starting point of metaphysical speculations. Everyone of the great idealists gave his own interpretation to the Kantian idea of pure apperception. It is beyond the scope of this study to write the history of the various interpretations and developments of Kantian thought. We want to point out only that this evolution was bound to lead to an increasing alienation of philosophy from psychology. It seemed evident that the object of psychology was the "determinable self," while philosophy had as its task to penetrate into the "determining self." If the psychologist has to be concerned with the study of the objective facts of man's internal life, then obviously the problem of philosophy will consist in a metaphysical explanation of man's subjectivity. Another consequence which became clear in the course of this evolution was an increasing "dehumanization" of philosophy. Cartesian dualism was promptly replaced by modern trialism. The germ of it may be found in Kant himself. Even in Kant the object of the inner sense differs from that of outer experience; on the other hand, transcendental self-consciousness contains the conditions which make both inner and outer "intuition" possible. "Consciousness in itself is not so much a representation distinguishing a particular object, as a form of representation in general."[8] Regarding the last-mentioned relationship, two wholly divergent interpretations may be found among Kant's spiritual descendents. According to one view, we must see in autonomous "consciousness in general" the "intellectual activity" of a super-empirical ego; the other view makes the ego participate in a super-personal transcendental mind in the most diverse ways. Notwithstanding the divergence of these two views, they agree in one point—the domain of "consciousness in general," "pure consciousness,"

---

[7] *Op. cit.*, p. 220.
[8] *Op. cit.*, p. 216.

"mind," lies in another metaphysical plane than the world of inner and outer experience. Thus the new trialism neglects the evidence of man's existential unity even more than was done by Cartesian dualism. For Descartes the "thinking thing" and the "extended thing" were two *realities,* even though they were totally heterogeneous. Since Kant, man in both body and soul is an object of experience, but at the same time he shares somehow in the transcendental consciousness, and it is this consciousness which makes it possible for him to think of himself as a psychical and a physical object.

The danger of a modern trialism is not imaginary, as we will show by examining the systems of three important contemporary philosophers. It is intentionally that we have chosen three thinkers who differ widely in their ideas and philosophical temperament. They are Heinrich Rickert, Max Scheler, and Edmund Husserl.

3. *The Trialism in the Philosophy of Heinrich Rickert*

Starting Point. The well-known neo-Kantian philosopher Heinrich Rickert took as the starting point of his speculation the dialectics of subject and object. It did not escape his penetrating mind that, although the concepts of subject and object always indicate an inner tension, a distance (and at the same time its bridging), nevertheless the pairs of opposites in which this tension is concretely realized are not always the same. In reality one must take into account a triple opposition—namely,

1) between my body and the world;

2) between my soul and my body;

3) between "the" consciousness and a content of *my* consciousness.

Conclusions. Starting from this statement Rickert is led to far-reaching consequences. He considers it evident that "the" consciousness mentioned in the third pair of opposites cannot be my consciousness, the consciousness of a concrete individual person, but must be a kind of "consciousness in general" of an "epistemological subject." This follows from the fact that "the" consciousness in the third pair of opposites is nowise marked by any concrete lived experience or any particular content of consciousness. Hence this consciousness is a concept correlative to a subject of which *only one* thing can be said—namely, that it is conscious of a content but not of any determinate content. In principle, this concept of subject excludes everything that is capable of becoming an object; therefore, it can be thought only as a concept indicating a limit. All individual psychical facts and therefore also everything which "the" consciousness makes my consciousness must be counted among the world of objects, for "consciousness in general" has no characteristics capable of being objectivized. It is not even permissible to speak in this context of a subject of perceptions, feelings, or volitions, because every further precision as this-individual-here is irreconcilable with the concept of "epistemological subject." Perceiving as well as the perceived, feeling as well as the felt, tending as well as the object which is tended to belong to the realm of the concrete contents of consciousness and therefore must be placed into the category of objects.[1]

Rickert applies the same method to the realm of practical philosophy. In an analogous way he constructs here the concept of a "transcendental duty in the epistemological sense."[2] Thus the sphere of the epistemological subject with its impersonal knowledge and its objectively undetermined will is, metaphysically speaking, wholly different and separate from the subject as a soul and the subject as a body. The human person participates in these three totally different spheres.

Critical Remarks. What remains incomprehensible in Rickert's speculations is by what right we may consider such a person as one and only one person. Rickert likewise neglects the question why we use the same term "subject" in the three above-mentioned cases. Certainly, it cannot be a pure coincidence that it is not only to our body, but also to our soul and our consciousness that we apply the term "subjective," although always in an analogous sense. Starting from this question it would have been easy to find a way to an existential kind of philosophy, but Rickert remained blind to the possibilities opened to thought by this perspective.

4. *The Trialism of Max Scheler*

Max Scheler's trialism is entirely different from that of Rickert. To understand that also with respect to Scheler we must speak of trialism it is necessary to describe more precisely a few important characteristics of his philosophy of man. For this purpose we will

---

[1]Cf. *Der Gegenstand der Erkenntnis,* 2nd ed., Tübingen-Leipzig, 1924, pp. 24 f.

[2]*Op. cit.,* p. 143.

begin with the picture of man displayed by him in his principal work FORMALISM IN ETHICS AND THE MATERIAL ETHICS OF VALUE.[1]

Ego and Person. To understand Scheler's philosophy of man we must take care not to be misled by his very unusual terminology. For instance, what we have called the object of inner perception is designated by him as "the ego." As he explicity states,

> Every ego is given only in the form of a unique perceptive modality—namely, the form of the act of inner perception and the form of diversity which corresponds with it by virtue of its very nature.[2]

In opposition to Kant, he emphasizes that the idea of the ego is not required as the condition which makes the existence of objects possible, but the ego is rather an object among other objects.[3] But concerning the concept of soul Scheler approves the critique of the philosopher of Königsberg. The supposition that the soul is the real supposit of the ego of individual lived events is not supported by phenomenological evidence. On the other hand, the ego which in its own way penetrates into all experience is an "indisputable phenomenon."[4]

When we apply the phenomenological reduction, the ego disappears from our field of vision, as well as the possible soul and the whole real human individual. What remains is the various acts and the nature proper to these acts. If we ask ourselves, What is the performer required by the essence of such diverse acts as perceiving, feeling, evaluating, loving, etc., we discover the idea of person.[5] It is to be noted that the person spoken of by Scheler is neither a psychical nor a physical reality. Scheler does not tire of stressing that his concept of person is psycho-physically indifferent. Person is that which is "required" by the essence of the various intentional acts, i.e. that which makes these acts and their "eidos" possible.

> Person is the concrete essential unity which unites essentially different acts in their being and which in itself (therefore not for us) precedes all the essential differences between these acts, especially the difference between inner and outer perception. . . . It is

---

[1]*Der Formalismus in der Ethik und die materiale Wertethik*, 3rd ed., *Jahrbuch für Philosophie und phänomenologische Forschung*, Halle a. d. S., 1930. Hereafter quoted as *Formalismus*.
[2]*Op. cit.*, p. 389.
[3]*Ibid.*
[4]*Op. cit.*, p. 391.
[5]*Op. cit.*, p. 395.

the being of the person which "is the basis of all essentially different acts."[6]

The person nowise is the permanent and temporally lasting element in the different lived experiences of the ego.

> Since the person effects its existence only in the living of its possible experiences, it does not make sense to try to grasp it in its lived experience.[7]

Only the person, but not the ego, effects intentional acts. Therefore, the person can never become the object of an intentional act. By its very nature the person is never "given."[8]

Act and Function. With the rigorous distinction between person and ego corresponds the distinction of "act" and "function." Acts, Scheler emphasizes, have nothing to do with functions.

> All functions are . . . functions of the ego and never anything belonging to the sphere of the person. Functions are psychical, and acts are non-psychical. Acts are produced, but functions produce themselves. Functions necessarily posit a body and a surrounding world to which their "phenomena" belong. But person and act do not posit a body; and what corresponds with person is a world, but not a surrounding world. Acts flow from the person into time; functions are merely facts of phenomenal time.[9]

Precisely because acts are psychologically indifferent, they are able to have as their object both psychical and physical realities. The intimate connection between acts and person Scheler explains by saying:

> [The person] exists only in the production of intentional acts. Thus by its very nature the person is not an 'object.' Reversely, every objective attitude, whether it be perceiving, representing, thinking, remembering, or expecting, immediately places the being of the person out of reach.[10]

Relation of Soul and Body; Soul and Ego. Scheler tries to establish phenomenologically the difference between psychical and corporeal modes of phenomena. As the criterion he uses the unextended

---

[6]*Op. cit.,* p. 398.
[7]*Op. cit.,* p. 401.
[8]*Op. cit.,* p. 405.
[9]*Op. cit.,* pp. 402 f.
[10]*Op. cit.,* p. 405.

character of the psychical.[11]   In proposing this criterion he develops a very interesting theory regarding the relationship between, on the one hand, soul and body, and on the other hand, soul and ego.

According to Scheler, the ego is a pure "reciprocal inclusion" of lived events, and not the successive or juxtaposed existence of psychical facts in space-time.   Such a "dispersed existence" arises only as the result of the dissociating action of corporeity.   "Regarding the fundamental determination of the relationship existing between the manifoldness of the ego and the body, there are . . . only two possible answers," says Scheler.   "The first is: the body dissociates the 'reciprocal inclusion' of the ego into that which is immediately given in the individual lived experiences of inner perception."   The other answer is that of the associationism of psychological atomism. Scheler rejects the latter, because there is "a psychical manifoldness . . . which represents a genuine 'reciprocal inclusion' in the ego, an authentic being of the lived event 'in the ego,' and not outside it."[12]

Accordingly, Scheler does not recognize any dependence of the functions of the ego upon physical causality.   In the sphere of the ego there rules only the psychical causality of motivation, which ultimately represents a kind of causality proper to the ego.[13]   We do not intend to delve deeper into this theory, but have mentioned it briefly only for the purpose of justifying the interpretation which follows.

Interpretation of Scheler's Ego.   Scheler's notion of the ego corresponds with what is usually called the psychical, but with the difference that he endeavors to eliminate everything which could give rise to a naturalistic conception of psychical reality.   For this reason the phenomena belonging to the ego have to be unextended; for this reason Scheler denies them the mark of "duration," as well as that of localization in space; for this reason also psychical phenomena are not subject to physical causality, but constitute a system *sui generis*, which is determined only by inner motivation.   Thus what remains of the world of lived events is indeed nothing but a pure "reciprocal inclusion" of immanent phenomena.

By means of this structure Scheler wants above all to justify the existence of an "understanding (*"verstehende"*) psychology" along-

---

[11]*Op. cit.,* p. 429.
[12]*Op. cit.,* pp. 433 and 435.
[13]*Op. cit.,* p. 438.

side a naturalistic "introspective psychology."[14] As is known, as early as 1894 Wilhelm Dilthey had demanded autonomy and independence for such an "understanding" psychology, as opposed to psychology which is "explanatory" in the same sense as physical science. Edmund Husserl also frequently argued in favor of "purely introspective psychological" research. The fact that Scheler often uses the noun "soul" ironically and usually in a negative context finds its explanation in this that the noun recalled to him the traditional thesis of the substantiality of the soul, which he felt himself obliged to oppose.[15] On the other hand, he does not hesitate to use even in a positive sense the adjective "psychical" (*seelisch*), as well as its derivative noun "the psychical" (*das Seelische*). This is easily understood if one keeps in mind that from his phenomenological viewpoint "the psychical" is simply the object of inner perception, i.e. the ego with the "manifoldness of phenomena external to its own body."[16]

Thus the disconcerting element in Scheler's philosophy of man lies in this that he has a very peculiar way of drawing the line of demarcation between soul and body, or better, between purely psychical and psycho-physical phenomena. However, if we abstract from this confusing element in his thought, the fundamental characteristics of Scheler's trialism will become at once apparent.

Main Characteristics of Scheler's Trialism. The highest region of phenomena is that of person and his acts. We may identify it with the sphere of the mind, for Scheler says explicitly:

> By excluding the acts (and *a fortiori* the person) from the psychical sphere, we do not want to claim that they are physical. In doing this, we are not in the least impressed by the old dilemma derived from Cartesian metaphysics that "everything" has to be either psychical or physical. . . . But we apply the term "mind" (*"Geist"*) to the whole sphere of acts . . . inasmuch as we apply this term . . . to everything which has the nature of act, intentionality, and meaningfulness.[17]

The next sphere is marked by the " 'reciprocal inclusion in the ego' characteristic of (purely) psychical acts"[18]—an inclusion which is preserved from every naturalistic interpretation. The "layer" farthest

---

[14]*Op. cit.*, p. 438.
[15]Cf. *Op. cit.*, pp. 390, 391, 394, 434.
[16]*Op. cit.*, p. 430.
[17] *Op. cit.*, p. 404.
[18]*Op. cit.*, p. 430.

removed from the mental center of acts is the one which is dominated by empirically verifiable psycho-physical causality.[19] This "layer" obviously corresponds with the sphere of the besouled body insofar as this body can become the object of scientific objectivation.

With this philosophical speculation about man correspond in Scheler's work other analogous distinctions, such as his "stratification" of affective phenomena which, as is known, play an important role in his philosophical thought. Because the class of "sensory feelings" serves merely for the transition from sensation to feelings in the proper sense, it may be omitted. Thus only three categories remain— bodily or vital feelings, purely psychical feelings (pure ego-feelings), mental or personal feelings.[20] With these categories correspond the three forms of love which, according to Scheler, can be distinguished— the spiritual love, which is proper to the person; the "psychical" love of the individual ego; and the vital or passionate love.[21] Scheler justifies this division as follows.

> Although vital, psychical, and spiritual acts are different and are experienced differently even in themselves and not only with respect to their supports, nevertheless they are essentially connected with these supports, the "body," the "ego," and the "person."[22]

From this it can be deduced as certain that Scheler's ego is nothing else than the domain of psychical phenomena conceived as purely immanent.

Scheler's whole theory of human levels clearly is connected with the phenomenon of possible [degrees of] objectivation. The more a thing can be objectivized, the farther removed it is from the spiritual center of man, the person.

> The person is the substantial unity of all acts which a being performs; the person is beyond theoretical knowledge and cannot become a datum of it; it is reached only by the individual's lived experience; hence it cannot be an "object" and still less a "thing." Accordingly, the only objects which can present themselves to me [in the presence of another human being] are 1) the other's body; 2) the unity of his body; 3) his ego and its corresponding (vital) "soul."[23]

---

[19]*Op. cit.*, p. 440.
[20]*Op. cit.*, p. 344.
[21]Cf. *Wesen und Formen der Sympathie*, Bonn, 1923 (hereafter quoted as *Sympathie*), p. 194.
[22]*Op. cit.*, p. 195.
[23]*Op. cit.*, pp. 192 f.

Scheler's classification of values corresponds with this hierarchy:

> All values attached to lifeless bodies *(Körpern)*, our own body and soul can be presented to us as objects . . . , but not as purely personal values.[24]

If we abstract from lifeless bodies *(Körpern)*, there will remain three realms of phenomena in which the philosophy of man is interested, viz., body, soul, and spirit. This division corresponds perfectly with the trialistic conception criticized above.

Critique of Scheler's View. The following remarks may be added to those made above. We have mentioned Scheler's ambitious effort to clarify the connection between the purely psychical and the psychico-physical.[25] But one would search in vain for similar efforts regarding the relationship between person and besouled body. The difficulty is all the greater within the framework of Scheler's thought, because this philosopher admits the metaphysical unity of all life. All forms of life are intrinsically connected, the realm of the living is a single *whole* which only from a morphological viewpoint is divided into different entelechies. Yet the mind is not the result of a biological evolution. Contrary to Bergson and Simmel, Scheler emphasizes:

> The mind is not an "efflorescence" or "sublimation" of life . . ., whether it be considered insofar as it knows and thinks or insofar as it is capable of emotion and volition.

> The person is superior to the body, and its purity loftier than the body, its own and every other "life," which are merely conditions for its terrestrial existence and at the same time matter for its external organization.[26]

Spontaneously the question arises here: If this is true, to what extent can the body still be the body of an individual person? Why is it that the person is so intimately connected with the sphere of the psycho-physical and vital functions? How can the spiritual person, as spiritual, by way of being embodied, act upon the world surrounding him and existing with him? Undoubtedly, Scheler has asked himself this type of question, but his answer is limited to the remark: "For us there is no substantial unity between spirit and life, person and center of life, but only a dynamic and causal unifying bond."[27] How-

---

[24] *Op. cit.*, p. 193.
[25] Cf. *Formalismus*, pp. 411-495.
[26] *Sympathie*, p. 88.
[27] *Op. cit.*, p. 89.

ever, this "solution" is disappointing, because it is wholly out of line with the main features of his philosophy. It indicates a return to the Cartesian viewpoint, which he had so explicit rejected. Descartes' philosophy of man is essentially based upon the thought that man's spiritual and material elements are not united by means of a substantial bond, but through a dynamic relationship. Descartes' "thinking thing" moves the vital center of the body, and reversely the movement of this vital center exercises influence upon the spiritual person. In this we may truthfully see the prototype of a purely "dynamic bond of mind and life." But the structure of Scheler's thought does not allow such an extrinsic connection to be considered even as an emergency solution.

Conclusion. We must conclude therefore that also Scheler's trialism does not take into account the fundamental evidence of man's unity. The opposition between besouled body and the vital soul on the one hand, and the spiritual person on the other, seems to be insurmountable. And as a result this contrast continues to play an important role also in Scheler's later works. We find it there in the form of the typical opposition: powerful drive—powerless spirit.[28] Nevertheless we think that in Scheler himself a first step in the direction of a true solution may be found, namely when he speaks of the spiritual acts which springing from the person develop in time.[29] Although this idea was nowhere developed by Scheler, it does not seem impossible to us to give more depth to this general thought and systematically to exploit its value.

5. *The Double "Split" of the Ego in the Transcendental Phenomenology of Edmund Husserl*

INTRODUCTION

Just as in Scheler's philosophy, so also has there been considerable evolution in the thought of Edmund Husserl. This evolution has left its mark upon his study of the questions which interest us here immediately, such as the problem of the ego, that of internal and transcendental experience, and that of psychology and phenomenology. To the difficulty caused by this evolution one must add the fact that it is impossible to determine Husserl's exact position with respect to a given doctrine without doing some violence to him. For in his

---

[28]Cf. especially *Die Stellung des Menschen im Kosmos,* Darmstadt, 1928.
[29]*Formalismus,* p. 403. German: "die aus der Person in die Zeit entspringen."

philosophical wanderings there is not so much question of a succession of clearly defined periods as of certain currents and undercurrents of philosophical thought of which at best one can say that at a given time a few were predominant.[1] Moreover, as Herman L. Van Breda has recently stressed, a special investigation would be needed to answer the question to what extent Husserl's own explanation of his method agrees with the method he uses as a matter of fact.[2] However, in this study we do not want to enter into a historical discussion and therefore we will limit ourselves to the interpretation of a single representative work of Husserl with respect to the problem that concerns us here. For this purpose we have selected his CARTESIAN MEDITATIONS,[3] because this work owes its origin to one of those rare efforts of Husserl to give a synthetic view of his thought. But, as should be evident from our warning, our critique does not aim at "the" philosophy of Husserl, but only at a single tendency of his thought which for a time predominated.

EXPOSÉ OF HUSSERL'S THOUGHT

Starting Point. As the title itself, CARTESIAN MEDITATIONS, indicates, the starting point of Husserl's investigations is related to that of Descartes. The problem which fascinates him is Descartes' demand for an apodictic foundation of the sciences. This demand can be filled only upon the basis of a "first philosophy" which itself judges and adequately vouches for its own validity. In his search for an apodictic evidence capable of proving the absolutely certain epistemological foundation of the first philosophy, Husserl eliminates successively the various realms of objects given in naive experience— things, men, one's own body, sciences and theories, briefly, *the* world which falls under the *"epoche."* However, this does not mean that Husserl considers the existence of these realms of objects as problematical, but only that he does not make use of these evidences; he puts them "between brackets," because *a priori* it is possible that further experience would unmask their presumed reality as pure appearance. This method he calls phenomenological reduction.

---

[1]Cf. above, Introduction, p. 4, footnote 3.

[2]Cf. the article "Phaenomenologie" in *Katholieke Encyclopedie voor Opvoeding en Onderwijs,* The Hague, 1954, vol. III, pp. 351 f.

[3]*Cartesianische Meditationen und Pariser Vorträge,* edited by Stephan Strasser, The Hague, 1950, vol. I of *Husserliana, Edmund Husserl, Gesammelte Werke,* pp. 41 f. Hereafter quoted as *Meditations.*

Obviously, Husserl follows a path which is related to that of Descartes, although it is not exactly the same. But he deviates from the Cartesian tradition in one important point. Descartes thought it possible to save a little island of philosophical certainty in the midst of an ocean of doubt. One piece of the world he kept, the *mens sive animus sive intellectus,* in a word, the mind. The existence of this "thinking thing" was for him an axiom beyond all attack. He thought that with the help of this axiom it would be possible to deduce all other truths mathematically and thus to reconstruct the universe of the sciences in a critical and rational way.

Descartes' Error According to Husserl. In Husserl's view, it is precisely in this that lies the tragic error of Descartes. He restrained the radicalism demanded by his intellect too soon. He did not study sufficiently the nature of the ego which makes the "epoche." This ego may not be simply identified with the real man, his soul and his consciousness. For when I reflect transcendentally upon myself,

> [I am] no longer . . . the man who grasps himself in his natural self-experience as man, nor the man who by abstraction is limited to the pure data of *'inner,'* purely psychological experience of the self and thus grasps his own *'mind.'* In this way of *'natural'* apperception, I and all other men are objects of positive or objective sciences in the ordinary sense of the term, such as biology, anthropolology and empirical psychology. The psychical life spoken of by psychology has always been conceived as psychical life in the world. Obviously, this applies also to my own life which is grasped and considered in purely internal experience. But the phenomenological 'epoche' inhibits the existential meaning of the objective world and thus completely excludes it from the sphere of our judgments. It does the same with the existential meaning of all objectively apperceived facts, as well as those belonging to inner experience. For me, the meditating ego, which, situated and dwelling in the 'epoche,' posits itself as the sole source of all objective affirmations and justifications, there is neither a psychological ego, nor psychical phenomena in the sense of psychology, i.e. as constituent elements of psycho-physical human beings.[4]

The Nature of Psychical Facts. We have quoted Husserl's own words in full, because they contain everything which is of importance for our question. It is really not difficult to prove that the psychical data, the lived events of consciousness, in one word, the soul spoken of by the psychologist, are given to us in a quite similar way as the other

---

[4]*Op. cit.,* First Med., par. 11, pp. 64 f.

facts pertaining to the world. As we have proved above, we stand *face to face* with these lived events, we consider them, judge them, assign them a definite place in our objective picture of the world. As we expressed it above, they are "at our disposal." The most radical way of disposing of them consists undoubtedly in abstaining from making any judgment concerning their reality. We actually are *a priori* fully able to suspend our judgment regarding the existence of psychical facts. Husserl's reasoning is perfectly consequent when he demands that, once the world has been placed "between brackets," we must do the same with the psychical realities belonging to our picture of the world. Thus we "dispose"of them in the sense that we make no use of our knowledge concerning their existence. We consider them merely as phenomena with which perhaps no reality corresponds. The psychical data are for me no longer anything but *cogitata,* thought things, of my *cogito.*

The Transcendental Ego. It is evident that thus their whole reality consists only in the fact that they are phenomena for me. It is only because of me that they have any meaning left, be it solely as simple appearances-to-me. But I, as the ego of pure *cogitata,* am not a man among men, a real subject, nor even a psyche capable of being objectivized. All this I have eliminated in the course of the reduction. The ego which remains is nothing but the "source from which all objective phenomena derive their meaning," i.e. the ego to which the phenomena appear as phenomena. This ego Husserl calls the *transcendental ego,* and he distinguishes it essentially from "me as a man in the world." For this "man in the world" is "placed between brackets" in the reduction. In his place we find an ego-phenomenon in the midst of a world-phenomenon, i.e. a percept among innumerable other percepts, all of which owe whatever they are to the *cogito* of the transcendental ego.

However, this interpretation of Husserl's teaching is still too succinct. Another detail has to be added, because it is very important for our purpose.

The Three Mental Attitudes. It is not possible to open an immediate and simple passage to the transcendental ego. To arrive at this ego we must assume successively three different "mental attitudes," each of which is made possible only by the preceding one. To explain the matter by means of a simple example, let us suppose that in an act of perception we see a house. As long as we remain in a naive attitude of mind, we "dwell upon the things, in this case upon the house," or as Husserl likes to express it, we "simply live turned towards the world."

The situation is different when we no longer pay attention to the house but to the perception in which the house is given. Husserl calls this mental attitude "natural reflection." In natural reflection that which first was nothing else than anonymous activity is made the object of our description and analysis. The *"id quo"* becomes an *"id quod,"* that through which an object is known becomes itself an object. We are no longer interested in the house. We do not care whether it really exists or is perceived only in a hallucination. What interests us is the lived events *as lived events,* as they are accessible to us in the acts of our own inner experience. If we carefully describe the phenomena of consciousness exactly as they appear to us, we are doing the work of purely descriptive "inner psychology." Even at this stage we must perform a certain "epoche," for we abstract from the dependence of our organism upon certain physiological functions, the existence of our body and that of the surrounding world, etc. In this sense, therefore, purely immanent psychology is a science which parallels transcendental phenomenology.[5]

It is only now that transcendental reflection can begin. The psychical fact of the "perception of the house" does not interest us any more than previously the physical fact of "the house." Where before, in the attitude of natural reflection, we said: what I am interested in is not the real house, but the real perception of the house, we now say, in transcendental reflection: what interests us is not the real perception but the transcendental act which has given reality to this perception. Again, we have changed an *"id quo"* into an *"id quod."* The real ego with its real perception of a house has become an ego-phenomenon and a perception-phenomenon of a house which together with other phenomena constitute the world-phenomenon. The question no longer is, How has a real ego performed a real perception of a house?, but, What is the transcendental activity to which the phenomenon "real ego," as well as the phenomenon "real perception" owe their value? The only possible answer is the constituent activity of the transcendental ego—this activity will have to be described phenomenologically with greater accuracy—for transcendental life is the source from which all "facts," whether psychical or physical, derive their power to be facts-for-me.

---

[5] Cf. 2nd Meditation, par. 14, *op. cit.,* p. 17.

It is only when we realize this that we can understand by what right Husserl identifies his transcendental phenomenology with the apodictic fundamental science or first philosophy.   Transcendental phenomenology is the "unfolding" of transcendental consciousness and its constituent activities in a twofold sense:

> first, as an unfolding of the self in the narrow sense, which systematically shows how the ego constitutes itself as the existence in and for itself of its own essence; and secondly, as the unfolding of the self in the wider sense, which show how the ego by virtue of its own nature constitutes also the other, the objective, and in general everything which possesses an existential value for the ego, be it in the "I" or the "non-I."[6]

Briefly, transcendental phenomenology is the systematic "self-unfolding" of the universal consciousness to which every reality owes the character of its reality.

The "Split" of the Ego.   This philosophical thesis is rich in consequences.   One of them is the fragmentation of man's unity.   Husserl does not try to conceal this, but frankly confesses it.   Nevertheless, his position in this respect is not quite clear.   For instance, in his lectures given at Paris, February 23 and 25, 1929, he characterized the split of the ego as follows.

> Thus a kind of a split of the ego takes place in the phenomenological reduction.   The transcendental spectator puts himself above himself, looks at himself and . . . thus discovers himself as man in the consideration of himself as a *cogitatum*.[7]

In the following months Husserl develops this idea.   He does not speak any longer of one split of the ego, but of two.

> If we say of the ego which naturally perceives the world and simply lives in it that it is the ego which is interested in the world, then the attitude which is phenomenologically modified and constantly adhered to will consist in this that a split of the ego occurs, insofar as the phenomenological ego will establish itself as an *uninterested* spectator above the ego which is naively *interested* in the world. That this occurs will then be accessible by means of a new reflection whose transcendental nature will once more demand the attitude of the *uninterested* spectator who is interested only in adequately seeing and describing.[8]

---

[6]Fourth Meditation, par. 41, *op. cit.,* p. 118.
[7]*Pariser Vorlesungen, op. cit.,* p. 16.
[8]First Meditation, *op. cit.,* p. 73.

Thus the partition of man into three distinct regions is completed. The first of these three regions contains the "ego in the world," i.e. man as a psycho-physical and positively social reality. The second is constituted by the life of consciousness which is free from all naturalistic apperception and in this sense "pure." The third is the region of the transcendental ego, to whose constituent activity both psycho-physical and purely psychical reality owe their existential value.

To this division corresponds the distinction of sciences into three classes—namely, "sciences which are positive or objective in the ordinary sense of the term"; purely introspective psychology, which is distinguished from sciences of the first class by the performance of the psychological "epoche"—also called by Husserl the "phenomeno-logical-psychological" or simply the "phenomenological" epoche—; and finally transcendental phenomenology, to which access is given by the transcendental phenomenological reduction.

Metaphysical Sense of the Ego Split. We would not have mentioned this division here if it had only a methodological value in the narrow sense of the term. But it is precisely in the CARTESIAN MEDI-TATIONS that one can see in Husserl a tendency breaking through to attribute to the results of phenomenology a value which goes beyond the purely phenomenological and becomes metaphysical. These meditations are an important milestone on the road travelled by this great thinker inasmuch as he endeavors to show in them how the systematic development of transcendental phenomenology must lead to a universal ontology.[9] For, according to Husserl's view, to every difference in my constituent intentional activities corresponds a difference in the existence and structure of the things and beings which for me rank as realities; in other words, an ontological difference. Husserl expresses this view in unambiguous terms as follows.

> So a rigorously consequent phenomenology constructs the forms of possible worlds *a priori,* but with a strictly intuitive essential necessity and generality; these forms, in their turn, are constructed within the framework of all possible forms of being in general and that of its hierarchy of levels; all this is done in an original way, i.e. in correlation with the structural *a priori* of the function by which they are constituted.[10]

---

[9] Cf. 5th Meditation, par. 64 *op. cit.,* pp. 178 f.
[10] 5th Meditation, par. 64, *op. cit.,* p. 180.

In the light of these explanations we can only say that to the various splits of the ego resulting from the different reflective attitudes of thought correspond as a matter of fact different ontological levels in the ego.

CRITICAL REMARKS

The question arises again, What happens to the unity of man in his concrete existence? At first, one is inclined to answer: the unity of the human person is safeguarded by the unity of the activity which constitutes the transcendental ego. But this answer is not satisfactory, for, as we have been told above, the ego constitutes not only "itself as the existence in and for itself of its own essence," but it constitutes "in general everything which possesses an existential meaning for the ego, be it in the 'I' or the 'non-I'."

Accordingly, to use the words of Roman Ingarden, there remains "the great difficulty, which to my knowledge no one has ever pointed out, *how one and the same subject can be at the same time the ego which constitutes and the real ego which is constituted,* when the characteristics attributed to these two egos are mutually exclusive and therefore cannot exist together in the unity of an object."[11] This objection of Husserl's former student and follower is fully justified. Within the framework of Husserl's metaphysics transcendental life possesses a creative power—we cannot avoid this term—; the various forms and levels of being, such as "world, nature, space, time, besouled being, man, soul, body, social community and culture,"[12] owe their existential value to the various constituent intentional activities. But then the question arises, Does such a creative mind still deserve to be called an ego? To what extent is this ego finite and limited? To what extent possesses it individuality? Is it still possible to qualify it metaphysically as contingent? Is there no necessity for this ego to exist, to be more than an individual nature, to be eternal and infinite? If the answer is in the affirmative, there will be an unmistakable relationship between the transcendental idealism whose essential characteristics are described by Husserl in his CARTESIAN MEDITATIONS and the objective idealism of the great systematic philosophers.

We may add that later, hitherto unpublished, manuscripts confirm this impression to the extent that the idealistic tendency reveals

---

[11]*Kritische Bemerkungen zu den "Cartesianischen Meditationen,"* quoted in *op. cit.,* p. 213.
[12]5th Meditation, par. 64, *op. cit.,* p. 180.

itself in them. Within the scope of this study it is not possible to analyze Husserl's philosophical unpublished works; so we will restrict ourselves to a single typical passage.

> Man must die, but transcendental original life, primordially creative life and its primordial 'I' cannot come from nothing or be reduced to nothing.[13]

To a certain extent this statement of Husserl answers the questions raised above. "Primordial creative life" manifestly exists independently of man's individual life. The "primordial 'I'" is a consciousness which creates the world. Still, on the other hand, the transcendental life in man somehow participates in the creative principle of the world, for otherwise the particle "but," which marks opposition in the second part of the sentence, would be meaningless. To this extent Husserl's primordial "I" shows a certain similarity with the "objective mind" of certain idealistic systems.

The individual human being, in his turn, belongs, as we have seen, to two different regions of being—that of the pure life of consciousness and that of animal reality. How these two levels of being coexist in the unity of an object we are not told.

Thus we see that what we consider as the human person is in Husserl split in two respects and broken into three parts—the psycho-physical "I," the "I" of immanent lived events, and the transcendental ego. It seems impossible for these three parts to constitute an existential unit. Therefore, we must label also Husserl's thought as the expression of a trialistic trend of philosophy.

6. *Metaphysical Aspects of Modern Trialism*

Neglect of the Unity of the Human Person. Without further comment it should be manifest that the above-characterized post-Kantian evolution of modern thought implies serious dangers. It tends to the complete ruin of the view of man pictured by perennial philosophy. We agree with Max Scheler when he says that one must

> consider as the greatest of all metaphysical errors since Averroes every doctrine which wants to conceive 'persons,' i.e. the concrete centers of spiritual activity, as 'modes' or 'functions,' of a universal mind, an absolute unconscious spirit (Hartmann), a

---

[13]*Fungierende Subjektivität und objective,* stenographic manuscript of the years 1934-35, designated in the Husserl archives as K III, 6. Page 399 of the transcription.

transcendental absolute consciousness (Husserl), or a transcendental reason (Fichte and Hegel's 'pantheism' of reason).[1]

Rickert's themes of thought also evidently must be assigned a place in the ranks of the intellectual movement of a resurgent Averroism.

The opposite procedure, however, seems to us equally open to objection. When Scheler cuts loose, as it were, pieces of the "panorganism through which a single life pulsates,"[2] in order to group them in an arbitrary way around spiritual action centers, he too impairs the metaphysical unity of man. The result in both cases is the same—the most fundamental egological evidence, that of the unity and wholeness of the human person, is neglected.

Source of This Aberration. We must ask ourselves how such an aberration could have originated. So many modern thinkers, who represent otherwise very diverse philosophical trends, admit one or the other form of trialism. This is a striking fact, which offers food for thought. It is irrelevant whether authors place emphasis upon the spiritual ego, as is done by those quoted above, or with Ludwig Klages consider "the mind as the antagonist of the soul."[3] The question which we must face is, What brings these philosophers to make such a sharp distinction between the concepts of "mind" and "soul"? Why do they all reject an idea which for many centuries has satisfied man—the idea of an *anima,* a soul, which at the same time is *intellectiva,* understanding? Why does their philosophical thought dissociate the principle which gives rise to the rational and volitional character of our life as persons from the consciousness given to us in the form of psychical facts?

The answer to this question has been anticipated in our preceding analyses. The evolution of man's picture in modern philosophy since the time of Descartes and Locke evidently has an intimate connection with the problem of reflection, internal perception, introspection. Now in internal experience psychical data, phenomena of consciousness and lived events are given in the form of objects. But what we find in ourselves as object cannot be the principle of our being-directed-to objects. This is a simple truth, which since Kant numerous thinkers have considered as fundamental. These philosophers were so deeply penetrated by this thought that they neg-

---

[1] *Sympathie,* p. 88.
[2] *Op. cit.,* p. 96.
[3] *Der Geist als Widersacher der Seele,* 3 vols., Leipzig, 1932-39.

lected the evident fact of man's unity. The difference between spiritual being and physical being appeared to them so evident that they did not pay attention to the fact that the human person is concretely a mind-and-besouled-body.

We see in this a confirmation of the wise old saying that a one-sided emphasis upon half the truth may become the occasion of a whole untruth. The task of traditional philosophy appears to lie in harmonizing both egological evident facts in one great synthesis. But, as we intend to show in the subsequent study, such a synthesis is not possible within the framework of an objectivistic anthropology.

THIRD STUDY

THE OBJECTIVISTIC CONCEPT OF THE SOUL

1. *Kant's Critique of the Paralogisms and Traditional Psychology*

INTRODUCTION

Underestimation of Kant's Critique by Some Traditional Psychologists. Is, after Kant's devastating critique, a philosophical psychology still conceivable? Has not the Sage of Königsberg conclusively shown that the presuppositions upon which such a science is to be built are untenable? Has he not made clear that every effort in this respect is doomed to failure? Our reply to this question will depend upon our ability to discover the approach to a genuinely metaphysical concept of the soul and a method by which this concept can be adequately justified in a philosophical way. In this respect we believe that a philosophical examination of conscience is necessary. We are far from subscribing to the view of Joseph Geyser, who says:

> We do not have to worry about this demonstration [of Kant], for we, too, profess most emphatically that one can never arrive at the real soul by means of the rationalistic method of research.[1]

Such language underestimates the scope of Kant's reflections. True, his critique of the paralogisms reveals *among other things* that rational psychology is untenable from the viewpoint of method; Kant wants to prove *also* that no conclusion can be drawn from a mere analysis of the principle "I think." But Geyser forgets that according to Kant the "physiology of the internal sense" is wholly incapable even of adequately *raising* the problem of the substantiality and unity of the spiritual ego, because there is question of "conceptions, the object of which cannot be given empirically."[2]

Other neo-scholastic philosophers show a more discerning mind in this respect. They understand the decisive importance which must be assigned to Kant's view of the problem. They know that the question regarding the reality of the spiritual ego coincides with that concerning the subsistent human soul, and that reversely the empirical as well as the philosophical concept of the soul is deficient if Kant's

---

[1]*Psych.*, vol. I, pp. 34 f.
[2]*Critique of Pure Reason*, p. 209.

critique is justified. Therefore, they rise courageously to the defense of their position. But in their zeal they are tempted to overlook the truths which Kant, notwithstanding his negativism, has taught us. As a result, their rejoinders do not always carry conviction. Let us show this by means of a single example, for which we will take Beysens' polemics against Kant.

A TYPICAL CRITIQUE OF KANT

The Basic Principles of Beysen's Procedure. Beysens' critique of Kant contains numerous useful arguments. He shows that Kant's argumentations are nothing but an application of his critique to psychology. He further combats Kant's formalism by drawing attention to the fact that the ego concept is applicable only to a single individual subject.[3] We can still agree with him when he emphasizes that "I think" is grasped only in an experience. But the question is: What is the nature of this experience? As far as Beysens is concerned, it is at once beyond dispute that experience in general and of necessity can have only objective data as its object. As he declares in the beginning of his psychology,

> Because every experience has as its object only facts, the direct data of psychological research will be those facts in which the life of the soul reveals itself, i.e. the concrete activities and states of the soul.[4]

Speaking about self-consciousness he again affirms

> The original internal experience gives . . . never anything else than concrete psychical facts, thoughts, emotions, etc.[5]

The Foundation of the Consciousness of My Ego. The consciousness of my ego reposes upon a similar empirical knowledge, although this experience is initially of an affective nature. Thus in every case my ego is part of the content of whatever is grasped as a fact.

> The content of every consciousness contains, apart from the knowledge of the psychical facts, also that of the psychical subject, the ego.[6]

---

[3] *Algemeene Zieleleer,* 2nd ed., vols. 1 and 2, Amsterdam, 1905 and 1911, vol. 3, Bussum, 1920, p. 20.

[4] *Op. cit.,* vol. 1, p. 4.

[5] *Op. cit.,* vol. 2, p. 181.

[6] *Op. cit.,* vol. 2, p. 173.

Moreover, the lived experience of the ego is equivalent to a consciousness of an affective nature. As Beysens expresses it,

> In our psychical life it is the sensation of the ego, the animal
> consciousness, which provides us with the first impressions of
> our self.[7]

Briefly, I am for myself a particular known (or co-known) object of
a very special nature. Initially the content of this datum is not yet
clearly distinguishable from that of other known data. The stage of
clarity is reached only by means of the considerations of the self and
the reflective analysis implied by this consideration. In Beysens'
view,

> self-consciousness arises through abstraction, in the wider sense,
> or through the analysis of psychical data which originally are
> purely objective.[8]

Concretely this takes places as follows. We compare our psychical
states and activities with one another and discover in everyone of
these psychical data the mark of the ego. If we do this, we will conclude to the real existence of the ego, for "we find ourselves in each
of them." We owe our clear conceptual knowledge of the self to the
reflective analysis of our consciousness of ourselves, which initially
is of an affective nature.

> By means of abstractive reflection upon the impressions of the
> common sense and the analysis of the elements contained in it, the
> intellect forms the idea of the ego.[9]

Others Share Beysens' View. We may point out here that to a
large extent Beysens' view agrees with that of outstanding theoretical
psychologists of his time. We think here especially of the viewpoint
expressed by Johannes Lindworsky, a well-known psychologist. Just
as Beysens, Lindworsky is of the opinion that

> [it is] the ability to abstract, i.e. ultimately the capacity to know
> relationships, . . . which allows us to grasp that our lived events
> belong to the ego.[10]

---

[7]*Op. cit.,* vol. 2, p. 195.
[8]*Op. cit.,* vol. 2, p. 181.
[9]*Op. cit.,* vol. 2, pp. 195 f.
[10]*Experimentelle Psychologie,* 5th ed., München, 1931, p. 201.

In his THEORETICAL PSYCHOLOGY Lindworsky goes even further and constructs a theory of laws governing the psychical contents of lived experiences by taking his starting point in the contents which are least distinguishable, such as colors, tone qualities and intensities, etc. which are barely discernible from one another.[11]

Among the various classes of such elementary contents of experience those pertaining to the ego (*"der Ichzug"*) constitute a special group; "then there follows the vast class of sensations; next that of sense affections, etc."[12] Briefly, for Lindworsky the difference between the knowing of one's own ego and a sense datum is not more profound and fundamental than e.g. that between a sensation and a sense affection.

The Reality of the Ego. However, let us return to Beysens. His arguments against Kant are based mainly upon the allegedly empirical views explained above. Against idealistic agnosticism Beysens emphatically declares

> If we *reflectively analyze* these concrete phenomena of consciousness, we will find in every fact of consciousness as distinct elements, first, the phenomena as such, but also alongside them the same ego which is the support and principle of each of these phenomena. The objective reality of this 'ego' therefore cannot be doubted, for it is an element revealed by the analysis of the data of experience.[13]

CRITIQUE OF THIS ARGUMENTATION

Does Self-consciousness Result from the Analysis of Experience? Beysens' method of argumentation leaves us rather sceptical. First of all, we ask ourselves whether phenomenologically speaking, it is correct that the becoming aware of one's ego takes place in the way described. Is it true that I first have before me a serious of conscious acts and states, then compare these acts and states with one another, discover in all of them as their identical "element" their pertaining-to-the-ego (*Ichzug*), and finally consider this element as the sign that these states are *my* states? In other words, is it true that self-consciousness is based upon experience, abstraction and analysis? Do the processes described by Beysens and Lindworsky correspond with the phenomenological reality? Has our self-consciousness its foundation in abstract processes of reasoning and induction?

---

[11]*Theoretische Psychologie im Umriss,* Leipzig, 1926, pp. 12 f.
[12]*Ibid.,* p. 13.
[13]*Algemeene Zieleleer,* vol. 3, p. 20.

Is Beysens' Theory Free from Contradiction? Moreover, the question must be asked whether or not this whole structure is free from logical contradictions. In this respect it appears rather strange that I should be capable of recognizing immediately one or the other trait as "pertaining to the ego." If I am able to grasp immediately the relevance of a psychical reality as such to the ego, then I must have "known" about myself from the very beginning and do not need reflections, analyses and comparisons.

Is the Ego Known Only Through Abstraction? Beysen's theory offers no explanation for the fact that the experience of being aware of ourselves is essentially an experience of something concrete. In his opinion, it is only through the abstracting activity of our ego that we are aware of ourselves. Of course, it is true that we possess *also* an abstract knowledge of ourselves and make use of it in the most diverse ways. But, as we will show later,[14] this knowledge is secondary and can be conceived only upon the basis of a more primordial consciousness of the ego. This primordial consciousness is undoubtedly a "knowing" concerning something thoroughly concrete, for with respect to my self it is impossible to "leave away" something of it, generalize it, or make it universal, without it ceasing to be my self. Hence it is no tautology when we say that everything I am immediately, I am. We cannot understand how such a "knowing" of the most concrete could be gained from abstraction.

Does Beysens Refute Kant? Finally, we must ask whether Beysens' argumentation can be considered as a refutation of Kant. According to Beysens, the ego is an object of knowledge, although originally this knowledge has a vague, affective character, and its content is not clearly distinguished from that of other contents of knowledge. The important metaphysical point is that according to Beysens we experience the ego as an "impression." We discover the ego through the analysis of objective facts. As if the dismemberment of a fact could ever produce anything but facts! As if the analysis of objective data could ever result in a subjective reality! Such a view is wholly untenable.

The Experience of the Self Differs from the Internal Experience of an Object. Let us demonstrate the point by means of two concrete examples. Take the sensation of pain as a state of consciousness. This sensation is given to me as an objective datum in internal experience, which can be effectively analysed by me. For example, I

---

[14]Cf. pp. 104 f. and 177 f.

can observe that the pain lasts a certain length of time, is localized in my finger, alternately is "burning" and "stabbing," etc. But we ask, Is the fact that it is *I* who have the pain known to me by abstractive dismemberment, as is the case with the duration, localization and kind of the sensation? Is not, on the contrary, the ego the condition which renders such experiences possible at all?

Let us examine the same question in connection with another example, that of an act of thinking. Suppose I want to raise the number 137 to the second power. It is not likely that at the same time I will be able to perform a reflective analysis, because this kind of mental activity does not allow it. However, we may leave out of consideration the fact that there are acts which exclude a simultaneous objective reflection, although this fact has a bearing on the question. In any case, the analysis of the objective data will give results of this kind: I calculated according to this method and not according to that one; first I had a wrong answer, then I corrected my mistake; etc. Such are the results which the dissection of the experience in question would teach me. But now we ask again: Is self-consciousness met in this analysis as an element *alongside* other elements such as the method used in calculating, the correct and the false answer, etc.? No one will seriously make the claim that this is the case. The truth, on the contrary, is that the ego, the "I myself," belongs to a wholly different metaphysical dimension than all *a priori* conceivable data of our objective analyses. The ego is not a fact among countless other facts. It is not an element which together with other elements constitutes the contents of a lived experience. Such an element must necessarily show the phenomenological character of the whole to which it belongs—it is a "this-here" which I discover, an "already there" which I come across. Here lies the weak point in Beysens' critique of Kant, which in other respects is so interesting. It escapes him that the inner experience of my own self differs metaphysically from internal experience whose intentionality is still objective.

Or to express it more accurately, it did not escape him completely. In a passage of his philosophical psychology, where he does not argue against Kant but against Wundt, Beysens remarks

The explanation of the undeniable subjectivation of the ego, which originates from secondary phenomena of a sensitive and affective order, . . . presupposes a previously acquired knowledge of the own ego which manifests itself most strikingly in these phenomena and is already intuitively given when these states are distinguished as 'internal' or 'subjective' from others that are external or objective. Thus every further explanation of this subjectivation is superfluous and impossible.[15]

This remark certainly contains many valuable elements. But if it is correct, it will mean that inductive inferences do not contribute anything to the genuine explanation of self-consciousness, since the development of the consciousness of the ego through the subjectivation of objective phenomena "presupposes a previously acquired knowledge of the own ego." Hence the ego is an aprioristic condition for the possibility of any objective knowledge, and any further explanation, i.e. empirical explanation, of this *a priori* is "superfluous and impossible." Thus it appears that Beysens and Kant are in agreement in this matter.

The Ego is Not an Intentional Object. In our opinion, Kant is in a very strong position when he points out the essential difference between the consciousness of the "determining self" and that of the "self determinable" through inner experience. Of course, Kant does not provide a phenomenological foundation for his thoughts. But this does not exclude that they can be completed in this respect. Phenomenologically speaking, it is immediately evident that any knowledge we have about a conscious being results from our experience of our own self. However, not everything which is usually called psychical, may be classified as self-experience in the strict sense. There are innumerable psychical states, processes and contents which merely "appear" to us, announce themselves, i.e. make themselves known to us. The pain in my finger, for instance, is an intentional object to which I am in a sense *"directed."* Within limits, I am able, as was said before, to "dispose" of it. Between me and the sensation of pain there is a kind of distance of subject to object; the same applies to all the unsubstantial moments distinguished in the sensation of pain which "appears" to me, such as its duration, localization, nature, etc. The sensation of pain, as well as any of its properties, can become an intentional pole. However, nothing like this occurs in the experience of my own self. I cannot at all "dispose" of my self; I cannot place myself at a distance from my self; I do not "appear" to myself in the way a perceived object appears to me; briefly, with respect to my own self, I am not an intentional pole.

Personal and Social Ego. The preceding statement needs to be made more precise. As Johannes Lindworsky remarks, the term "I,"

---

[15]*Zieleleer,* vol. 2, pp. 189 f.

ego, is used in very different senses.[16] Modifying his terminology somewhat, we may speak of a "social ego," a "personal ego," and an "originating ego." By the term "social ego" we mean the person himself insofar as he is a center of social relations. My social ego is determined, for instance, by the fact that I am the father of a family, a citizen of this State, the chairman of that organization, etc. The *personal ego* is nothing else than the sum total of the objective facts which make it possible for a man to form a certain picture of his own person in the physical, psychical and moral sense.[17] I know, for example, of myself that I am of medium height, a bad tennis player, endowed with a lively temperament, etc. The personal and the social ego can "appear" to me in the above-mentioned strong sense of the term. For instance, I can picture to myself how I look when I preside at the meeting of my organization. My social and personal ego are thus made the object of my own cognitive activity. In an analogous way the same applies to my volitional acts. For example, I can ask myself why I am such a bad tennis player and then try to improve my game, etc.

As the just-quoted examples show, the boundary between the personal and social ego is vague, and their distinction is not based upon any essential difference. With Bruno Petermann we can bring together these two egos that are subject to experience under the term "the lived double" *(erlebensmässige Gegenbild),* i.e. "the actual concrete lived form in which the personal structure enters into the realm of lived experience."[18] This "double" I am able to observe, compare and judge; I can determine its value; be satisfied or dissatisfied with it; attempt to change it; etc. By its very nature it can also be eliminated by me; for instance, when I try to raise 137 to the second power, I am not conscious of my social or personal ego. This ego, of which I can "dispose" in a way, which by its very essence I can find and seize as an intentional object, may be compared with Kant's "determinable self."

The Primordial Ego. Nevertheless, this analysis is one-sided, for even my intellectual activity implies a kind of lived self-experience. This primordial grasping of the self, which linguistically is couched in such simple words as "I calculate," or "I have pain," etc., is con-

---

[16]*Experimentelle Psychologie,* p. 200.
[17]Thus our division does not coincide with that of Lindworsky.
[18]*Wesensfragen seelischen Seins. Eine Einführung in das moderne psychologische Denken,* Leipzig, 1938, p. 91. By "lived double" is meant my objectivised (personal and social) ego such as it is experienced by myself (Tr.).

cerned with the "originating ego" *(das entspringende Ich)*, hereafter also called the "primordial ego" and the "ego-source," i.e. *the ego-logical reality from which originates my whole concrete being myself* with all its activities and passivities, its powers and dispositions, its properties and states. This primordial ego is the source of our personal life. It was concerning this ego that the remark was made above that we cannot "dispose" of it, set it aside, get rid of it. This "originating" ego is the subject of the lived experience of the self which dwells in all our acts.

The term "ego-source" should not be misunderstood. Among other reasons, we have chosen this term because it expresses that the "originating" ego is *not* the ego-person with the fullness of his personal life. The very picture implied by the term "ego-source" indicates this, for the source of a stream is not yet the stream, but that from which the stream comes forth. In the same way, the "originating" ego is the *principium fontale,* the fountain head,[19] of everything which the personal and social ego is, accomplishes, and undergoes. It is the *root* of my human existence as ego with the fullness with which it displays itself in its vital surroundings and social environment, but it is not this ego itself. It is related to the personal and social ego as a metaphysical *id quo.* From the logical and ontological point of view, but not from that of genetic psychology, it is "prior," i.e. it is that through which my being-situated-in-the-world-as-ego arises and is made intelligible.

The Primordial Ego is Not an Intentional Object. Thus it becomes clear that the primordial ego cannot be to me an intentional object. If nevertheless I try to make it an object of objectivizing cognitive and volitional acts, e.g. by saying "I have pain," or "As a professor I ought to calculate faster," the personal or social ego is at once substituted for the anonymous source. The social and personal ego may constitute the content of a lived experience or contribute to it. To what extent they do so depends upon the age, cultural conditions, inclination to self-reflection and other qualities of the subject. The "ego-source," on the contrary, is always present, but never as a special object or an objective element. It is not the content of a lived experience, but the "ego living the experience," of which Husserl says that it "refers not to any proper phenomenological datum."[20] In other words, a lived experience is neces-

---

[19]Cf. *Summa theol.*, p. II-II, q. 26, a. 3 c and *Contra gentes,* bk. I, ch. 68.
[20]*Logische Untersuchungen,* 4th impr., Halle a. d. S., 1928, vol. II, Part I, p. 353.

sarily the lived experience of an ego and for an ego, but it is not necessarily the lived experience of the "double." Therefore, only the "originating" ego belongs to the material *a priori* of all contents of consciousness, but not the objectivized or objectivisable ego.

The Primordial Ego and the Soul. We may even go further and say that if such an egological *a priori* can be established in the form of a "source of my thought and action" (Karl Jaspers), it will deserve to be called the "soul." For this hidden root of my human existence is that from which arises my being self-subsistent, living, spiritual, person, etc.; it is this root which makes me possible as an ego-situated-in-the-world; it makes me exist as a psycho-physical reality. Thus my "ego-source" is the active reality (*"Wirk-lich-keit"*), and the only reality with which my human existence as the self fully coincides.

For this reason we think that the question of the primordial ego is intimately connected with that of the philosophical concept of the soul. The correctness of this view will be shown in the course of subsequent investigations.[21]

All this implies that no abstractive analysis of psychical facts will ever be able to lead to the discovery of the "anonymous" ego. This is immediately evident, for it will never be possible to deduce from an analysis of the phenomena a proof for the existence of a subject to which these phenomena appear; it will never be possible to conclude from any kind of impressions to the existence of the ego which receives these impressions. As long as one holds fast to this kind of objectivistic postulates, every effort to show the reality of our spiritual ego will be doomed to failure.

Conclusion. The conclusion to be drawn from our critical considerations may be best summarized in the following alternative. Either my soul is the substantial support of all my contents of consciousness, and then it is not given to me in the way of a content of consciousness; or the soul is given to me in the way of such a

---

[21]Let us state at once that in our investigations we must abstain from entering into a discussion of the philosophical theory of faculties. This does not mean that we consider this theory unimportant. On the contrary, it is our intention to prepare a special publication dedicated to the difficult and delicate problem regarding the relationships of the traditional *potentiae animae* to certain empirical concepts. Provisionally, the term "ego-source" is sufficiently justified here by referring to the Thomistic doctrine that the soul is the formal principle of the besouled being (Cf. *Summa theol.*, p. I, q. 77, a. 6). Introducing here the faculties as intermediary principles would render our explanations extremely complex, without resulting in any change in the principles upon which our views are based.

content, and then it is not the substantial support of all my contents of consciousness.

Passing from the static to the dynamic view, we may formulate the alternative in this way: If my soul is the substantial being which gives a further determination to the psychical data, it itself will not be a psychical datum subject to further determination; if, on the other hand, my soul is a psychical datum that is further determinable or contained in such a datum, it will not be the substantial being which further determines the psychical data. In other words, if I identify the intentionally knowing ego with my soul, then I may not do the same with the object intentionally known by my ego; if, on the other hand, I identify the object intentionally known by my ego with the soul, I will have to seek my intentionally knowing ego in another metaphysical dimension. Unless we want to persevere in uttering ambiguities, we will have to make our choice here.

2. *At the Limits of Intentional Knowledge*

The Crucial Question in Philosophical Anthropology. In the preceding pages we have explained the reasons for our critical attitude. However, as soon as we endeavor to draw positive conclusions from our critique, we find our way blocked by an antinomy of capital importance. Let us assume that, contrary to the objectivistic view, we identify the spiritual ego with the "determining self" and not with the "determinable self." It is easy to express this assumption, but it leads us to the question: How do we know that there is such a thing as a determining self? If our knowing is a more-precisely-determining, how is it that we are able to make judgments concerning that which by its very nature does not belong to the determinable? If we can know the existence of a reality only by means of an intentional orientation to "this" or "that," where do we find the basis for our certainty with respect to the existence of some-thing which in principle is not a possible pole of intentional orientation? With Husserl, we may ask:

> How would we be able to ascertain that 'fundamental fact of psychology' without thinking it, and how would we be able to think it without making objects of the ego and the consciousness aimed at in this ascertaining?[1]

---

[1] *Logische Untersuchungen,* vol. 2, part 1. p. 360.

Nevertheless it is a fact that we mentally possess our "ego-source." If there is anything at all which is necessarily exercised in every act, it will be this internal affirmation of the self, which is, as it were, the egological "cantus firmus" resounding through all our conscious activity. As de Raeymaeker remarks,

> Consciousness of self is nothing outside of the living ego, which feels itself living. . . . I lay hold of myself from within, in the interior clarity which I call up within myself, thanks to the identity of the conscious ego and the real, living ego. I *am* and precisely of this I am *conscious.*[2]

However, metaphysically speaking, what is the basis of this elementary certainty regarding the identity, unity and substantiality of my ego? This question, with all its philosophical consequences, must be raised. It is the crucial point of philosophical anthropology in its entirety.

The Question is Insoluble for the Objectivist and the Idealist. The objectivistic realist is unable to answer this question. If in the realm of the egological nothing else is given to us than objects and facts, the road to an immediate grasp of the ego will be blocked forever; consequently also the necessary conditions for a mediate grasp of the own ego will be lacking.

The question is a stumbling block also for the idealists. If the typically idealistic assertion of Le Roy is true that "an 'outside or beyond thought' is wholly unthinkable,"[3] the idealist will have no objective knowledge regarding thought, consciousness, "transcendental reason"; briefly, he will have no objective knowledge with respect to the transcendental condition for the possibility of objectivity. But, as all sceptics, Le Roy contradicts himself *in actu exercito*, in his actual thinking, because he makes the "beyond thought" the object of a judgment whose truth he affirms.

The Problem Is Not Solved by Rickert, Scheler, or Husserl. Rickert, Scheler and Husserl likewise do not offer any assistance in solving the puzzle. If "consciousness in general" is the condition for the possibility of any concrete act of consciousness, how will it be possible for this consciousness in general to be known concretely in an act of consciousness?

---

[2] *The Philosophy of Being,* p. 13.
[3] *Le problème de Dieu,* Paris, 1930, p. 251.

If Scheler's "person" can never become the object of an intentional act, how is it possible for Scheler himself to make a judgment regarding this "person"?

The dilemma reveals itself most pointedly in Husserl. The simplest way of illustrating it is provided in a comparison made by Husserl himself.[4] According to this comparison, the psychical ego is an objective observer of the animal ego, just as the transcendental ego is the "uninterested spectator" of the psychical ego. But in that case, who will watch the transcendental ego? On whom are the phenomenological analyses based? How will we be able to describe, for example, the constituent activity of the transcendental ego if it is precisely this activity which makes possible the existence of both us, the describing subject, and the objects to be described? Does this not require, as it were, the choice of still another higher observation platform? And would there not be need of a fourth still more distinterested observer who analyzes what the third does? How can we escape in this way from a regress to infinity?

The Road to the Solution of the Problem. Notwithstanding this apparently invincible difficulty, we may assert with feelings of gratitude that nowadays much preparatory work towards the solution of this crucial problem has been done by modern thinkers of both scholastic and non-scholastic trends. This may be illustrated here by means of a single quotation taken from H. Thielemans' study entitled KANT AND SCHOLASTICISM. The quotation reads as follows.

> I am able to consider myself in a way which has neither the empirical nor the objectivized ego as its object, but permits me to grasp myself as the being which is the source, at least the possible source, of acts that are mine. . . . This real noumenal ego may be best described in the words of Jaspers as 'the source of my thought and action.' Here we are no longer concerned with a concept, but with an elementary apperception, which is not knowledge in the proper sense and which coincides perhaps with what we may call the consciousness of our radical spontaneity, of our certainty, definite and indubitable certainty, that something depends on me and on me alone. This ego, then, appears to us as the autonomous and self-conscious source, as the self-possessing source of its actions.[5]

---

[4]Cf. above, p. 52.

[5]"Kant en de Scholastiek," *Bijdragen v. d. phil. en theol. faculteiten der Ned. Jezuieten,* vol. 1, 1938, p. 323.

Here we find the direction indicated in which we must seek the answer to our problem. The alternative proposed at the end of the preceding section applies only to *one* way of knowing—the knowing of "this" or "that," the knowing which at the same time is always a "being-orientated-towards," a "more precise determination of," the knowing which makes explicit. It seems to us that it cannot be subject to doubt that the "ego-source" can never be given to us in the way of a datum of consciousness which "appears" explicitly and therefore can be intentionally seized. Perhaps, however, there is still *another form of knowing than the actual or possible "fulfilling" of a cognitive intention by a particular object-pole.* This is the point which will have to be investigated now.

3. *The Metaphysics of "Being and Having" and the Concept of the Soul*

The Characteristics of "Having." Our position can be justified also by taking different metaphysical views as the starting point. Manifestly, that from which my personal existence in all its fullness unfolds itself must be ascribed to the realm of what I *am* and not to that of what I *have*. What is the difference between these two metaphysical categories? For the answer to this question we may refer to the profound considerations of the well-known existentialist Gabriel Marcel. He writes as follows:

> Ultimately, everything is reduced to the distinction between what one has and what one is. Only it is extraordinarily difficult to express this in a conceptual form. Yet it must be possible to do it. What one has evidently presents a certain exteriority with respect to the one who has. Nevertheless this exteriority is not absolute. In principle, what one has are things or that which can be assimilated to things, and to the precise extent that such an assimilation is possible. I am able to *have* in the strict sense of the term only something which has to a certain extent an existence that is independent of me; nay, the fact of being possessed by me is added to other properties, qualities, etc. belonging to the thing I have. I have only that of which I can dispose in some way and within certain limits; in other words, [I have only] to the extent that I can be considered as a force endowed with powers. Only that which one has can be transmitted.[1]

---

[1] *Être et Avoir*, Paris, 1935, p. 225.

So, according to Marcel, the essential characteristics of "having" are the following:

1) The object of my "having" exists independently of me, at least to a certain extent.

2) It exhibits with respect to me a certain exteriority and foreignness.

3) I am able to have everything to the extent that it has the character of an object (we intentionally widen here Marcel's description of "that which can be assimilated to things, and to the precise extent that such an assimilation is possible").

4) Within certain limits, I can dispose of everything I "have."

5) According to Marcel, I can cede to another only that which I have. We would like to formulate this characteristic somewhat more carefully and positively by saying: in principle, I can get rid of what I have.

I Do Not "Have" My Own Ego. It is evident that this phenomenological description of the reality which in general can become the object of my "having" does not at all apply to my primordial ego. We may say even that *a priori* none of the five enumerated characteristics can be a property of my "ego-source" or my soul. My soul is not foreign to me or independent of me, because it is the metaphysical *principium fontale,* the fountain head, of my personal subsistent being. My soul, moreover, does not have the mode of being of an object, for I cannot "dispose" of it or get rid of it since it is precisely the soul which makes possible all my acts of "disposing" and getting rid of.

On the other hand, we must admit that because of the third essential characteristic I am in principle able to "have," at least intentionally, i.e. in the way of a "filling of an empty intention,[2] everything in so far as it has the character of an object. But, as we have shown definitely, my soul does not have the mode of being of an object; therefore, it cannot be something which I can "have" in any way. However, there is something which I have, namely the psychical phenomena. Thus it follows that my soul is not a lived event of consciousness, not a psychical datum, not an element resulting from the dissection of psychical phenomena, not a structure consisting of

---

[2]German: *Erfullungsbewusstsein.* In Husserl's terminology a purely formal assumption without concrete content is called "empty." The intention is "filled" when it obtains a material content (Tr.).

psychical elements. It is manifest therefore that we must not seek for a solution of our problem in the direction of "having," but in the direction of "being." Contrary to everyday usage of language, we therefore assert: my soul is not *my* soul because I "have" it. My "ego-source," my originating ego, *my soul is that which primarily I am.*

The same result may be reached in another way. To Marcel's analysis of the essence of "having" we may add a sixth eidetic point, which can be formulated as follows: *a priori* I can "have" an endless number of relatively subsistent beings, but *a priori I can "be" only a single subsistent being.*

We do not have to examine here how this *a-priori* is connected with general metaphysical truths, insofar as it gives expression to the absolute value of the principle of *ens et unum,* being and unity. Our statement is immediately evident because of its eidetic character. However, we would like to add the following remark. The data of consciousness always present themselves concretely in the plural. They belong to the objects which I am able to "have" in the above-indicated sense. So the temptation is great to attempt to construct somehow a "psychical ego" out of the manifoldness of the psychical phenomena. But any such attempt will inevitably meet the same difficulties which stopped Hume.

Hume's Error. The critics of Hume have accurately gaged his error and sharply condemned it. Konstantin Österreich, for instance, is quite correct in asserting:

> The explanation of Hume's mistake is that he looked in consciousness for the ego as a separate, independent, and isolated content which somehow stands in the same line as all other contents. But the ego does not do that. It stands outside the line.[3]

However, it is easier to criticize Hume than positively to solve the anthropological problem raised by him. It is not sufficient to speak in this connection of "wholeness," "structure," or "gestalt." From a metaphysical view point such an answer does not solve the question. The view, for instance, that the ego is to be considered as a complex of "gestalts" satisfies philosophers no more than the theory of "bundles" or "collections" of the English sceptic himself. Fundamentally Hume speaks the strict truth when he says that "we have no impression of self or substance, as something simple and individual."[4] The only

---

[3] *Die Phänomenologie des Ich,* vol. I, Leipzig, 1910, pp. 11 f.
[4] *Treatise of Human Nature,* Oxford, 1896, vol. I, appendix, pp. 633 f.

suitable answer here is: do not look among your "impressions," your "ideas," or any contents of consciousness whatsoever which you have. Pay attention to the fact that you *are*. What you have is always a plurality; what you are is necessarily an identical self-subsistent unity. And this is precisely what we mean when we speak of "substance."

The only methodical attitude which will safeguard us from Hume's typical error in our search for the soul is not to start from physiological, psychological or sociological facts. The only possibility to stay outside the "line" mentioned by Österreich is not to join the line. In other words, whoever looks for the essence of the soul must primarily try to investigate what he *is*. One who does not investigate directly his existence does not look for the essence of the soul but for something else.

I am Primarily Soul. This elementary truth may be expressed also in this way. That which I am primordially, i.e. in such a way that no exteriority, foreignness, disposability, plurality and real composition breaks its existential immediacy, that is my soul, my spiritual soul. We have called it the "ego-source," because the soul is that which I am primarily. In other words, I am spiritual soul inasmuch as I am myself absolutely.[5]

This statement applies to the dynamic aspect of my primordial life as ego just as well as to that of its identity. Precisely as "originating" ego I am the same at every moment of my existence; and precisely as "ego-source" I am another at every moment of my life. Metaphysically this fact can be explained only through the meta-phenomenal relationship of two transcendental principles—namely, the "principle of self-subsistency" and the "principle of accidentality."[6] The following text of Gerard Verbeke seems very appropriate to explain the ontological structure with respect to the egological realm.

My *whole* being has a dynamic character. As a self-subsistent being *and* as an accidental being I am constantly modified. But

---

[5]The expression "I am primarily soul," which we have used repeatedly in this connection must not be confused with the more or less Platonic theses "I am only a soul" or "As soul, I have a complete being." In the subsequent investigations we will have an opportunity to inquire in what sense I am also essentially my body.

[6]With these expressions we want to indicate the meaning of the Thomistic concepts of substance and accidents, which are free from all physicalism. To prevent another source of misunderstandings, we will distinguish hereafter also between the self-subsistent being, the "being-in-subsistence" (the *substantia* as *id quod*) and the "principle of self-subsistency" (the *substantia* as *id quo*). In an analogous way, we want to distinguish the "accidental being" and the "principle of accidentality."

this cannot be explained through the principle of self-subsistency but only through the principle of accidentality.

My *whole* being has a character of permanence. As a self-subsistent being *and* as an accidental being I am always the same. But this cannot be explained through the principle of accidentality but only through the principle of self-subsistency.[7]

These expressions correctly indicate the metaphysical structure and at the same time are phenomenologically justified.

It is a misuse of the traditional categories when one claims that the self-subsistent being is found by detaching from it what is accidental being in it.   It is likewise doing violence to metaphysics when with Theodor Lipps one claims that the psychical data are the empirically observable accidents of an otherwise unknown substantial support. As de Raeymaeker emphasizes, "What is given in experience is the real, particular being, and not its accidents."[8] If we want to apply this truth to our egological problem, we will have to say: I *am* the self-subsistent being and I *am* the accidental being. I *am* also the "accidents," namely, insofar as I, the self-subsisting being, am at the same time of a dynamic nature. I *am* they and therefore I do not *have* them, not even in the form of psychical phenomena which can be grasped intentionally.

What, then, are, metaphysically speaking, the contents of consciousness, psychical facts, objects of inner experience? What is that which is spoken of by the introspective psychologist? What is the basis of his idea of the soul? These questions can be answered only at the end of our investigations, for the answer presupposes the solution of a whole series of more profound problems. We will therefore first try to give an essential description and definition of the phenomenon of the "besouled body" (Studies Four and Five) and circumscribe metaphysically by way of reduction the genuine interiority of consciousness (Study Six).   Only then will we be sufficiently prepared to grapple with the epistemological problem which was the starting point of our studies (Study Seven).

---

[7] *Noten by de cursus van Metaphysica,* Louvain, 1945/46.
[8] *The Philosophy of Being,* p. 177.

PART TWO

PHILOSOPHICAL INVESTIGATIONS
OF THE
SOUL AND THE BESOULED BODY

FOURTH STUDY

THE PHENOMENOLOGY OF THE EGO AS THE AUTHOR OF ITS ACTS

1. *The Methodical Elimination of Problematic Concepts*

Any understanding of the essence of the soul presupposes a philosophical clarification of the concept "my body." The reason is that this clarification will have to show whether the familiar distinction between "body" and "soul" is based upon concretely demonstrable phenomena or the "living ego" comprises in undifferentiated unity everything which is traditionally split between the categories of body and soul. If the second alternative is true, man will have to be considered only as a vital whole.

The Inner Tension of the Ego. It would make matters very easy for the philosophical anthropologist if he could make use of the second alternative. But everyone feels that this view is an illegitimate oversimplification of the problems faced by philosophical anthropology. Our life as persons runs its course in a state of inner tension whose philosophical meaning must be explained. This tension can be characterized in different ways, although such a characterization would be at least in part very inadequate. We may speak, for example, of something "internal" and something "external," something "intimate" and "strange," "conscious" and "unconscious." We may try to explain our lack of indifferentiation by means of all kinds of hypotheses, such as the assumption of different substances, different atoms, different chains of causes and effects. But we cannot deny the problem of soul-body, although we are capable of putting it aside in favor of other questions. We can, for example, study how the existing being adjusts itself, grasps itself, "projects" itself, reveals itself, understands itself, etc. Such a suspending of work at the solution of one difficulty for the purpose of devoting oneself to another may be wholly justified from the methodical point of view. We ourselves will repeatedly make use of this liberty. But in doing so one should not forget that the avoided antinomy still remains an antinomy. In the present case the antinomy appears again as soon as instead of investigating the ontological status as a whole of the one who adjusts himself we pay attention to that of "adjusting" and "being adjusted," "grasping" and "being grasped," "revealing" and "being revealed," etc. Manifestly, these expressions indicate nothing else than two poles between which personal existence runs its course in a tension which may assume many forms, but remains essentially identical with itself. It is precisely here that lies the ultimate foundation of the old problem regarding the body-soul.

Anyone who is somewhat at home in the history of psychology knows the numerous and sometimes ambitious efforts made to give from the viewpoint of positive science or philosophy an interpretation of the dualistic and unitary character of our life as a person.[1] The thinkers of Antiquity, the Middle Ages and modern times, but especially the philosophers, phenomenologists and psychologists of the last three generations,[2] have spared no trouble to give a scientific foundation to the concept of the soul. In the critical studies which form the first part of this book we have tried to show why this search of modern thinkers for a satisfactory distinction between the two forms of human existence were bound to remain fruitless. Because of the lack of precision in the fundamental categories it is not surprising that the discussions and exchanges of views give the impression of a Babylonian confusion of tongues. One feels inclined to exclaim: *quot capita tot sententiae,* so many heads, so many opinions.

The Search for an Incontrovertible Starting Point. Because of the innumerable obscurities, ambiguities and the misunderstandings and contradictions resulting from them, philosophical prudence demands that we begin with a viewpoint which is not controverted, a starting point which itself is not a part of the above-mentioned problems. This is a precaution that is taken also by those engaged in research in other rigorous sciences. When doubt arises regarding the meaning of a datum, these men of research ask themselves very sensibly: How did we arrive at it? What was our procedure? What did we measure? and other similar questions. Such a procedure is,

---

[1]For a first orientation we may refer to M. Dessoir, *Abriss einer Geschichte der Psychologie,* Heidelberg, 1911; J. Brederveld, *Het Object der Psychologie,* Groningen, 1933; R. E. Brennan, *History of Psychology from the Standpoint of a Thomist,* New York, 1946.

[2]Concerning these, cf. e.g. L. Binswanger, *Einführung in die Probleme der allgemeinen Psychologie,* Berlin, 1922; R. Müller-Freienfels, *Die Hauptströmungen der gegenwartigen Psychologie,* 2nd ed., Leipzig, 1930; J. C. Flugel, *A Hundred Years of Psychology,* 1833-1933, 5th ed., Duckworth, 1945.

we think, justified also from the phenomenological point of view, for it consists in a regression from the deduced to the original evidences. In an analogous way we want first to secure a starting point that is not subject to doubt by saying: the meaning and scope of concepts such as body, soul, matter, spirit, psyche, consciousness, etc. are subject to debate. Therefore, we will provisionally abstain from making use of these categories, which are part and parcel of the very problems facing us. Evidently, in the search for a definition one cannot appeal precisely to that which itself must be defined. Therefore, for the present we will put "between brackets" such couples of concepts as body-soul, unconscious-conscious, physical-psychical, etc., i.e. we will act as if they were wholly unknown to us. Instead, we will prefer to ask ourselves how we have obtained these concepts. Obviously, this question will be asked in essential generality. Thus it may be formulated in this way: *What in general is required that I may be able to form a concept which is concerned with my concrete being and essence as ego?* What makes it *a priori* possible for me to arrive at egological statements? What condition must be fulfilled before there is such a possibility?

The answer to this question is without ambiguity. To make such judgments *I must be a priori capable of performing acts of which I myself am in some way the source and the object.* This is a fact which has not yet actually been doubted by anyone. Whoever would attempt to doubt the truth of this statement, would come in contradiction with the reality of his own existence. Anyone who were to assert: I cannot perform actions of which I myself am the object, proves precisely by this negative judgment regarding himself that he is very well capable of it. Accordingly, our statement presents itself as primordially evident, i.e. any attempt to deny it leads to the reappearance of the structural relation itself which it is supposed to deny.[3]

However, the scope of this primordially evident statement must be very carefully examined. It is not unintentionally that we have formulated it with so much discretion. We may not assert without any further ado: I am the *sole* source and the *sole* object of my "retroverted" acts.[4]

---

[3]Cf. the author's "Beschouwingen over het vraagstuk der apodicticiteit," *Tydschrift voor philosophie,* 1946, pp. 226 ff.

[4]The author uses here and in other passages the terms *rückgerichtet, ich-gerichtet* and *rückzielend,* which I have rendered by "retroverted," "directed to the ego," and "retro-directed." Translator's note.

It is not even evident in the ordinary sense of the term. Immediately open to understanding is only that the act which "aims" is in a certain sense my act and that my own activity is to some extent exercised upon myself. But for the time being I do know neither whether I am the sole source of this activity nor whether I am its sole recipient. Special analyses would be needed to otbain clarity in this point.

"Retroverted" Acts and Reflection. A second remark is connected with this. Acts of the kind described above are often called *reflective acts.* This term, which is derived from the Latin *reflectere* indicates a kind of "turning back," "bending oneself backwards," "bending backwards over oneself." As we will see, it is not unintentionally that in the philosophical tradition especially thought and the activities of consciousness are indicated as reflective. The term "reflection" is accompanied by the idea of "bending oneself over oneself in thought," "thinking of oneself," "becoming conscious of oneself." But provisionally we do not yet know what consciousness, thought, etc. are, for we have put these ideas "between brackets." Moreover, it is not yet clear to us whether and to what extent the idea contained in the term "reflection" is applicable to our activities. For this reason we prefer to speak of acts that are *"directed to the ego," "retroverted,"* or *"retro-directed."* With these terms we want to indicate the phenomenological appearance of the structural relation that there is something in the act which originates in me and something which reverts to me.[5]

Obviously, in this way our considerations are bound to encompass a much wider area. The expression "acts turned towards the ego" in the above-described sense embraces also such activities as "looking at oneself," "moving oneself," "washing oneself," etc. The essential difference between "looking at oneself" and "thinking about oneself" is not immediately evident. In the present phase of our studies we will not be able to clarify the distinction without making use of concepts that have not yet been justified. We will therefore consider actions turned towards the ego in their entirety and ask ourselves whether in spite of their diversity they have certain com-

---

[5] We do not want to dispute the right of others, especially Thomists, to use a different terminology. Yet the question must be asked whether the limitation of the problem to absolute categories does not result in an oversimplification. In our opinion, the *"reditio completa,"* the complete return, of St. Thomas points to the possibility in principle of a *"reditio incompleta,"* an incomplete return.

mon traits. Is it possible for such disparate phenomena as "looking at oneself" and "thinking about oneself" to show common characteristics? Do they obey definite essential laws? A phenomenological analysis will show that this really is the case.

2. *Phenomenology of "Retroverted" Activities*

A retroverted act is an act of which somehow *I* am the source and at the same time the recipient. I am the reality from which the act goes out, i.e. its subject, and at the same time the reality upon which the act is exercised, i.e. its object. In a mysterious way I am divided without ceasing to be a unity. Something in me functions as subject pole and something else as object pole. We must now subject to a closer examination this ego which is the source and the recipient of retroverted acts.

The Unity of the Subject Pole. The subject pole, as we notice immediately, is always identically the same ego. When I say '*I* look at myself,' '*I* wash myself,' '*I* think of myself,' the term "I" indicates the author of all these activities, who remains all the time the same. The activities may be very numerous, extremely variable and diversified; yet their variation and manifoldness does not impair the identity of their source. In this respect there is no difference between acts turned towards the ego and acts whose orientation is directed towards the "world." Without hesitation, I will say, for instance, that I have washed myself, dressed myself and gone out, without anyone being in doubt whether the subject of the washing and dressing be the same as that of the going out. Manifestly, it is one and the same ego pole which turns sometimes to its surroundings and sometimes to its own person. Even when the immediate support of the activity is a definite organ, we do not doubt for even a single moment that the action itself goes out from the subject as such. No one will get the idea of saying 'my hands wash me,' or 'my legs move me,' but it appears to be evident to us that *I* wash myself and that *I* move myself. The stream of activities goes out from me and in its course runs through different channels—including my own members and organs. My hands do not wash me, but *I* wash myself *with* my hands; my feet do not move me, but *I* move myself *with* my feet. We believe that we know this "I" already. It is the familiar, simple, everyday ego from which spring my being and my acting; it is the ego of undivided subsistence, the numerically identical subject pole; briefly, it is the primordial ego. Accordingly, for the time being we say that *the subject of retroverted activities is always "I," the identical primordial ego.*

The Plurality of the Object Pole. A wholly different picture is presented by the object pole of retroverted acts. Here the matter is not so simple. To give an approximate description of it we will have to draw attention to a whole series of essential characteristics.

In the first place, we notice that here we have to do with a plurality of object poles. The immediate object of 'I move myself' can be identified only in part with that of 'I wash myself'; and the object of 'I think of myself' seems to be still more extended. The multiplicity of the various object poles forces itself upon us. Sometimes their mutual relationship can be considered as a partial or total inclusion of one in the other; sometimes one object pole is "outside" or "alongside" the other. The object of 'I brush my teeth' is not included in that of 'I wash myself' and vice versa. These objects therefore present, at least with respect to my retrodirected activities, a certain independence of each other. Later this relative independence will have to be characterized more closely. Provisionally, we may limit ourselves to this statement: When I consider myself as the object of actual or possible retrodirected activities, I discover in myself something which at first I did not even suspect—namely, an aspect of multiplicity. I become aware of the fact that the numerically identical subject pole is faced with a plurality of different object poles. *I am a unity insofar as I perform an act, and I am a plurality insofar as these acts are exercised upon myself.* We do not yet know how this phenomenological condition must be explained, but later we will see that a great difficulty lies concealed here.

The Foundation of this Plurality. If we try to find on what this aspect of plurality is founded, we will soon discover a certain mutual exteriority of the object poles. One is not the other; one is *at a distance* from the other; one is *outside* the other. This being-at-a-distance assumes sometimes the mode of a spatio-temporal distance, and at other times that of a purely temporal dispersion. As L. van der Horst remarks, "when I turn my regard to my interior, I find *contents of consciousness* which are at a distance from each other."[1] For instance, the idea of writing an article which I had yesterday is not the same as that which I have today. I have modified or perhaps even given up my intention to treat the matter in this or that way. Let us suppose that I really have come back upon my decision to treat the problem in *this* way. This fact does not reduce my first plan

---

[1]"Tijd onder psychologisch aspect," *Tijdschrift voor Psychologie*, vol. 3, 1948, p. 337.

to nothing, for in a sense it continues to exist "alongside" my new plan. I can still recall it; I can compare it with my new thoughts; I can confirm or come back upon my change of plan; etc. Briefly, my former plan still constitutes a possible object pole. However, the term "former" expresses that it is no longer actual and thus indicates a temporal distance.[2] Again, we can see in a sense which is not just figurative but *analogous* that one object pole is not the other; one is at a certain "distance" from the other; in a sense, one is foreign to the other. Thus *the "originating" ego which is always and wholly present to itself is faced by a plurality of object poles which are dispersed in a spatio-temporal and temporal way.*

3. *The Objectivisable Ego as Multiple Unity*

A further precision of the foregoing statements remains necessary. These statements should not be understood as if we consider the ego, insofar as it can become the object of retroverted acts, as a plurality and mutual exteriority of elements without any further qualification. In this respect we must carefully distinguish the situation which exists on the part of the subject from the one which characterizes the objectivisable ego. At once it seems evident that I as the performer of my acts am always the same, undivided, numerically identical subject. But the same cannot be said of the object-ego, for *retroverted acts do not reach me immediately but only mediately.* Everyday language clearly expresses this. Certainly, it is no accident that we usually say 'I shave myself,' and not 'my hand shaves me,' while on the other hand we may say also 'I shave my beard,' but not 'I shave myself in the area of the beard.'[1] What I want to indicate by the words "my beard" is not, at least not primarily, a possessive relationship, for I do not possess my limbs and organs in the same way as I possess three or four pairs of shoes. By putting "my" before "beard" I want to express this: the retroverted activity of shaving is exercised immediately upon the beard, but insofar as this beard belongs to my person, i.e. insofar as it is *my* beard, the activity concerns me in a mediate way. This assertion applies universally to all egological object-poles. No matter how numerous and diverse they may be, how clearly they reveal that they are outside one another and diverse, they all share

---

[2]Concerning the possibility and the good right to disengage such object poles by abstraction, see section 5, pp. 94 ff.

[1]I have changed the original example *"sich kämmen"* to one which can be used reflexively in English (Translator's note).

in the unity of the primordial ego. In this sense the beard I shave is "my" beard; the representation I form is "my" representation; and the decision I came back upon is still "my" decision. The immediate objects of my retroverted acts are sometimes *this* and sometimes *that;* they are divided, ordered and arranged now in a spatio-temporal way and then in a purely temporal respect. But what I reach in this way is always *my* object poles. Thus the plurality and dispersion of my retroverted acts is limited and contained by the unity of my primordial ego. What I attain immediately with my retroverted acts is diverse realities that are "outside" and "alongside" one another, but the mediate recipient of all these acts is I myself as their anonymous ontological center. Accordingly, we may characterize the phenomenological situation as follows. *As subject pole I am a unity, and as object pole I am a plurality in a unity, a "unitas multiplex,"* i.e., as we will say from now on, a multiple unity (W. Stern). Here again, it is manifest that a great conceptual difficulty lies hidden behind these words. However, provisionally we will limit ourselves to the description and analysis of what is given in itself. Phenomenologically speaking, the object-ego appears divided into many diverse realities, although, on the other hand, these realities are connected and united into a whole.

4. *The Objectivisable Ego as Imperfect Interiority*

"Actio" and "Factio." The preceding static analysis needs to be complemented by an investigation of the dynamism of retroverted acts. In this connection we will have to raise the difficult question which was avoided at the beginning of this chapter—namely, whether the retroverted act belongs to the category of immanent acts or to that of transcendental acts. Is the ego-directed act, in the words of St. Thomas, an *actio,* a doing? Can we say of it *"sistit in operante,"* it stays in the agent? Or is it a *factio,* a making, and must we say of it *"transit in exteriorem materiam,"* it passes over into external matter?[1] Is the retro-directed act a *reditio completa,* a complete return, in the strict sense of the term, i.e. an act which is produced by me alone and has its one and only object in me? Am I, the source from which it springs, at the same time its recipient? Or is such an act comparable with the motion of a billiard ball, which transmits its impetus to another ball? Does such an act end by being "lost," "absorbed" by "the other," by that which is outside me?

---

[1] *In II sentent.,* d. 23, q. 2, a. 4, sol. 1, *ad* 4.

A Retroverted Act Is Not a "Factio." Let us examine the problem first from the side of the object-ego. Manifestly, we may not identify our retroverted acts with *facere*, making, for a characteristic of the kind of act investigated here is that it is not directed towards the "world" and "worldly" objects. Its effect is, as we have noted before, evidently experienced in ourselves. Accordingly, we may claim of the ego-directed act that "it does not pass over into external matter."

Does the retro-directed dynamism remain wholly within us? Does its effect not radiate around us? Does it reside wholly in the performer of the act? Is its source at the same time its term?

The Case of Self-Motion. To answer these questions let us take the case of a simple self-motion. It is true that *I* am the one who moves as well as that I am the one who is moved. But is this description not somewhat too summary? When I raise my arm or stretch out my leg, I have to overcome a resistance which clearly does not come from me, i.e. not from me as the performer of this act. For I am the one who wants to perform this motion, and therefore I am not the one who resists its execution. Does this resistance originate from another being or perhaps many other beings? I do not know, but in any case it comes from the "world." It is a non-ego which I meet in my ego. Insofar as the overcoming of this resistance belongs to the execution of my motion, my action is concerned with the world and does not remain in me. Thus with respect to the retroverted act we may not simply affirm that it "remains in the agent." Physiologists, anatomists and physicists will be able to give all kinds of learned explanations for it by calling the inner resistance muscular tension, friction, inertia, gravity, etc., but from our phenomenological viewpoint all these explanations are irrelevant. The only thing of importance for us is that we must partly disavow our previous affirmation. In the broad sense in which the formula is used here, we must now say that the retro-directed act "passes over into external matter."

Objective Self-Knowledge. What has been said above with respect to self-motion applies also to other retroverted acts, such as objective knowledge of oneself. Is it not true that in our effort to arrive at objective intentional knowledge of ourselves we encounter difficulties that are similar to those which oppose our knowledge of the world? When, for instance, I look at myself, I can reach with my regards only a part of myself, and even this part I can see only from a definite angle. Moreover, it is clear to me that one seen part is not the other, that one is "at a distance" from the other. I do not see myself in my entirety; I am not wholly "transparent" to myself; I am unable to obtain an integral knowledge of myself. As an objectivisable ego I "appear" to myself always in a definite "perspective." Although this "perspective" is not like that of "worldly" objects, it shows a genuine analogy with it. In an analogous sense we must speak of "perspective" with respect to intentional self-knowledge. *Later* I will no longer see myself as I appear to myself *now,* in this light, in this posture, in this vital and social situation. At a different moment I will necessarily receive a different impression of myself. Of course, I never consider myself in the same way as an entirely foreign thing, and it is true also that my objective self-knowledge will always be complemented by another source of self-knowledge. Nevertheless, to the extent that my ego-directed cognitive effort aims at "objects," it realizes itself under "worldly" conditions, such as dispersion, perspective, "profile," etc. Accordingly, even in the realm of self-knowledge I encounter the non-ego in the ego.

Temporally Dispersed Acts. It is to be noted that the same is true if the objects of my self-knowledge are not dispersed in a spatio-temporal way but merely temporally. Everything that is temporally given changes, fades and disappears in time. As we have pointed out before, a perception, a representation, or a decision—insofar as such phenomena can be isolated by abstraction—change in form and character, as it were, before our very eyes. This is primarily an effect of the continual change of temporal perspectives. The "now" overshadows and covers the "now" which was a moment ago and opposes itself also to the clear grasp of the "now" that is coming. The actual temporal object pushes aside the object which is no longer actual, and this, in its turn, exercises pressure upon the object which has barely become actual, etc. And what is becoming actual, already throws "its shadows forward" upon that which actually is. What they used to express by the old term "stream of consciousness" is nothing else than the result of this dynamism of the actual. For an illustration of these essential relations we may refer again to our analysis of decision. Our actual plan slides, as it were, over the previous decision which was given up; yet this project that is pushed into the background somehow remains present to me—namely, as the possible object of a retroverted act.

Emotional "Relief." The dispersion in time plays an important role in the formation of a "relief" of actualities, but it is not the only determinant factor. We may not present matters more simply than they are. In reality, apart from the temporal "profile," there is also an emotional profile. However, the phenomenology of emotional life is so complex and has been given so little systematic exploration that we must restrict ourselves merely to drawing attention to it. We want to state simply that it is not always necessarily the last lived event which possesses the greatest actual strength. For example, I can continue to add numbers "mechanically," while this activity is completely overshadowed and emotionally dominated by an irritating event which took place some time ago. Suppose someone has threatened me in a brutal way. In such a case, my anger, my shame and my fear are the factors which dominate, even when some time has passed since the threat. A whole series of objects has kept me busy since, but in a peculiar way they lack the strength to capture my attention. The emotional shock has disturbed my former hierarchy of degrees of actualities and replaced it by a new one. It has contributed decisively to change the character of all possible objects of retro-directed activities. Clearly, temporal perspective and emotional perspective cross and contribute independently to the formation of the "relief" of my egological actualities.

An "Idol" of Self-Knowledge. We will abstract here from the problems of affective and emotional life, which would require a special study. They have been mentioned here only in order to contradict Husserl when he asserts

> The *lived event* does not present itself . . . by perspective. This implies that the perception of a lived event is the simple vision of something which in its presence, in each moment of its 'now,' is given (or can be given) in perception as 'absolute,' and not as an identical aspect which detaches itself from its modes of appearance through one-sided perspective.[2]

It seems to us that this assertion is not in agreement with the phenomenological situation. Let us return once more to our analysis of the project that has not been executed. In the various moments of its "now" this spiritual lived event (my plan to write the article) appears to me in my "perception of the lived event" now as useful and then as useless, now as profound and then as shallow, now as too extensive and then as too short, etc. Similar remarks can be made with respect

---

[2] *Ideen zu einer reinen Phänomenologie und einer phänomenologischen Philosophie*, Vol I, edited by W. Biemel, vol. III of Edmund Husserl, *Gesammelte Werke*, The Hague, 1950, par. 44, p. 101. Hereafter quoted as *Ideen.*

to the lived experience of being threatened. The threat, which yesterday seemed so fearful to me, today appears perhaps as ridiculous, etc. Nevertheless, it remains the same emotional lived-event, just as the plan or decision remains identically the same this-one-here to which, as we have seen, I can always come back. It is the same, not in spite of but *because of* the continual change of form and *because of* the continual alteration of affective timbre. Accordingly, we think that it is necessary to widen our concept of "perspective." Contrary to Husserl's assertion that what is "given in perspective" is "in principle possible only as spatial,"[3] we assert that it is possible also as temporally dispersed and in general as something which is not, not yet, or no longer, wholly present with itself, as something which fits in with the possibilities of a "worldly" situation. For this reason we would like to say of the lived event exactly the same as Husserl observed with respect to the thing—namely, that by virtue of an essential necessity there corresponds to it an empirical consciousness of the same [event], as perceived under all its aspects, which in a continuous and unified way confirms itself, and that this empirical consciousness is based upon a complex system of diverse forms of appearances and perspectives.[4] The privileged gnoseological position of so-called immanent phenomena is therefore at most a question of degree and not one of principle, and gnoseological optimism here is not supported by a philosophical analysis. Not without reason did Max Scheler warn us against such "idols of self-knowledge" and declare emphatically:

> There is perhaps nothing which constitutes such a fundamental obstacle to knowledge of the soul in any form as the opinion, which is commonly accepted by many men of research and philosophers of our times and the recent past, that in contrast to the external perception of nature, internal perception cannot be deceptive, and that lived events coincide with the evident and adequate knowing of these events.[5]

In passing we may mention that all objections which have been raised against the introspective method of the "pure psychology of immanence" can be fully reduced to two topics. First, the question is whether an object pole of self-knowledge, notwithstanding its deformation by its temporal perspective, can be described correctly

---

[3]*Ideen,* vol I, par. 41, p. 95.
[4]*Ideen,* vol. 1, par. 41, p. 93.
[5]*Die Idole der Selbsterkenntniss,* in *Vom Umsturz der Werte,* vol. II, 2nd ed., Leipzig, 1919, p. 7.

enough to become the object of strictly scientific judgments. Secondly, it must be determined whether the formation of emotional profiles does not prevent objective observation. Nearly all arguments which since Auguste Comte have been adduced against the introspective and retrospective methods draw their strength from these two considerations. However, we will not examine these questions here. They were mentioned only to show that our problem is neither incidental nor new, but results from the very essence of retro-directed acts of knowledge.[6]

5. *The Objectivisability of the Temporal Ego*

TWO EXTREME VIEWS

Bergson and Münsterberg. It is time to mention certain objections which perhaps can be raised from the standpoint of the psychology of totality. A proponent of this type of psychology may point out that we have no right to speak of temporal objects. What is a continuous flux, he will assert, what is subject to a total change of character, what steadily flows by and finally disappears, *is* not; at least, it does not exist in the manner of an object. By speaking of temporal objects we make "things" out of the phenomenal world of the interior. Temporal reality consists exclusively of a Heraclitian stream in which everything changes into everything. Probably such a psychologist will quote Henri Bergson's words:

> The apparent discontinuity of the psychical life is due to our attention being fixed on it by a series of separate acts. . . . True, our psychic life is full of the unforeseen. A thousand incidents arise, which seem to be cut off from those which precede them, and to be disconnected from those which follow. Discontinuous though they appear, however, in point of fact they stand out against the continuity of a background on which they are designed, and to which they owe the intervals that separate them; they are the beat of drums which break forth here and there in the symphony. Our attention fixes on them because they interest it more, but each of them is borne by the fluid mass of our whole psychical existence.[1]

H. Münsterberg goes even further. According to him,

> [The psychical] in a way is the residue which remains when one has disengaged and abstracted that which in the various experiences can be identified and consequently has a causal interconnection.[2]

---

[6]Cf. K. Oesterreich, *Die Phänomenologie des Ich,* pp. 274-305.
[1]*Creative Evolution,* New York, 1911, pp. 2 f. Cf. also *Essai sur les données immédiates de la conscience,* Paris, 1889, pp. 104-108.
[2]*Grundzüge einer Psychologie,* vol. I, *Die Prinzipien der Psychologie,* Leipzig, 1900, p. 88.

Haas. Diametrically opposed to these ideas is the view of W. Haas, who without the slightest hesitation speaks of a world of psychical objects.

> We are born into a psychical world, a world of psychical things, which we find waiting for us and simply take over. These psychical things belong to our immediate and more remote surroundings, i.e. the ideological and affective orientation and complexes of family, social environment, country, time, etc. We take them over 'ready-made,' accepting them consciously or unconsciously, and begin by living in them. By modifying and changing them we build *our own* psychical life, i.e. ourselves as psychical existences.[3]

Our own psyche, "i.e. the things which are the property of our ego and constitute its psychical body,"[4] are not more than a part of the objective world of psychical reality.

Can Temporally Dispersed Realities Be the Object of Retroverted Acts? Against these two extreme views we have to determine our own position. In doing so, we want to leave out of consideration the question of psychical causality, intensity, etc. As should not be forgotten, we do not yet know what is meant by "psyche," "psychical," and other similar terms, because provisionally these terms have been "placed between brackets." Likewise, we do not have to determine here in a theoretical way the nature of consciousness. Our question is simply: Can temporally dispersed and extended realities be the object of retroverted acts? Can such objects be identified? Are they real or possible object poles of repeatable acts of the same or of a different quality?

Equivocity of the Term "Object." Before attempting to answer these questions, we must clear away a misunderstanding. It is to be noted that the term "object" may be used in different senses. For many thinkers an object is necessarily a thing, something which is quantitatively determinable and measurable, something material. As we have explained elsewhere,[5] this usage of the term is not to be recommended. For us an object is any reality which *a priori* is capable of becoming the pole of an intentional orientation for a subject. Thus an object does not necessarily have the mode of being of a "thing." All that is needed is that it can play explicitly the role of an intentional pole. Obviously, even in this wider sense, an object

---

[3] *Die psychische Dingwelt,* Bonn, 1921, p. 42.
[4] *Op. cit.,* p. 90.
[5] *Objectiviteit en Objectivisme,* Nymegen-Utrecht, 1947.

is identifiable, for otherwise it would be impossible for us to become or to remain intentionally directed to it. We would not be able to recognize the object as the *same,* orientate ourselves internally to it, and return to the *same* object after we have performed other acts. But the *a priori* possibility to identify the object includes the possibility to distinguish it. It belongs to the essence of an object to be really distinct from other objects, for it is able to function as an intentional pole for me only because in some respect it "stands out" against other objective realities. Only a *"this-here"* which delineates itself against a *"that-there"* is *a priori* capable of becoming the object of an internal orientation.

The Distinction of the Objects of Retroverted Acts. In this sense it can be asserted, we think, that all possible objects of my retro-directed acts are phenomenologically distinct or distinguishable from one another, for they all stand out against their spatio-temporal or purely temporal environment. The proof of this assertion is not difficult. Münsterberg would hardly have succeeded in writing books if he had not been able to retain an idea, a representation or a train of thought, to return to such an idea etc., combine it with others, and synthetize them. But all these activities presuppose as a first and most elementary condition the identification of the idea, representation or train of thought in question. Accordingly, realities which are given in a purely temporal way are certainly capable of being identified, and not at all fused together into a single "amorphous" mass of lived events. The so-called "stream of consciousness" likewise is not an all-engulfing chaos. True, this stream reminds us of Heraclitus' problem, because it puts the phenomenon of becoming before us in the clearest possible way. But do we meet this phenomenon only in the objects that are given in a purely temporal way? Is it not true that we encounter them also in the spatio-temporal world? Would we have any possibility at all of knowing anything concrete if what is in the process of becoming is not identifiable? In reality, we grasp developing and changing objects because of their relative self-sub-sistence. Everything which in any respect possesses a certain in-dependence stands out against the rest and can be identified as such as long as it retains this relative self-subsistence.[6] For this reason it is possible to draw relatively distinct "waves" out of the stream of consciousness, to identify them and to make them objects of inten-tional acts.

---

[6]An analogous assertion applies with respect to relatively distinct accidents which are found "in" or "on" the self-subsistent being.

CRITIQUE OF THE EXTREME VIEWS

Bergson. In the preceding part we have already indicated our position with respect to Bergson's views. The importance of his "lived duration" will be evaluated later. Meanwhile it seems undoubtable to us that relatively distinct phases, forms and structures are delineated in continuous development. Of course, these distinct, relatively independent unities may not be compared with the individual pearls of a necklace. It is only by means of abstraction that we are able to single out definite stages and characteristic moments in the continuous process of becoming. However, this does not mean that the singling out is arbitrary; that the really given does not offer a motive for such an abstractive act. True, it is only through abstraction that we can distinguish the child from the boy, the boy from the young man, and the young man from the adult. Nevertheless, this abstraction is not accidental but motivated by definite typical moments in the course of the development itself. It is an *abstractio cum fundamento in re,* an abstraction with a foundation in reality.

In an implicit way Bergson himself acknowledges this. To limit ourselves to his own example, when we fix our attention upon the drum beats, we do not do so accidentally, but for definite reasons. The drum beats stand out against all other sounds of the symphony, for instance, because they are louder, have a different timbre, or accentuate a special part of the rhythmic flow. Briefly, they really distinguish themselves from the other sounds of the symphony. In a similar way it happens continually that in the course of "real duration" important moments and phases stand out which are distinct from others as relatively independent phenomena. Nowadays most psychologists readily admit this. As Buytendijk expresses it,

> Although we are not able to know subjective *qualities* in an objective way, nevertheless we know so much about contents of consciousness, thoughts, motives, phantasms, dreams, etc. that they can become objects of our intellect. In this sense there is an objective psychical world, which we are able to correlate with our own psychical experience and with the perceptible physical world.[7]

The facts to which Buytendijk appeals here are all familiar to us. *Ab esse valet illatio ad posse,* from the fact we may conclude to the

---

[7] *Algemene theorie der menselijke houding and beweging,* Utrecht-Antwerp, 1948, p. 53. Hereafter abbreviated as *Houding.*

possibility. It is of no use to deny the possibility of something which we are doing all the time.

However, we can agree with Bergson insofar as he took a stand against the naturalism and physicalism of his times. With him we want to emphasize that the relatively subsistent of which we are speaking consists neither in "psychical elements" nor in "atoms of soul." What we are speaking of are entities which are "detached" (*Abgehobenheiten*) but not "things." Their ontological value will have to be determined later.

Haas. For the same reason we must reject also the view proposed by Haas. The very term "psychical thing" itself seems very misleading to us, for the essential marks of a *res,* a thing, are totally different from those of temporal objects. The thought also that I can "take over" such psychical things, that they should belong to my "possessions," just as realities of the world, makes a strange impression. How untenable such a conception is has been shown above in our phenomenological analysis of "having."

CONCLUSION

Summarizing, we may say that the romantic psychology of Bergson and Münsterberg agrees with the data of phenomenology as little as do Haas' reifications. We want to abstain from all one-sided views and merely describe faithfully what appears. But then we must observe that temporal reality is differentiated, formed and structured in many ways; that it reveals a relief of actuality which changes all the time, as well as changeable temporal and emotional perspectives; and that the transition from one perspective to another takes place by means of innumerable figurations. This structural complexity of temporal reality allows me to turn myself internally towards a definite "delineated object" and later to revert to this same object. As we had suspected from the very beginning, the objective aspect of the ego includes, alongside spatio-temporal poles of actual and possible retroverted acts, also others which are dispersed merely in time. Accordingly, in this sense we may speak of temporal objects.

6. *Phenomenology of Quasi-Objective Reality*

The Non-Ego in the Ego. Let us now return to the problem which was our starting point. The multiplicity of mutually distinct real or possible temporal objects allows us to make these objects the terms of retro-directed acts of knowing and willing. On the other hand, this plurality of distinct realities which present different profiles in a temporal perspective is not given to me at once. We encounter here the phenomenon of mutability, distance and foreignness, and, as we have seen, this phenomenon is genuinely analogous to "worldly" phenomena of the same order. Here again we have to say: if I am the self-exploring ego which tries to arrive at a sharp delimitation of temporal objects and to retain them unchanged in its grasp, then I am not the ego which gives rise to the kaleidoscopic variations of temporal and emotional perspectives, to the ceaseless changing, the fading and blending of innumerable nuances. Insofar as my cognitive act has to overcome these resistances, it is struggling against "wordly" obstacles. Here too, I encounter the non-ego in the ego. My endeavor to know myself does not remain wholly "in" me; there is always something of it which is directed to the realm of the "world."

Something analogous applies to the ego-directed acts of willing. They also encounter a particular resistance, which does not seem to originate "properly" in me. When, for example, I want to "pull myself together" for a certain purpose, I have the impression that my task consists in trying to overcome the non-ego in the ego. This is a well-known familiar experience. Accordingly, our retro-directed effort always and necessarily meets in ourselves something of the "world" and "worldly" laws that are foreign to the ego.

Quasi-Objective Reality. It is time, however, to characterize somewhat the objects of retro-directed acts, for obviously the categories *subjective-objective, immanent-transient, and primordial-reflective* are not sufficient to give an adequate description of the facts. We ask ourselves therefore what these peculiar objects are which belong to the ego, but also to the non-ego. What shall we call something which is no more an object of an *agere* than of a *facere?* What sort of beings are these realities which constitute a plurality, but also a multiple unity? realities which reveal themselves somehow as self-subsistent, but only in a relative sense? realities which possess a certain foreignness and strangeness to the ego, but not the same foreignness and strangeness as the things and beings of the surrounding world? A term is needed to characterize this special mode of being which is proper to me insofar as I am the object of retro-directed acts. Manifestly, this mode of being lies midway between the domain of *agere* and that of *facere.* It cannot be considered as either immanent or transient, but shows certain features of both. In many respects it seems to be "worldly," yet it cannot be simply ascribed to the "world." It is clear that I am never an object for myself in the same sense as another being or thing; nevertheless with my retro-directed acts I do not reach my primordial ego immediately. I am for myself an as-it-were-object, an as-if-object, an almost-object, or, as we shall say it from now on, a *quasi-object*. Accordingly, all concrete intentional poles of my real or possible retroverted acts are quasi-objects. As "originating" ego I have with them a quasi-objective relationship.

7. *Characterization of the Subject Pole of Retro-Directed Acts*

The Dependence of the Ego on the "World" in its Retroverted Acts. We will now raise the question whether within the framework of a metaphysics of finite being the subject of retroverted acts can be considered as their absolute source. An examination of the question shows that this is not the case. The ego is not the absolutely creative source of retro-directed acts. All the time it is forced to seek support, aid and complementation in the realm of objects and quasi-objects. Activities such as looking at oneself, washing oneself, moving oneself, etc. are possible only in a surrounding world, a living space, and with the aid of "worldly" objects. Even the apparently pure act of thinking of oneself cannot be performed without the ego appealing continually to objects and quasi-objects. When I think of myself, I try to form an image, of myself in the form of a synthesis, made of all kinds of impressions, representations, thoughts, etc. In addition, I have apprehended myself in all these representations and thoughts as a personal and social ego in function of my corporeity, my surroundings, my fellow men. If, for example, I take the resolution "to improve myself," I will do so because of an experience, an occurrence, or an advice, which ultimately are an experience in the world, an occurrence in a social situation, an advice of another being. We must therefore admit that for all our retro-directed acts we count on a contribution from the non-ego. Thus I am not the one and only foundation from which my retroverted acts originate. To indicate their origin with greater precision I will have to say: I bring them forth insofar as I am enmeshed in quasi-objects and objects. Of course, as primordial ego I am the true source of these acts, but not without the necessary relations I have to non-ego realities. Accordingly, I am the original author of my retroverted acts, but not in a sovereign way.

Man Is a Relatively Immanent Being. Therefore, in this way also we arrive at the conclusion that retro-directed acts are not of a truly immanent nature. True, there is always something in them which goes out from me, and something which returns to me. But we must not forget the correlated truth that in every retro-directed act there is also something which goes out from the "world," and something which returns to it. Clearly, concrete man is no more a closed monad than he is a simple moment in a steady flow of development. He is neither *actor,* doer, nor *factor,* maker. The expression *"sese movet,"* he moves himself, cannot be applied to him in the strict sense; likewise, the cosmological principle *"quidquid movetur ab alio movetur,"* whatever is in motion is moved by another, does not apply to him without qualification. The performer of retro-directed acts stands somewhere midway between these two absolute categories. To a certain extent, he shows himself closed, yet in a way which allow a measure of receptivity. He unites self-sufficiency with want; his independence is mixed with dependence. How these contradictions can be reconciled we do not yet know. Provisionally we restrict ourselves to the statement that man as the performer of retro-directed acts must be considered as an *imperfect interiority,* a *relatively immanent being.*

8. *Quasi-Objective Processes*

The phenomena which characterize the quasi-objective ego are extraordinarily complicated and offer many aspects. Our description would be one-sided if this complexity were not taken into consideration. So to complete our analyses we will have to discuss the quasi-objective processes.

Processes on the Borderline of the Ego. Till the present we have considered the world of quasi-objects exclusively from the intentional standpoint of the ego. This could give rise to the impression that these objects are purely passive. This, however, is not the case. The primordial ego is not always the immediate support of all activity. Of course, as we have pointed out before, it is true that '*I* walk with my legs' and that no one will assert 'my legs walk.' But, on the other hand, it cannot be denied that everyone says 'my heart beats' and not 'I beat with my heart.' Here we have an event whose origin cannot be simply identified with the primordial ego. It is only insofar as this heart is *my* heart that this mysterious activity also somehow belongs to me.

We have to do here with certain automatic processes. The heart beats whether I want it or not. Its dynamism takes its course independently of my will and knowledge. On the other hand, however, this dynamism has a quasi-objective character; I do not face it in the same way as the ticking of my watch. The heart is capable, for instance, of expressing something of myself, which the ticking of my watch cannot do. Yet even this expressive function of the heart beat escapes my will and usually also my knowledge. In this sense I must consider these automatic processes as belonging to the non-ego in the ego. Undoubtedly, such "self-activated" processes exhibit a great foreignness and exteriority; they lie, so to speak at the outskirts of ego. Yet they do not simply belong to the realm of "worldly" phenomena. I exist *also* in the beating of my heart and also in the thousands of mysterious functions and processes described by the physiologist, the biologist, the chemist, etc. Generally, however, I exist "in them" only in a very mediate way. By its very nature the quasi-objective process belongs to the realm that is most remote from the ego.

Nothing authorizes us to assume that the domain of physiology is the only one in which we encounter quasi-objective dynamism. The empirical psychologist is accustomed to come across analogous phenomena. As everyday experience shows, often temporal objects also obey their own laws. To give a few examples, something I want to recall does not come to my mind, but when I *no longer* think of it, I suddenly know it again; a chain of associations takes a course which I do not like, but when I try to get rid of them, I do not succeed; an emotion, affective state, or passion "dominates me." Something of which I am not simply the source by its own spontaneous action determines my whole personal life.

These Processes Are Not Suitably Described by "Passivity." This is the reason why a quasi-objective process is often called passivity. The expressions *"passio," "affectio," "trahi,"* etc. point in this direction, as well as Husserl's qualification of the associative process as a "passive synthesis." But the question must be asked whether this terminology is suitable. Something which takes part in considerable— often even violent—dynamic processes may not be simply disposed of as passivity. To the contrary, in their own way, associative syntheses, the structural formation of the contents of my memory, the fit of passion, etc. are expressions of activity just as much as the beating of my heart. Only this type of activity is not immediately, and generally not in its totality, *my* activity.

Quasi-Objective Processes and Retroverted Acts.   Nevertheless, I exist *also* in the quasi-objective process.   It can even happen that I exist *only* in it.   In conditions such as unconsciousness, sleep, dreams and hypnosis the quasi-objective functions take over.   Of course, the primordial ego is still at work, but it does not rise above the level of its connection with quasi-objects and objects.   So when we spoke of the ability we have of detaching ourselves from the quasi-objects and of facing as subjects the quasi-objective process, we were not concerned with an actual possibility but with a possibility in principle.   *In principle* I am capable of making all quasi-objects the object of retro-directed acts.   Whether and to what extent I *de facto* make use of this essential possibility is something for the empirical psychologist and the physiologist to decide.

Accordingly, there is no question here of a sphere of passivity, but of a domain in which the ego seems to border upon the non-ego. I am the origin of these processes, but in such a mediate way that I experience them almost as "happening" to me.   It is in this sense that we call them quasi-objective processes.

9. *Definition of the Concept "My Body"*

"My Body" Is the Whole of Quasi-Objects.   A first contribution to the elucidation of the above-described egological situation can perhaps be given by a more precise determination of the concept *"my body."*   Starting from our analyses of retro-directed acts we may say that my body is *the whole of my real and possible concrete quasi-objects.*   In other words, everything which concretely can be the object of a retro-directed act belongs to the phenomenal domain of corporeity.   My body therefore is characterized by this that *a priori* it can become a quasi-object for me with respect to all its levels, organs and structures.   Evidently, this concept of the body includes much that usually is classified as belonging to the realm of the psychical.   However, we do not worry about this deviation from customary terminology, which will be justified later.

I Neither Simply "Have" Nor "Am" My Body.   This conceptual definition may be completed with another, for which the way has been prepared above in Chapter Three.[1]   My body is the reality which I have and am.   Better, it is the totality of all realities which I do not have in the absolute sense because I am they, and those which

---

[1]Section 3, pp. 71 ff.

I am not absolutely because I have them.[2] Let us recall the essential characteristics of "having" described by Gabriel Marcel. Why do these characteristics not apply in the absolute sense to my body? Why do the various parts of my body, my limbs and organs, present a mutually *restricted* independence, a *lesser* exteriority, a *limited* diversity? Why can I "dispose" of them only within certain limits? Why can I not simply "set aside" my body? Obviously, the reason is that I am *also* this body. That "in" which I exist cannot be really independent and foreign with respect to me; I cannot "dispose" of it as I want; I cannot "get rid" of it without putting my very existence in jeopardy. In other words, my body with all its different levels, organs and structures is neither an object nor a complex of objects. On the other hand, it is *not simply* "I myself." The mode of being of my body appears to lie midway between "being" and "having," in the same way as it constitutes the transition from being-subject to being-object, from being-as-ego to "disposable" being.

My Body is Quasi-Objectively. The preceding characterization of my body is to a large extent negative. Perhaps we may complement this description in a more positive way as follows. My body is the extension of my "originating" ego in the direction of the "world." It is the bridge which connects the ego with "worldly" things and beings. It is the continuation of my subjectivity in the realm of the objectivisable. It is the link between what *a priori* I can only be and what *a priori* I can only have. All this may be summarized succinctly in the formula: the mode of being of my body is quasi-objective.

10. *First Reflection on the Metaphysical Contrast: "My Body"— "My Soul"*

The Inner Tension of the Ego. We are now sufficiently prepared to express conceptually, at least in a provisional way, the inner tension of our personal life, which constituted our starting point. The preceding descriptions indicate essential characteristics of our total existence as human persons. They are no constructural hypotheses, fancies or speculative flights of the mind. Nevertheless, one would be inclined to consider them such, for what we have discovered in our investigation is a series of contradictory statements.

Summarizing briefly the most important ones, we have successively asserted the following—

---

[2]Cf. H. Plessner, *Lachen und Weinen*, Arnhem, 1941, p. 39: Man "neither *is* nor *has* merely a body."

1) I am a subject, and I exist "in" my quasi-objects.

2) I am numerically *one* being, and I am a plurality in a unity.

3) I am simple, and I am a plurality of relatively independent, juxtaposed and mutually external quasi-objects.

4) My retro-directed acts have their origin in me, and these same acts originate in the "world."

5) I am the recipient of my retro-directed acts, and the "world" receives these acts.

The last two contradictory pairs of statements may be formulated also in this way: I am an immanent being, and I am not an immanent being.

6) I execute acts, and I offer resistance to these acts.

The Non-Simplicity of the Ego. We are faced here with a series of contradictory judgments, all of which are valid at the same time and with respect to the same object—namely, my ego. These judgments, moreover, are made from one and the same standpoint, which is that of my concrete retro-directed act. Finally, all these judgments are based upon genuine phenomenological evidences. If we do not want to end in absurdities, we will have to make up our mind and admit: *I am not simple;* I am "composed." How this composition has to be conceived I do not yet know. I know only that in my human existence the modes of being of two realities reveal themselves. These realities I call, in deference to a very old and venerable tradition, *"my body"* and *"my spiritual soul."*[1]

The Explanation of My Contradictory Character. In the light of this distinction we can explain the contradictory character of our affirmations as follows. I am body insofar as I exist "in" my quasi-objects. As a body, I am a plurality in a unity. Insofar as I am body, I consist of a plurality of relatively independent, juxtaposed, and mutually external quasi-objects. As body, I am relatively immanent. Insofar as I am body, I offer resistance to my own acts.

Opposite this series of judgments we place another contrasting series. Insofar as I am spiritual soul, I am subject. As spiritual soul, I am unique and simple. My life as spiritual soul runs its course in genuine immanence. My spiritual soul is the source of all my acts.

---

[1]The concept of spirit as such will be developed later, in Ch. VI, pp. 164 ff.

Some of these points will have to be more fully explained. But first we must make a remark of fundamental importance.

11. *Metaphysical Consequences*

Because of My Spiritual Soul I am Primordially an Ego. If our preceding analyses are correct, the difference between "my spiritual soul" and "my body" is essential and irreducible. It is quite possible for one part of my body to take over the functions of another part, but it is unthinkable that my body or a part of it, say, a finely tuned organ, take over the place of my soul. Without any further comment this conclusion follows clearly from our analyses. The reason is that my body with all its members, organs and structures has essentially a quasi-objective character. Thus my body can exist only insofar as it is a *quasi-object for me*. In other words, my body with all its parts must necessarily be a "body-for-me," a "body by means of which I . . ." Briefly, it can be only "my embodiment." Thus my body is unthinkable without something which is the subject with respect to all real and possible quasi-objects of this body. This is the aprioristic condition under which the existence of an ego is possible in the world. In every person therefore there must be something which cannot be changed into a quasi-object, something which in principle does not function as the pole of intentional acts, something which does not appear to me as just a fact among other facts. *In the emphasis given to this partial truth lies the indisputable merit of those metaphysicists* who since Kant, as we have tried to show above,[1] have influenced modern thought about the spiritual ego. It should be clear now also in what consists the error committed by these philosophers. The reality which makes us spiritual beings, patently is not a super-individual "general consciousness," a non-human transcendental ego, a person in Scheler's sense. To characterize this reality we do not need anything else than the concept of the spiritual soul, provided that we take care to safeguard it from false interpretations. Above all, we must emphasize therefore that the spiritual soul is not the object of the research of empirical psychology; that the soul does not appear to us as a "detached" entity among other "detached" entities;[2] that the soul therefore does not function as an object or quasi-object with respect to ego-directed thinking or willing. Because of my spiritual soul I am primordially an ego; and in it lies the basis

---

[1] Cf. Part I, pp. 35-57.
[2] *"'Abgehobenheit' immitten von anderen Abgehobenheiten."*

for the condition which makes possible all the data, facts and states which interest the empirical psychologist, the psychiatrist, the sociologist, etc.

My Spiritual Soul is the Principle of My Existence as an Ego. Perhaps this metaphysical thesis may be completed by the following considerations. The relation of my soul to my body is essentially irreversible. Otherwise man would not be essentially different from other more or less closed physical, chemical, or biological systems. What makes such a "multiple unity" into an ego or person is precisely the subjective element which does not belong to the organized multiple unity. In other words, just as it is impossible to be the son of one's father and at the same time this father himself, so also one and the same reality cannot be the body of something and at the same time that which is embodied in it. For this reason we say that *this relationship is irreversible.* From this irreversibility flow the above-mentioned relationships. If my body is essentially a *"quasi-object for. . .,"* my soul cannot be a *"quasi-object for. . ."* But in that case we must admit also that my soul is not the object of explicit intentional self-knowledge, not a phenomenon among other phenomena, not an object to be treated by the psychologist or the psychiatrist. Here lies the reason also why all objectivistic efforts to understand man as the resultant of certain physiological, biological, psychological, or sociological facts must necessarily fail. It is impossible in principle to explain man as any kind of a "system of equilibrium." The result of any effort to do it anyhow, is inevitably a manikin, a robot, a machine in the Cartesian sense, but never a person. What is always lacking is precisely the principle of absolute egological being, which we have called the spiritual soul. My spiritual soul is that which distinguishes me from a biological system; it is the ultimate reason why I am more than just a phase in a cosmic process of evolution. Briefly, my spiritual soul is the principle of my existence as an ego.

"My Soul" is Not an Abstract Aspect of My Ego. From this it follows that what I call my spiritual soul does not represent an abstract aspect of my personal existence.[3] The proof of this assertion does not seem difficult. Abstraction is possible only where we have to do with one or more concretely given data. This applies also when

---

[3]Even recently, Alexis Carrel claimed: "In reality, the body and the soul are views taken of the same object by different methods, abstractions obtained by our reason from the concrete unity of our being. The antithesis of matter and mind represents merely the opposition of two kinds of techniques." *Man, the Unknown,* New York, 7th ed., 1935, p. 118.

there is question of different degrees of abstraction. Even the most complex system of abstraction is ultimately based upon the solid foundation of concrete facts. Such a concrete datum is, for instance, the phenomenon "my body." Reflecting on my body I can abstract, for example, from its color, shape and weight, and form the universal concept of "one's own body." I can eliminate also the aspect of animation and thus change "my body" into the general concept of "corpse." But I cannot abstract from my spiritual soul. Evidently, the condition under which an abstractive act is possible is not fulfilled —namely, that the reality to be abstracted be something given. For, as we have seen, my spiritual soul is not a fact among facts, but that through which facts are facts. In other words, I am capable of abstracting from every particular reality, but unable to grasp adequately in a universal concept the principle of my own existence.[4] No matter what I think, represent to myself, or imagine, I will always be this unique individual existence which is "there," together with the represented, thought, or imagined object, as the one to whom these objects "appear." Whether I think of the origin of the terrestrial globe or the air traffic in the year 2000, I am always "there with it" as the singular ego. Somehow I am present, not as a human being with two hands and two feet, not as the person called by this or that name, who is the father of a family and a citizen of this State. I am present neither as a personal nor as a social ego, but as the anonymous and primordial ontological center, i.e. as the subject which faces the different objects and quasi-objects in an objective or quasi-objective way. This is also the mysterious reason why in Husserl's philosophy, after all kinds of reductions—whether they are called psychological, phenomenological or transcendental-phenomenological—there always remains an irreducible ego for which the reduced reality is a phenomenon. The "last spectator" necessarily escapes from every kind of "world nihilation."[5] What has been described here as the ultimate

---

[4]Undoubtedly, we cannot do without an inadequate conceptual symbol of the reality which cannot be grasped objectively. However, such a symbol is not introduced because of an intentional consciousness of contents, but only because of a "directional" consciousness. Cf. Ch. VI, pp. 179 ff.

[5]However, it seems wholly illicit to us to conclude from this to an ontological priority of the ego which cannot be "placed between brackets" with respect to world, reality and being, or even to attribute to it "constituent" (i.e. creative) forces. Let us not forget that even this "last" subject is an ego which "discovers" its existence in the midst of the universe of being. Therefore, it is a finite, contingent and limited being. We may speak here only of a metaphysical relationship between ego and world, a relationship which must inevitably be thought by a being endowed with a finite intellect.

subject is manifestly nothing else than the *principium fontale,* the fountain spring, of my personal being, i.e. my soul. I cannot leave my soul out of consideration, because my soul is that which considers. I cannot "raise" it to universality, because for me the soul represents a center of the universe which cannot be compared with anything else. In other words, my soul is not a possible object of abstractive thinking. My soul is for me the unique and incomparable reality through which *my* being is rooted in being *itself.*[6]

---

[6]By this we do not deny that the *distinction* between my body and my soul is based upon acts of abstraction. The immediate datum is obviously man in his concrete unity. The distinction can be made only insofar as we, as it were, "eliminate by abstraction" everything which in the immediately given personal unity is not soul. Here again the irreversibility of the body-soul relationship shows itself. Concerning this question, see pp. 169 ff.

FIFTH STUDY

TOWARDS THE PHENOMENOLOGY OF THE CORPOREAL EGO

A CONTRIBUTION TO THE PHILOSOPHY OF NATURE

1. *Introduction to the Problem*

Multiplicity in Unity. The scope of our preceding investigation was to circumscribe the phenomenon "my body." This circumscription was to remain of a strictly eidetic nature, and consequently the forms under which corporeal existence reveals itself were characterized exclusively from the standpoint of the intended methodological demarcation. Undoubtedly, it would have been desirable to develop more fully the material *a priori* of this realm. However, such analyses would go beyond the limits of the strictly methodical development of our investigations. We shall therefore be satisfied with a mere reference to the valuable descriptions given by other phenomenologists, such as Husserl, Scheler, Buytendijk, Merleau-Ponty and Plessner. Nevertheless, we would like to define more precisely the mode of being of the corporeal ego in one respect which is important for the problem facing us. We mean that we would like to consider from the phenomenological standpoint the problem of *the unity and multiplicity of the corporeal ego*. Our preceding explanations are too sketchy in this respect. What are we to understand by the formula: "I exist 'in' my quasi-objects"? What is the meaning of the expression "multiplicity in unity"? How can many relatively self-subsistent things constitute *one* self-subsistent being?

An Insufficient Answer. At first, one may have the impression that the answer is quite obvious. The statement 'I exist in my quasi-objects' seems to signify nothing else than 'the whole exists in its parts.' If this is the case, then I will exist *in* my quasi-objects just as a village "consists" of several houses or a forest of a number of trees. But is this an adequate comparison?

Even a brief reflection on this question will show that we have used values such as "whole," "part," "to compose" and "to divide" in an equivocal sense. Prescientific, scientific and even philosophical terminology is so uncertain and fluctuating in this respect that there appears to be an urgent need for a phenomenological clarification of the problem. The limited scope of our investigation forces us to restrict ourselves to the description of a few important broad lines.

But an elementary orientation seems absolutely indispensable, for we cannot work with obscure, vague, or equivocal terms. If we want to reach our goal, we must have at our disposal the necessary intellectual tools.

Purpose of This Study. Before beginning our work, we want to state clearly what our purpose is. What we are concerned with is above all a *phenomenology* of unity and multiplicity. This implies that we must take our starting point from concrete wholes, concrete parts, concrete composition, unification, division, etc. Hence we may not raise these problems on the level of the formal and aprioristic sciences. But logic, arithmetic, geometry, the theories of groups and sets are concerned with abstract wholes and parts and with ideal composition and division.

Other Philosophers Offer No Help. We would like very much to make use of the investigations of philosophers of repute. This course would seem to be all the more the right approach because in the twentieth century serious efforts have been made to arrive at a theory of order. But to our regret we are forced to state that these efforts can hardly be of any use for our purpose. This applies especially to the order theory conceived by Hans Driesch.[1] In a typically Kantian attitude of mind Driesch carefully distinguishes his "theory of order" from the "theory of reality."[2] In his view, the order theory has nothing to do with reality, but is related to logic. As he assures us, "in any case, there exists a philosophical domain—it may be called logic in a broader sense, but we call it correctly the theory of order."[3] What we need, however, is an order theory which at the same time is a theory of reality and consequently an explanation of reality.

It would seem obvious to think here in the first place of Edmund Husserl and his "theory of whole and parts."[4] But we must not forget that, although Husserl's explanations contain valuable hints for our purpose, they are a part of his LOGICAL INVESTIGATIONS. This fact partly explains the formalistic, abstract and "un-real" character of his considerations. As an example we may refer to the following definition: "We call 'piece' every part which is independent with respect to a whole W."[5] Husserl makes no distinction between "cutting

---

[1]*Ordnungslehre. Ein System des nicht-metaphysischen Teiles der Philosophie*, Jena, 1912.
[2]*Wirklichkeitslehre. Ein metaphysischer Versuch.* Leipzig, 1917.
[3]*Ordnungstheorie*, p. 2.
[4]*Logische Untersuchungen*, bk. II, part 1, pp. 225-293.
[5]*Op. cit.*, p. 266. I have substituted the letter *W* for the original *G* (*einen Ganzen G*). Tr.

into pieces" and "dividing," between a heap of pieces and a whole which is made up of real parts.

Paul Häberlin's STUDIES IN THE PHILOSOPHY OF NATURE[6] likewise offer no help, because this author starts from the concept of the "in-dividual" while the questions we have to raise are concerned with the foundations of this concept, as they are to be found in a theory of order.

The Positive Sciences Provide No Assistance. Do we have to turn, then, to the positive sciences? We are not blind to the fact that, because of the failure of philosophy to provide the necessary theory, the proponents of the moral sciences and descriptive branches of learning have often tried to arrive at the desired goal by their own efforts. Unfortunately, nowadays the opposite tendency manifests itself—the tendency to define everything which is presented by the phenomenon "order" exclusively in a quantitatively exact and therefore abstract way. Others, such as Hellmuth Plessner[7] and F. J. J. Buytendijk,[8] have concretely seen the phenomenological problems which arise in this domain and have treated them in part. But their descriptions refer at once to very special phenomena which are connected with being-alive, being besouled, being in motion, being conscious, etc. Neither Plessner nor Buytendijk intended to construct a theory of order. So we must conclude that the authors whose work is systematically general remain in the abstract, while those who give concrete descriptions do not aim at the connection of their problems with the fundamental questions of unity and plurality.

Limited Scope of this Study. As a result, we are obliged to blaze our own trail. But we must repeat that we want to give only an elementary orientation. Moreover, we prefer to limit the problems to be considered as much as possible. We shall therefore speak only of whole and parts which possess a relative self-subsistence. The question of unity and plurality with respect to accidents has less interest for us. This is the reason why in the following pages we will consider unity and self-subsistence in a way which presupposes the connection of these two concepts.

---

[6]*Naturphilosophische Betrachtungen. Eine allgemeine Ontologie,* 2nd ed., Zurich, 1939, vol. I, *Einheit und Vielheit.*

[7]Cf. *Die Stufen des Organischen und der Mensch. Einleitung in die philosophische Anthropologie,* Berlin and Leipzig, 1928. Hereafter abbreviated as *Stufen.*

[8]Especially in his latest work *Algemene theorie der menselijke houding,* Antwerp-Utrecht, 1948.

2. *The Concept of Relative Self-Subsistence*

The Distinction of the Individual from its Surroundings in the Static Order. It is usually assumed that a being which exists independently is distinct in all respects from all other real and possible self-subsistent beings. It is, so we think, wholly undivided in itself (*"indivisum in se"*) and wholly separated from all other beings (*"divisum ab alio"*). However, phenomenological research shows that reality often appears quite different to us. However strange it may seem, the more the being in question has the ontological status of a thing, a *"res,"* the less the above-mentioned assumption is justified. A thing or a complex of things does not appear to us as an absolute "this-here," i.e. it is not in all respects distinct from other things. True, in everyday life I may say 'this cloud is white,' and 'the sky is blue,' but these statements are extremely summary. If I consider the cloud carefully, I will find that it is not only white, but also cream-colored, yellow, grey and at the edges bluish; I will observe that this bluishness becomes darker and darker till it imperceptibly fuses into the blue of the sky. Between white and blue in the strict sense there is a zone which may be attributed as well to the cloud as to the sky. Borrowing Husserl's terminology, we may say that the cloud has a *horizon*. It is not absolutely distinct and separated from its surroundings. There is also differentiation in it, and this internal division is precisely what makes possible the imperceptible transition into the other, the external. Nevertheless, the cloud appears to us as a certain unity and as the self-subsistent support of certain properties, so that I can justly make the judgment 'the cloud is white.'

Perhaps one will object that the example of the cloud is an exception and that similar assertions cannot be made with respect to the letter I write or the table at which I am seated. It is true that for practical reasons we try to limit as much as possible the horizon-like fusion of things into one another. But we have only to see in bad light, from too far away or too near, and we are faced again with the phenomenon of the ill-defined, the vague and the indistinct. In principle, we are obliged to admit that the *optimum* to which we naturally tend, and which consists in this that the self-subsistent is as much as possible allowed to appear as such, is always of a transitory nature. Another remark has to be added—*now* we try to grasp the table with our eyes as clearly as possible, and the forms of this piece of furniture stand clearly out against the dark room; *then* we consider the grain pattern of the table top, and at once the contours of the thing are fused together with the horizon "table-room," while a detail of its internally differentiated structure comes to the foreground. What first was a "part" changes into a "whole"; what previously was a whole is now considered as belonging to the horizon of the whole. The material thing is always and of necessity experienced in this way. This would not be possible if it were wholly "divided from the other" and in the strict sense "undivided in itself." The material thing therefore is not absolutely simple: it is complex, really differentiated, structured and organized. It is precisely because it is to a certain extent internally divided, and the surrounding things likewise do not show themselves wholly "closed," that a zone of transition arises which can be considered to belong to one thing as well as to another.

The Distinction of the Individual from its Surroundings in the Dynamic Order. The dynamic aspect of the concrete thing gives rise to analogous remarks. Whatever action may be attributed to it, we are never able to conceive it independently of its surroundings. The table, for instance, exercises pressure on the floor, and the cloud in the sky moves. Yet it does not occur to us to consider this pressure and motion as "acts"[1] or "deeds" of the table or the cloud. In scholastic terminology we could say 'a thing is not a *suppositum.*' In other words, it does not "do" anything, but *something happens to it,* and what happens is a result of the definite constellation "thing—surroundings." From the dynamic viewpoint, we likewise observe a horizon-like fusion between the action exercised by the thing and the action which it undergoes from other things. In philosophical generality we can state only that the thing is capable of undergoing actions and "transmitting" these actions in a causal way. But we cannot determine with absolute certainty where the boundary lies between the dynamism proper to a thing and the dynamism that is external to it. As de Raeymaeker writes,

> In things the 'distinct from every other' is never found perfectly realized; they are not 'supposita' in the strict sense of the term. Nevertheless animals and even plants manifest a relative unity.[2]

---

[1] The German *"Handlung"* and *"Tat"* indicate actions of persons (Tr.)

[2] *The Philosophy of Being,* p. 243. Obviously, the phenomenological situation will be different if activities are found which must be attributed to the being in question itself. In such a case the being stands out from its surroundings in an entirely different way. These phenomena have been described by Plessner and Buytendijk under the title of "positionality." Cf. *Stufen,* pp. 80-185 and *Houding,* pp. 47-54.

Relative Self-Subsistence. Briefly, the concrete material self-subsistent thing, with which we are primarily concerned here, constantly supports itself on the things surrounding it with respect to its being and nature, its activity and passivity. Nevertheless, it constitutes a certain unity in the sense that *in one or more definite respects its being "divided from the other" is more pronounced than its internal differentiation.* So in a certain respect it is *one* being, but not in another. Such a reality we call a *relative unity* or a *relatively self-subsistent thing.* In scholastic terminology we may characterize such a reality by saying that it does not constitute a unity *simpliciter* but only *secundum quid.* To this kind of reality we would like to apply the words of St. Thomas: "There is nothing that prevents something which is divided in one way from being undivided in another way."[3]

Accordingly, material being is not merely a "weak unity." Its weakness is more fundamental and lies in this that in a certain respect it does not even constitute an independent unity with respect to its surroundings.[4] Positively speaking, this means that every relatively self-subsistent being has its own way of constituting a unity, i. e. its own *modus unitatis,* mode of unity. As a result, it can be the support of properties and states; it is able to undergo and exercise actions; and is capable of standing in a definite relationship to other relatively self-subsistent things.

Thus the line our investigation must take is indicated. We are going to describe and analyze several relatively self-subsistent realities, and upon the basis of these phenomenological analyses, we will try to arrive at a conception of a certain typology. We will compare several modes of unity with one another, and formulate certain eidetic laws. In doing so we will not lose sight of our proper goal, which is to establish how it is possible that I, this living whole, am a plurality in a unity.

3. *The Accumulation*

The question raised is what, phenomenologically speaking, is the form under which the relatively self-subsistent being appears to us? What experiences do we have with respect to its concrete wholeness, its real parts? How does the phenomenon of "wholeness"

---

[3] *Summa theol.,* p. I, q. 11, a. 1, *ad* 2.
[4] In their characterization of vital material reality Viktor von Weiszäcker and Erwin Straus call this phenomenon "coherence" and "symbiosis." Cf. *Der Gestaltkreis. Theorie einer Einheit von Wahrnehmen und Bewegen,* 3rd ed., Stuttgart, 1947, and *Vom Sinn der Sinne,* Berlin, 1935.

arise? This question cannot be answered immediately. There are innumerable kinds of internally more or less differentiated wholes. A group of trees, a utensil, a flock, a geometric figure, an organism, a human society, all of these can be imagined under this title. Perhaps, however, it will be possible to discover definite types in this plurality. Perhaps there are certain phenomenological laws which govern this matter.

Phenomenology of the Accumulation. Let us being with what is probably the most simple case. Why, for instance, do I speak of a "flock of sheep"? Obviously, because I have perceived the animals in mutual proximity and thus grasped their numerical plurality as a plurality enclosed in a certain unity. If I had seen one sheep here, another there, and a third far away, I would not have perceived a "flock." The accidental mutual proximity of the animals was the concrete phenomenon which made me distinguish this plurality from the landscape and grasp it as a relative unity. I proceed in the same way when I perceive a "group of trees" as such. Here also the decisive factor is the circumstance that the trees are in mutual proximity. Accordingly, if there had been just a few sheep or trees, the plurality would not have been seized phenomenologically as a whole. Each of the animals or trees would have appeared to me as a being with its own self-subsistence. The phenomenon of group evidently arises from the fact that similar beings are dispersed somewhat restrictedly. As soon as individuals of the same kind are not isolated but reciprocally connected, they lose, phenomenologically speaking, something of their independent character. They become elements of a relatively independent unity, in the sense indicated above. The various sheep, for instance, are biologically, physiologically and psychologically self-subsistent beings; yet from the viewpoint of their spatial proximity I can consider them as mutually connected, i.e. as "parts" of a flock. In this case it is easy to define the unifying principle—it is nothing else than the relative absence of dispersion in space-time.

So we see that from our analysis of the phenomenon "group" we have become acquainted with a first mode of being relatively self-subsistent. To indicate this type of relatively complete reality, which is met e.g. under the guise of "pile," "mass," "herd," "group," etc., we will use the term *accumulation*.[1] We call an accumulation *any relative unity of similar elements which are reciprocally connected by*

---

[1]Häufung.

one and the same accidental relationship. Because the accidental relationship of the elements is absolutely uniform, no single element plays a special role with respect to the formation of the unity.

Characteristics of the Accumulation. Although a more penetrating analysis would be necessary, we will have to restrict ourselves to indicating three characteristics which distinguish this way of being relatively self-subsistent. First of all, the nature of an accumulation is essentially dependent on the kind of elements composing it. An accumulation of leaves is quite different from an accumulation of stars or men. Everyday language clearly expresses this, for we do not speak of an accumulation or group without further qualification. If no qualification is added, the listener will ask at once, What kind of an accumulation? What kind of a group? These questions find their phenomenological foundation in this that *accumulation intrinsically refers to the elements by which it is constituted.* Secondly, *the accumulation depends on the number of its elements.* A flock of ten sheep differs from one of ten thousand sheep; a hundred thousand trees constitute another relative unity than a hundred trees. Evidently, the quantitative element plays a decisive role here. Thirdly, with respect to an accumulation, we may say that *the whole is equal to the sum of its component parts.*

Is "My Body" an Accumulation? Let us now ask the question, Is this kind of "multiple unity" related to the phenomenon "my body"? Without further ado it would seem to be clear that we have to do here with the opposite extreme. As the old scholastic saying goes, *Socrates non est acervus,* Socrates is not an accumulation. Nothing is so different from our bodily being as the external, accidental, and often random heaping of similar elements. The internal unity of my quasi-objects manifestly is of an entirely different type.

4. Homogeneous Coupling

The Homogeneous Whole. Let us now take another mode of relative self-subsistence, in which the unitary character of the being reveals itself more clearly. Think, for example, of water in a glass, a straight line, a protracted sound, or a piece of butter. None of these things makes the impression of "multiple unity," but rather that of a simple unity. This impression prevails until I decide to divide these apparently simple unities. Then I make the remarkable discovery that I can, for instance, divide and subdivide the straight line, and that the result will always be a straight line, no matter how small the line may be. Exactly the same happens when I interrupt the sound: every tone, no matter how short, has the same properties as the protracted tone. In an analogous way I can scoop a spoonful of water out of the glass, and then I will observe that the part is of the same nature as the whole: it consists of the same colorless, odorless liquid, and reveals the same slightly concave surface as the water in the glass. In the same way, I can convince myself that the smallest piece of butter is still butter. St. Thomas expresses this truth as follows:

> In every homogenous whole the whole is constituted of parts having the form of the whole, as e.g. any part of water is water; and it is in this way that the continuous is constituted of parts.[1]

Husserl's definition also could be quoted here:

> When a whole can be cut into parts in such a way that the pieces are by their very nature of the same lowest species as the undivided whole, we call the whole an extensive whole, and its parts extensive parts.[2]

One cannot help thinking here of an extensive homogeneous unity or the continuous in the mathematical and geometric sense of the term.

Undoubtedly, such concrete, relatively self-subsistent beings have served as models for the ideal unitary forms considered by the mathematician. From the phenomenological viewpoint, however, there exists a difference here, which can be sufficiently demonstrated by means of the following consideration. It is true that the phenomenon "part" is always the same, but the way of calling it forth, the act of "dividing," is different. The line was divided in space, the sound was interrupted in time. I can cut the butter, but I have to scoop the water. Why this difference? What is the meaning of the term "to divide" in this connection? How do I explain the fact that e.g. one half of a straight line is likewise a straight line?

The Mode of Unity of the Homogeneous Whole. The *concrete* phenomenon "straight line" is undoubtedly based upon a definite spatial disposition of extended and localized objects. Whenever I perceive something which is spatially disposed and arranged in this way, it will appear as a "straight line," whether it consists of houses, trees,

---

[1] *Summa theol.,* p. I, q. 11, a. 2, *ad* 2. The parts spoken of by St. Thomas are potential parts; hence he gives here a philosophical explanation of the fact that a homogeneous coupling is infinitely divisible.
[2] *Logische Untersuchungen,* bk. II, part 1, p. 266.

rails, or tiles. Evidently, these things have to be united in a definite way to "constitute a straight line." In what, then, consists the division of this line? In this that I disrupt, break, or suspend somewhere the regulative principle or rule by which the things are interconnected. If, for instance, I remove from a row of houses or trees one or more houses or trees, I will have disrupted the mode of unity at a definite place. I do the same when I interpose a pause in the temporal continuity of a tone. Likewise, the division of a piece of butter or that of water consists in nothing else. To cut or scoop evidently are special activities by means of which I tend to interrupt a definite interconnection. Thus we see why such diversified actions are understood by the term "to divide." The way of dividing must necessarily always be adapted to the mode of unity proper to the relatively self-subsistent being which is to be divided.

Thus it becomes clear that what characterizes the above-mentioned relatively self-subsistent beings must be sought in their special "bond of unity." The parts, for example, of a line have all one and the same structure, which in the idealization of Euclidean geometry is characterized as the shortest distance between two points. The parts of a tone, of water and butter are subject to physical laws—presumably very complex laws—which give them their particular way of being connected. Such a relatively self-subsistent being owes its unity to a definite connection of its constituent parts. For this reason we indicate such a being in our theory of order as a *homogeneous coupling* (*"Einung"*).

Characteristics of the Homogeneous Coupling. One of the most important essential characteristics of homogeneous coupling consists in this that in it *neither the part refers to the whole nor the whole to the part.* It is even doubtful whether in this connection one may speak of a "whole" and "its parts." These concepts have only a quantitative meaning here—in the sense that the whole is always greater than the greatest of its parts—, but no phenomenological datum corresponds with such a quantitative relationship. The water in my glass is a whole just as much or just as little as the water in the ocean. I could just as well consider it as a part. This phenomenon is expressed in some Romance languages by the use of the partitive particle, as e.g. "je bois *de* l'eau"; in many Germanic languages the same is indicated by the omission of the article whose function it is to indicate unity and self-subsistence, as e.g. I drink water, and not: I drink *the* water or *a* water.

The homogeneous coupling, moreover, is not determined by quantity alone. The mode of unity also has to be taken into consideration. Incidentally, this is the reason why we do not find Husserl's expression "extensive whole" very fortunate. Suppose I have to compose a "whole" line of 10 cm. by means of three straight segments of 6, 3, and 1 cm. The whole could be constituted, of course, just as well of $3 + 6 + 1$ cm. as of $1 + 3 + 6$ cm., etc. What is presupposed here as obvious is that I am aware of the correct disposition of the segments. If I assemble the three pieces in such a way that they cross in one point, I will not obtain the whole of 10 cm. I will have to arrange the parts in accordance with a definite rule which is always presupposed. "To compose" presents here a very special character.

We conclude from this that in the homogeneous coupling, apart from the kind and number of the component parts, the *formal principle* plays an important role. *It expresses itself in an internal law which is the norm according to which the parts are to be connected.*

Is My Objectivisable Ego a Homogeneous Coupling? If the question is asked again whether the mode of being of my objectivisable ego as a multiple unity shows any relationship with the homogeneous coupling, our answer will have to be a definite denial. To justify the answer it will be sufficient to draw attention to a single point. If, as an objectivisable ego, I would be a homogeneous coupling, I would exist "in each of my parts," for instance, in a pulled tooth or a lost hair, just as well as in the rest of my body. Moreover, even if beheaded, I would still be a human being, albeit somewhat smaller. Evidently, the whole of my quasi-objects constitute a relative unity of a quite different type.

5. *The Ordered Whole*

Still another type of differentiated unity is known to us, and it is this type that normally draws our attention much more than other more primitive kinds of order. We grasp, for example, a plant, an animal, or a tree immediately as self-subsistent being. We are even so much inclined to grasp such independent beings separately that, as the saying goes, we often "do not see the forest for the trees." Everywhere in nature around us we come across this phenomenon. Those mountains have a typical form; these stones show a crystalline structure; this constellation appears to me as a shape. Although I do not understand all the biological functions of even the lowest kind of animals, yet I grasp them as self-subsistent beings of a special kind. Which kind? This is the question which we must now examine.

The Most Elementary Ordered Whole. The most elementary of all the examples given above is the constellation. In it, we have to do with a limited number of simple data. Let us have a look e. g. at the Little Bear. The first question to arise is, What makes me single out this group from the silvery swarms in the starry sky as something relatively independent? Why do I consider this group as a special unity? By what right do I speak of a "form" in this constellation? There is no question here of color, shades, or motion. What characterizes the constellation as such is nothing else than the form. The form alone allows me to grasp and identify the Little Bear as something special in the midst of millions of stars. What I call the Little Bear are four stars which by the imagined connection of straight lines form a trapezoid, and three stars that are the prolongation of one side of the trapezoid in such a way that this prolongation slants more and more to the right. The fact that I picture the stars as interconnected by straight lines is characteristic; this procedure evidently makes it easier to grasp the form as such.

An Objection. Perhaps one will object that we are speaking all the time of form, formal principle, etc., without indicating what is meant by it. If one wants to cling to the immediate appearances and describe them as simply as possible, we will have to say that what is concretely given to us is seven shining points and nothing else.

Without entering for the time being into the metaphysical concept of form, we may assert phenomenologically that the view which gives rise to this objection is based upon an abstractive simplification. The concrete phenomenon is much richer and more complex. What is given in reality is the following:

1) Seven shining points;

2) The relations of each of these points to its neighbors;

3) The relation of each of these points to all the relations stated in 2) taken together.

If we had to describe only the first-mentioned relations, we could describe it simply as a homogeneous coupling. Only the third point contains the characteristic trait. There is no question here of parts which have a relation to other parts, but of parts that in addition possess a relationship to the fact that they have a certain reference to other parts. We discover in them a certain respect to their own being-related. Briefly, we meet here a relationship of order in a superior degree, so to speak, a relation in the second power.

Solidarity Resulting from this Relation. This point deserves a more profound examination. We just spoke of a trapezoid. A trapezoid is a geometric idealization whose function it is to designate both a definite spatially differentiated unity and the internal law governing this unity. Trapezoid means, among other things, four straight sides, of which none can be greater than the other three together; four angles whose sum must be 360 degrees; etc. Trapezoid means a definite law which is the norm governing each of the parts, i.e. the part itself, its connection with the neighboring parts, *and* its relationship to all parts of which the figure is composed. I can imagine four sides, four corners and four angles also arranged in a different way, so that they obey another law, for instance, that of the square or the rectangle. But then they would not be the sides of the trapezoid formed by the Little Bear, have these characteristic properties, these typical angles, and these definite mutual relations. If I cause a *single* element to vary, the nature of the whole will be modified; if I change the whole, I will alter the elements and their mutual relations. Accordingly, there is a very special kind of *solidarity* between the whole and its parts, a solidarity which is not to be found in either an accumulation or a homogeneous coupling. Here the inner law applies to the whole as well as to its parts. So we will call such a relatively self-subsistent thing an *ordered whole*.

As should be clear, we are thinking here of the phenomenon which under the names "form," "structure," "totality," and the adjectives derived from these terms plays such an important role as a descriptive and explanatory principle in philosophy, psychology, biology and many other positive sciences. However, neither the experimentalist nor the thinker always indicate exactly what they mean by these concepts. This is all the more reason for us to proceed very cautiously.

Investigation of this Solidarity. To simplify matters, let us take an ordered whole which consists of four concrete parts, *a, b, c,* and *d;* for example, a constellation formed by four stars. We speak here of an ordered whole if the reciprocal relation of the parts—of *a* to *b, c* and *d;* of *b* to *a, c* and *d;* of *c* to *a, b* and *d;* of *d* to *a, b* and *c*—is determined by the relation of each part to the connection *a-b-c-d.* Thus there rules here an *internal law which determines the way in which each part in particular is connected with all other parts, and this in function of the union of the parts in general.* This is what above we have called a reference to a relation or a relation in the second power. At the same time the way is indicated how the whole is formed "out" of its parts. It is because of the mutual dependence that the above-mentioned phenomenon of solidarity arises.

However, the expression "relation in the second power" should not be allowed to deceive us. We are far too much inclined to misjudge the profound metaphysical meaning of this phenomenon. Being one-sidedly tuned to abstract operations, we consider a "relation to a relation" as something trivial. An algebraic expression, such as $(a+b)-1$, a simple syllogism, a logistic formula, such as $p+q \rightarrow p$, all are expressions of a relation to a relation. But we overlook something here—namely, that the "relation in the second power" of which *I* am speaking here is not a construct of thought but the expression of a concrete mode of being. The reference of the elements to the fact of their own connection and the law flowing from it, in principle, simply express that the being in question is somehow *closed* with respect to its surroundings and imperfectly *refers "back" to itself* with respect to its own inner self.

A comparison with another type of relative unity may be instructive. A simple respect of order, a homogeneous assembly, is essentially an open relation, for in principle it can be expanded indefinitely by adding new elements. Reversely, the homogeneous assembly can be deprived of many elements by division, while the remaining parts will continue to reveal the same properties and formal qualities as the undivided assembly. But the whole which refers back to itself does not allow any arbitrary lengthening or shortening. If it is attempted anyhow, one has no longer to do with the same thing, but with something entirely different. If one divides or increases the whole, the character of the ordered unity will be changed at the same time.

Foundation of this Characteristic. Obviously, there is a reason for this characteristic. From the analysis of the example given above, we may conclude at once e.g. that *a* is connected with *b, c* and *d* by means of "if . . . then" relations which in principle do not link it with any other reality. In their interconnection, *a, b, c, d* have something proper, special and unique; in a sense they constitute a *little world of their own.* There are various ways in which this special character can manifest itself. In the simplest case the proper nature of the ordered whole will express itself in a certain spatial independence and closedness. Faced with such a spatial form of order, a generation which has grown up under the spell of exact physical science will exclaim in surprise that "the structured whole (*Gestalt*) is more than the sum of its parts." Later we will have to evaluate and interpret this and other similar formulas. Provisionally, we restrict ourselves to the more cautious statement that the relative independence of an ordered whole reveals essentially less relativity than an accumulation or a homogeneous assembly.

Terminological Clarifications. Of course, here again one may speak of a "whole," a "part" and "composition," but then these expressions are given a third meaning which is essentially different from the others. However, we think that it is desirable to use a terminology which is as unequivocal as possible. For this reason we prefer not to speak of either parts or elements with respect to the ordered whole. In view of the fact that *a, b, c, d,* each for itself and in its own way, possess a special relation to the totality to which they belong, and that this relation is comparable with the one existing between the members of an organism, we will from now on call them *members.*

What is meant by this term becomes clear at once if we separate a member from the ordered whole to which it belongs. Through this separation the member evidently becomes essentially different. An isolated star is something else than a constellation. A leaf or a limb of a body refer us immediately to the vegetative or animal organism to which they belong. Regarding an isolated datum of consciousness, it is only by abstraction that we can speak of such a thing. All this goes to show that when we separate a member, it ceases to be a member, i.e. embodiment of the internal law which gives form to the totality.

To complete our terminology we will have to find a term expressing the special relation of each member to the other members. No long search, however, is necessary, for the term has been known and used for thousands of years. When the relation between two or more members is determined by the relation of each member in particular to the whole, we are faced with the phenomenon of *order.* In such a case we say that the members in question are "ordered" or "in order." In this sense we are justified in considering every totality, structure, etc. as an "ordered whole."

6. *The Dynamism of the Ordered Whole*

The concepts of order thus far described enable us to give a correct description of a crystal or a constellation. But as soon as we pass from the world of really or apparently invariable forms to the ephemeral modes under which our infinitely variable quasi-objects appear, we experience that these concepts still need to be complemented in many respects. It is an age-old truth that the corporeal ego is a whole, not merely in the static order but also dynamically. It was expressed long ago in the well-known fable of Menenius Agrippa. Some body functions run their course automatically; others are based upon instincts and tendencies; others again are exercised in a more or less conscious way. All, however, adapt themselves in their action to the frame of the whole that I, as a corporeal being, am. All contribute to the vital activity of the whole, and all profit from the activity of the whole. For this reason, as Menenius Agrippa shows in his fable, the defect of one member of the functional totality has repercussions on all the other members. Thus in the dynamic order we encounter the same solidarity between the whole and its parts as we have met in the static order. Evidently, there are analogous conditions here, which may best be characterized by saying that *the reciprocal functional relations of the members depend on the contribution of each member to the total work*. The functional interconnection of my quasi-objects therefore is conditioned by the way in which they contribute to my life as ego. From this it readily follows that with respect to number, size, distribution, and proportion my members are ruled by an internal law, and that every increase or decrease in number or size, every modification and interference with their functioning can jeopardize the total act, i.e. my life as corporeal ego. This is the reason also why the quasi-objective ego cannot be constructed by joining together diverse functions into a sum-total. On the contrary, the quasi-objective ego will have to be understood by starting from the vital center that I am as the originating and dynamic ego. In other words, the body is *my* body as long as its dynamism runs its course in such a way that it is an embodiment of my ego. This is the case with all healthy members, organs and parts of the body; all my quasi-objects function as if they were interested in the purposive embodiment of my personal life. It is precisely by means of this solidary participation that these parts are distinguished from diseased and dead members and organs. In this sense St. Thomas emphasized:

"One does not speak of the eye and the flesh of a dead man, except in an equivocal sense."[1]

Modern Expressions of this Dynamic Solidarity. Nowadays the above-mentioned essential relationship is often expressed as follows:

The whole-phaenomena disclose properties and influences that are more than the sum of their parts.[2]

This description is not very satisfactory because its term "more" does not have a concretely definable meaning. Where there is question of a "more," there must be a possibility also of a "less." In principle, the difference between "more" and "less" must be subject to measuring, counting or calculating. But it is precisely of a difference which is beyond everything quantitative that there is question here.

The formulation of Max Wertheimer seems to be better. He says:

There are wholes, the behavior of which is not determined by that of their individual elements, but where the partprocesses are themselves determined by the intrinsic nature of the whole.[3]

In this formulation the distinctive characteristic of an ordered whole— its referring back to itself—is at least implicitly expressed. The mutual functional relationships of the members ("the partprocesses") depend on the dynamic relation of the members to the whole as determined by an inner law ("intrinsic nature of the whole"). Unfortunately, Wertheimer's definition contains a *petitio principii,* a begging of the question, so that it would appear to be less useful in philosophical research.

7. *The Participation of Members in the Formative Act*

We now encounter a difficulty which from the metaphysical viewpoint, as we will soon see, is of the greatest importance. This difficulty is so great that we prefer to consider it here in connection with relatively simple phenomena, rather than later when we will be concerned with complex ordered wholes. The reason is that, in our conviction, precisely the authentic metaphysical problems lie concealed in the simple facts of everyday life, and that the complicated complexes of problems are relatively easy to solve, once the foundations of their solution have been rendered secure. For this reason it

---

[1]*Contra gentes,* bk. II, ch. 72.
[2]W. Köhler, *Physicalische Gestalten* (3rd selection in *A Source-book of Gestalt-Phychology,* London, n.d., p. 17).
[3]*Gestalt-Theory* (*op. cit.,* first selection, p. 2).

is useful for the philosopher to start from the analysis of very simple phenomena.

Does the Ordered Whole "Have" Its Parts? The difficulty facing us here shows itself even in the homogeneous assembly, but much more clearly in the ordered whole. In the ordered whole we observe a very special relation between the totality and its members. Let us take the most simple of such ordered unities, e.g. a trapezoid or a triangle.

First, however, we must emphasize again that we are not speaking here of ideal spatial figures, *entia rationis* or beings of reason, but of concrete things, real forms, such as the wooden triangles used in drawing. The possible objection of the mathematician that accurate measurement may show such a thing not to correspond with the ideal triangle, does not impress us at all. The immediate appearance of the wooden triangle to us is a triangle, and this prenomenon above all demands an explanation. What is "self-given" and as such concretely perceived is more fundamental than all "more accurate measurement," because even the most accurate measurement is ultimately based upon such a grasping of the "self-given."

In daily life we say simply that the trapezoid *has* four sides, and that the triangle *has* three sides, etc. As philosophers, we must ask ourselves whether or not such expressions are correct.

Gabriel Marcel has devoted some attention to this problem. He calls the relation of the triangle to its sides an "implication of having": ". . . a category of having, insofar as it is implied for the subject in the fact of having [including, allowing] predicates."[1] However, we are unable to follow this philosopher of existence in this matter. Rather, it seems to us true that the triangle *has* its three sides in an entirely different sense than a tone has its pitch, or a color its degree of saturation, for the sides of a concrete triangle are not dependent and inherent accidents. Moreover, with his "implication of having" Marcel indicates a formally logical relation, while we are trying to grasp the essential laws of a phenomenological relation. Hans Driesch, in his treatise of the organic form, endeavors to characterize this particular relation between the ordered whole and its members by saying that "the organism has parts as properties."[2] This paradoxical statement shows that Driesch realized the difficulty encountered here.

---

[1]*Être et Avoir,* p. 216.
[2]"Der Begriff der organischen Form", *Abhandlungen zur theoretischen Biologie,* vol. 3 (1919), pp. 39 ff.

Let us ask ourselves first whether or not the essential characteristics of *"having,"* which have been analyzed in a previous chapter, can be found in this relationship.   Concretely speaking, does the triangle "have" its three sides in the same sense as I have a fountain-pen? Evidently, this is not the case. To point out only a single aspect of the impossibility of such an equation, we cannot take away one of the sides of the triangle without making it cease to be a triangle. The triangle is what it is because of its members.

"Is" the Ordered Whole Its Parts? Does the triangle *consist* of three sides? Is it its three sides? Does its being coincide with the being of these three straight lines (or straight things)? This too, we may not affirm without any further ado. These three lines could be drawn, or the three things could be arranged, also in such a way that they do not touch one another, cross in one point, or form a single straight line. The triangle exists "in" the three sides, but it *is* not its three sides. Looking at it from the viewpoint of the whole, we may say: The triangle is its three sides *and a formative act* which makes its triangular existence real. From the standpoint of the members we may say: they are members because they are subject to the norms of the formative act; it is because of this subjection that they participate in the formed character, the significance, the closedness, and the relative self-subsistence of the whole. All sides participate in the being of the triangle, but only to a limited extent. Although the triangle exists "in" its sides, it does not exist totally in any one of them. All sides participate to a limited extent in the being of the triangle, and this partly in the same way, and partly in a different way for each of the sides.

Let us assume that we have before us a rectangular isosceles triangle. It should be evident that in the whole of this figure the hypotenuse plays another role than the sides of the right angle. The hypotenuse has its own way of participating in the structure, and this way is different from that of the two sides forming the right angle. All three sides are to a limited extent triangle, but not in exactly the same way or in ways that are merely different degrees of the same way. The hypotenuse does not become a side of the right angle by changing its oblique direction. All three sides are *analogously* members of the same whole, i.e. the character of being a side of a triangle is formally adjudged to them partly in the same way and partly in a different way. What we have called the inner law is nothing else than the order and hierarchy of the different "participations" in the act which makes them real.

Dynamic Complement of this Analysis. It is not difficult to complete this analysis from the dynamic angle. To take again the most simple case, let us assume that our triangle performs a rotating motion with the hypotenuse acting as the axis. All three sides participate in the rotation, but in different ways. The hypotenuse merely turns around itself, while the other sides describe definite paths. All three sides *are* to a limited extent the rotating triangle; all share in the rotation of the triangle, but in analogous ways—the term "analogous" being taken here in the strict philosophical sense.

The Metaphysical Import of "More." Thus the superficial formula "the whole is more than the sum of its parts" conceals a very profound metaphysical meaning. However, we may not connect with this "more" any quantitative or even any objective sense. This "more" is not a thing, not a measurable magnitude or proportion, not a real quality or property; it is not something existent. In the terminology of scholastic philosophy we would say that it is not a *"quod"* but a *"quo."* It is the act which makes real, which confers actual being on that which is predisposed to being. It is at the same time the "formative" act, i.e. the act which imposes upon the whole and its parts a specific law governing their nature and operation. In other words, we may not seek behind this mysterious "more" anything else than the existential principle which scholastic philosophy used to indicate by the old and often misunderstood term "substantial form."

8. *The Hylomorphic Method Applied to the Problem of Unity and Multiplicity*

Our Problems Extend Beyond Human Existence and Life in General. A brief reflection shows that the problems hitherto raised in this fifth study are not at all limited to the domain of human existence nor even characteristic of the phenomena of life. As a matter of fact, we are confronted by them whenever we come into contact with material nature. Thus it is not a coincidence that our preceding analyses referred to the world of material things. For even the most simple spatially extended object shows the typical bifurcation described in the preceding pages—it is one and many, subsistent and non-subsistent, ordered and unordered. Of course, it is true that these notions cannot be applied to man without undergoing a characteristic modification, for unity, subsistence, and order are analogous concepts. However, this does not exclude that fundamental problems connected with these notions are primarily problems of material being as such. We will raise them here, because as a corporeal ego I am also material and participate in material nature. Accordingly, these problems must be investigated in the light of a philosophy of nature.

The Central Idea of the Aristotelian-Thomistic Philosophy of Nature. The central idea of Aristotelian-Thomistic philosophy insofar as it is a philosophy of nature is undoubtedly the doctrine of form and matter. The question, therefore, is whether or not hylomorphism contains methodical principles which allow us to overcome the difficulties encountered above. Note that we say *principles* and not explicitly formulated theses, although, as everyone knows, the problem of unity and multiplicity has repeatedly occupied the attention of both Aristotle and Thomas Aquinas.[1] Thus what will follow here is not to be found explicitly in the texts of either Aristotle or Thomas. On the other hand, to a large extent, the principles that have guided us in these thoughts exist embryonically in these two philosophers.

Relative Unity, Subsistence, and Order. Whatever is is one; therefore to be and to be one are the same, or as the Scholastic thinkers used to express it, *ens et unum convertuntur,* being and one are convertible. However, in reality we meet things that are not perfectly one. As appears from our descriptions, they are differentiated, structured, divided. Thus we are forced to describe their unity of being as a multiple unity.

In an analogous way, we may say that subsistent being is the primordial mode of being, that it alone is fully being. For the accident possesses only a derived being, it is only an *ens entis,* a being of being. Within the limits of a metaphysics of the finite, we may say that whatever is fully subsists, i.e. abstracting from its dependence on an infinite being, finite being does not depend for its existence on any other finite being. However, experience shows that genuine subsistence in this sense remains far from being general in concrete realities. True, *to a certain extent,* concrete things possess independence in being, for otherwise they would not really be. But their independence is mixed with dependence. With respect to their

---

[1]Cf., e.g., *Metaphysics,* bk. X, chs. 3 and 6.

unity and subsistence, material things have to rely on the being and nature of their surroundings. If the character of these surroundings undergoes a change, they disintegrate.

Finally, whatever exists is ordered. The absolutely chaotic is absolutely unthinkable. It does not exist as an actual reality. Whenever the idea of an "absolute chaos" is introduced in philosophy as a concept of limit, such an intellectual operation is based upon a directional consciousness and not upon that of an object.[2] Nevertheless, our experience shows that the objects encountered are ordered only to a certain extent. Different types of such order have been described in the preceding pages: the partially primitive and imperfect, and the partially refined and relatively more perfect. Thus we have shown that the concrete objects of our direct experience are ordered from a certain viewpoint, but unordered from another (superior) point of view. The material thing is constructed according to a certain inner principle of order, but excludes another superior principle of order.

Hylomorphism Offers the Metaphysical Explanation of this Relativity. Terminologically speaking, we may take refuge in using the terms relative unity, relative subsistence, relative order. For descriptive purposes such terms are adequate. However, the situation becomes different when we realize that being and being one are the same, that only the subsistent being fully exists, and that a partially unordered order is a contradictory concept. Thus it appears that the material thing somehow does not possess fullness and completeness of being. The philosopher who realizes this will feel himself forced to seek a metaphysical explanation for the "lesser-being" of material objects. As he will say, the material thing cannot at the same time be one and many, subsistent and non-subsistent, ordered and unordered. The absoluteness of being does not allow it. In this way a metaphenomenal reality appears to speak to us in the language of the phenomena. As philosophers, we can draw only one conclusion from our descriptions—the material thing is metaphysically composite. The way in which it is (is for me, is for us) reveals that two principles are at work, for a single principle cannot explain contradictory phenomena. These two principles, however, are not mutually incompatible as fire and water, for such incompatibility would lead to a kind of dualism. On the contrary, they are primordially related to each

---

[2]Cf. pp. 175 ff.

other. One is the principle of being determined, which traditionally is called the *formal principle*. Insofar as the thing is one, subsistent, and ordered, it owes this to its form of being. The other is the principle of being determinable, also called the *primary matter principle*. Insofar as the thing is multiple, non-subsistent, and unordered, it reveals the working of the primary matter principle. Because the concrete thing exists in reality by virtue of the reciprocal penetration and mutual limitation of these two principles, in general it will show the characteristics of determined being as well as of undetermined being. In other words, the *whole* thing will be formed matter, and the *whole* thing will be materialized form.

Another Approach. Perhaps it would be possible to arrive at the same truth in a different way. We have acquired the conviction that whatever is material consists of parts—the accumulation of actual parts, the homogeneous coupling of potential parts, the ordered whole of actual and potential parts. The metaphysical problem connected with this conviction reveals itself in the expression "to consist of." Why, we may ask, does the term "to exist" convey something different from "to consist of"? " To consist of" means "to exist as composed of," and thus implies two opposite aspects. Accordingly, we have to admit that there are two principles at work. The first accounts for *"existing* as composed of parts," the second for "existing as *composed of parts."* The latter, which is the principle of "parts outside parts," appears to be a principle of determinability, while the former, the principle of existing, expresses a determination of being. In this way we arrive at the same conclusion as above—the concrete thing in all its structures is materialized form and formed matter. It owes its unity, subsistence, and order (both static and dynamic) to its form of being. On the other hand, in its being not-fully-one, not-fully-subsistent, not-fully-ordered, the principle of indetermination of being expresses itself. The thing as it is given in experience shows how the form is limited by its materialization.

We want to emphasize that our considerations do not claim to express *the* theory of matter and form. Important conclusions from this philosophical doctrine have been intentionally omitted. However, in our opinion, we have sufficiently shown that certain fundamental principles of Aristotelian-Thomistic philosophy offer a solution also for the special problems which concern us here. Perhaps the point may be clarified by expressing the whole matter in this schematic form:

Metaphysical principles by which material being is		the material being
primary matter (*prōtē hylē*)	substantial form (*morphē, eidos*)	(*to synolon*) **is**
1. principle of potency for unity	principle of unity	a multiple unity
2. principle of potency for self-subsistent being	principle of self-subsistent being	relatively self-subsistent
3. principle of **potency for** order	principle of static and dynamic orders	ordered in a certain respect

9. *The Multiple Unity of My Members as a Structured Whole*

Thus far we have spoken only of the order which members have to the whole formed by them, and we have assigned to our body a place in the order category of the whole, while our limbs and organs were placed in the order category of the members. However, evidently this way of representing matters is still far too loose and simplistic.

Sense of the Term "Mine" with Respect to the Parts of My Members. A brief analysis will show this clearly. When, for instance, I look at my hand, the hand appears to me first as an organ by means of which I touch, grasp, and handle "worldly" objects. But after a closer look at this organ of touch and grasp, I become aware of things which I had not noticed before. The ends of my fingers are covered at the top with a smooth and hard horny mass, but the back of my hand looks different. On the back I see at regular distances pores from which small hairs grow, and these pores are interconnected by means of a system of tiny skinfolds. The philosophical question that arises here immediately is as follows. There is no doubt that these nails, pores, hair and folds somehow belong to my quasi-objects. But are they "members" in the same sense as my hand or my leg? Do I live "in" such a little hair on the back of my hand in the same way as I live "in" my hand? May I call them "mine" in the same sense?

Anyone will feel that this is not the case, and this negative feeling can be justified phenomenologically. We have already investigated the sense which the term "mine" has in this connection. The hand is *my* hand, because everything which happens to it or by means of it touches me immediately or is to my immediate advantage. But my relation to the nails and the hair of my hand is different. Of course, it is "I" who feel every contact with these little hairs, but I feel them in the way of "something that touches *my* hand," and insofar as this hand is "mine" it touches me. There is a respect of mediacy, a more indirect, more remote egological relationship. *A priori* speaking, the number of degrees of mediacy is unlimited, and one can conceive even a ramified hierarchy of mediate relationships. Perhaps the microcosmos of our quasi-objects is ruled by such a network of indirect relations.

Plurality of Principles of Order in One Ordered Whole. Let us carefully consider the phenomenon which presents itself to us. The pores are regularly distributed over the back of my hand. Together with the special network of tiny skinfolds they give the impression of a "picture" in exactly the same sense as we speak of a "picture" in the case of the Little Bear. Undoubtedly, a principle of order reveals itself in the system of pores, hair, and skinfolds. The nails of my hand and the rims of skin around them present a definite order, which manifestly is different from that observed on the back of my hand. Biologists and physiologists assure us that there are still innumerable other systems of order—visible and invisible, macroscopic and microscopic, biological, biochemical, and physical. All this does not change the essence of our problem, which is: how is it possible for one ordered whole to contain more than one principle of order? How can such a whole maintain itself? Why does it not collapse?

Fundamentally, this problem is similar to the one just considered. While the difficulty then encountered was to show the *a priori* possibility of a multiple unity, here the problem of **unity and multiplicity** arises on the level of principles of order. The solution, then, will be likewise similar. Just as all differentiated multiplicity is thinkable only in function of a unity, so also can there be a plurality of principles of order in one ordered whole only if these principles are, as it were, ramifications of one and the same general internal law. Let us clarify what this means by means of our analysis. As we have seen, my fingernails form in a sense a special system. This system is integrated into the general order of my bodily being, but in an indirect way. My nails belong immediately to the being and nature of a member, namely, my hand. In the dynamic aspect they have the function of giving support to my hand in its action as a grasping organ. The nails therefore are my nails insofar as they are integral parts of my hand, i.e. insofar as they are members of a member.

Structure. These essential relations have to be taken into account when we want to give an adequate description of the multiform and complex microcosmos of our quasi-objects. In the construction of a house it may happen that because of their special disposition and connection several component parts function as a single building block. It is likewise possible that several subordinated members together represent a single member of an ordered whole. These subordinate members constitute, as we will say from now on, the *structure* of a member. In our terminology therefore *a structure is a whole composed of subordinated members which in connection with one or more superior members functions as a single member, equal in rank to the other superior members.* Regarding the case analysed above we will say: certain subordinated members, such as the skin, nails, muscles of the hand, etc., contribute to the construction and operation of a single superior member (the hand). Briefly, we speak of a structure when we find a subordinate principle of order among the members of a whole.

In this sense we may speak of structures of equal, lower, or superior rank which all together constitute a hierarchy of structures. The various subordinated principles of order in it are simply the derivations and applications of one and the same internal fundamental law which guarantees the being and activity of the whole as such.

Structural Union of Two Ordered Wholes. Perhaps it will be useful to touch in this connection the question of the way in which two ordered wholes may be structurally united. It seems to me that two—and only two—forms of union can and do exist. Either each member of one structure in principle is capable of entering into a connection with every member of the structure, or one or more members of one or both structures have the special function of securing the connection and collaboration. In the first case we will speak of a *conjunction (Beiordnung)* ; in the second of an *adjunction (Zuordnung)*. The more differentiated way of union is the adjunction. In wholes that are more richly articulated and hierarchically constructed, the development of special adjoined members corresponds undoubtedly with an internal necessity. For instance, the system of my fingernails is adjoined in a very definite way to the construction and working of my hand, for several structural elements of my hand are made in such a way that they integrate the nails into the general organization and activity of the hand only at these definite particular spots and only in this or that definite way.

Terminological Clarifications. To prevent misunderstandings a terminological clarification has to be added to our explanations.

"Structure" has become a fashionable term. In present-day prescientific and journalistic usage of speech this term plays an important role. Often it is just because of its vague and indistinct character that the term is used, so as to conceal a lack of insight into and understanding of the situation.

Bona fide philosophers and psychologists use the term "structure" where we would speak of an "ordered whole." In this sense, for example, the Gestalt psychologists speak of a structure of the whole, a "field structure," and in this sense also Maurice Merleau-Ponty speaks of a "behavior structure." In passing, we want to draw attention to the significant fact that Max Wertheimer translates the term "the laws governing the inner structure of the whole" by the expression "the intrinsic nature of the whole." Many definitions of philosophers reveal the same idea. Louis de Raeymaeker, for instance, describes a structure as

> [a whole] whose principles are adequately defined by their correlation, so as to borrow all their value from their synthesis and all their meaning from the place which they there occupy.[1]

Eduard Spranger's famous definition likewise shows a certain relationship. According to Spranger,

> [a structure] presents an image of reality if it is a whole of which each part and each partial function accomplishes a task that is meaningful for the whole, and this in such a way that the construction and task of each part, in its turn, is conditioned by the whole and therefore intelligible only from the viewpoint of the whole.[2]

As should be clear, the conceptual content of these definitions partly coincides with what we have called an "ordered whole." Felix

[1] *The Philosophy of Being,* p. 106.
[2] *Psychologie des Jugendalters,* 11th ed., Leipzig, pp. 53 f.

Krüger, however, and the psychologists of the School of Leipzig are a special case. For them "structure" is "an artificial concept, used in the construction of psychological theory," whose function is to indicate the dispositional foundations of the whole system. These permanent dispositional foundations, of course, are less copiously articulated than the actual content of lived experience with its manifold patterns. So the adherents of the School of Leipzig indicate by the term "structure" that which is relatively simple; by "patterns," "pattern-like traits," "formations,"[3] etc. that which is relatively complex.[4]

It is not at all our intention to add to this prevailing confusion of terms. But we ask ourselves whether it is advisable to speak always of a structure in connection with behavior or a psychical totality. Structure is derived from the Latin *struere,* whose original meaning is "to pile up in superposed or juxtaposed layers." It seems to us that the image of a plurality of articulated complexes or systems of order is to be connected with the concept of structure. This was also the usual sense of the term before it became fashionable, as is exemplified, for instance, in such terms as the "structure of wood," "molecular structure," and "chemical structure." For this reason it is perhaps useful to make a distinction between an "ordered whole" that is governed by a single principle of order and a structure in which the internal law of the whole has ramifications in several different unities of order. Thus, for instance, a constellation, a syllogism, a figure, and a rhythm are ordered wholes for us, while an organism is, in addition, a structured whole. Although we keep in mind that many eminent thinkers and men of research deviate from this terminology, we are of the opinion that this terminology has to be used systematically in this study.

10. *The Quasi-Objective Multiple Unity as a Fluid Whole*

The Flux of Life. Another difficulty, to which an allusion has already been made, remains to be overcome. As we have previously pointed out, the unity of my quasi-objects possesses a changing and fluid character. This is true with respect to all levels of my quasi-objective life. My breathing, for instance, is part of my experience of the vital. What is breathing? It means to receive and to expel something in a rhythmically alternating motion. This continuous renovation of the self keeps my life as a bodily ego going. It is like-

---

[3] *"Gestalten", "gestalthafte Zügen", "Geformtheiten".*
[4] Cf. e.g. B. Petermann, *Wesensfragen seelischen Seins,* Leipzig, 1938, pp. 53 f.

wise to such a ceaseless change that I owe my continuous temporal life. The state in which I will live tomorrow is already in preparation today, and the disposition I have now is the result of *my* past. However, it must not be thought that this flux is exclusively a physiological phenomenon. The phenomenon appears much more clearly in the psychological realm. In my consciousness I am always directed to something; ceaselessly I gather new impressions; continually old contents of consciousness are pushed into the background by new contents. My present behavior is the result of my most recent actions, and what I am going to do in the next second is already now being decided. "Nature does not make any leaps." Nowhere is there a rift or a jump. One thing passes imperceptibly into another.

The Character of the Vital Flux. To describe this trait which characterizes all forms under which life appears use is made, in accordance with a twenty-five hundred year old tradition, of the image of a stream. What constitutes the point of comparison in this case is manifest: it is the continuity of change which one tries to characterize in this way. However, it must be emphasized that Heraclitus' metaphor cannot unqualifiedly be applied to vital phenomena. The flux of the living is something else than the course taken by a mass of water or an electric current along a pre-established path. Likewise, this vital flux may not be compared with a rainbow, whose various colored arcs are formed by ceaselessly renewed billions of droplets. None of these comparisons takes into account the phenomena of activity receiving into the self or actively expelling from the self. But vital functions are a living stream precisely because while flowing they keep their own flux running. They constitute *a flux which refers back to its own flow.*

Continuity is Not the Sole Aspect of the Quasi-Objective Ego. Continuity characterizes only *one* aspect of the forms under which life appears. To show this we too will have recourse to a comparison, which will be taken from the realm of sociology. But we want to point out emphatically that it is merely a *comparison.* In our opinion the meaning of the terms "whole," "member," "related to the whole," "organic," etc. in the domain of sociology is essentially different from that of the biological categories. However, we want to abstract here from this difference.

The Family as an Ordered Whole. Let us take, for instance a family. Although in a different sense, the family may be considered as an ordered whole. The family is ruled by an inner law that has generative, physiological, psychological and sociological aspects, which, however, do not concern us here. At present it is sufficient to note that every family has a definite character of its own. Not only is a working man's family different from that of a peasant or a royal house, but there are also profound differences between families of the same social class. What interests us here is this: the family is a unity, a whole possessing a certain character of its own, which I can trace and identify through the course of centuries. In speaking of the House of Burgundy or that of Orange, I always understand by this the same reality. Yet deaths occur all the time in this family, and new members are constantly added to it.

Identity of the Family. One would be inclined to argue: the identity of the family lies wholly in its continuity. If more members die than there are born, the "family dies out." If constantly many more births occur than deaths, the family will cease to be a family and will become a kinship or tribe. The existence of a fluid whole depends therefore on the equilibrium between accession and loss. Where approximately the same amount is added as is lost, there is continuity. It is because of this continuity that we are able to identify the House of Orange or that of Burgundy throughout the course of history.

This consideration is true, but it is not complete. Emphasis on this aspect alone makes one forget that the family is an ordered whole. The comparison with a stream breaks down here. In this respect we must recall an essential law of the ordered whole—namely, that every change in the relation of the members results in a change of the whole. Evidently, the addition of a new arrival or the departure of old members must be considered as profound changes.

Requirements to be Met by New Members of an Ordered Whole. There are definite reasons for this. In order that an element may become a member of an ordered whole, this element must first of all show a certain suitability. It must have a certain *ordinabilitas,* a capacity to be ordered, with respect to a definite order.[1] This, however, is merely a condition. The element in question must also be actively taken into the whole, which requires two kinds of activities. The new element must assimilate *itself* to the whole and finally integrate *itself* into the whole. This means that it must take the place and exercise the functions which belong to it by virtue of the order of the whole. Concretely speaking, to a certain extent and in a

[1]Cf. St. Thomas, *De potentia,* q. 7, a. 11.

certain respect it must become like the other members—namely, insofar as is required by the inner law of unity. On the other hand, the members which are already fully members must assimilate the new element, i.e. they must act in such a way that it becomes fully suitable for the place and the function for which it originally showed a certain *ordinabilitas*.

Application to the Family. The meaning of all this may be illustrated by means of our comparison. "Naturally" the members of a family will not behave in just any way with respect to the new-born child. They will feed him, care for him, raise him, etc. In time, they will show him the place which belongs to him within the framework of the family. All this belongs to assimilation and integration as a transient activity. The infant, on the other hand, will have to make a strenuous effort to become like the others. He will have to learn how to feed himself, how to move, etc., how to make his the habits, customs and norms of the family. For at the end of his development he will have to occupy a position and to exercise certain functions. Therefore, he has to adapt *himself,* assimilate *himself,* integrate *himself.* This whole active and passive process we indicate by the term "insertion" (*Einschaltung*). *In an ordered whole a new element is not simply added but "inserted."*

Evidently, the order previously existing in the family is modified by the appearance of the new-born baby. There are physiological, psychological and sociological changes. We will use the term *"commutation"* (*Umschaltung*) to indicate all these modifications of the total order, which may also be structural shifts, although not of necessity. No insertion takes place without commutation, for, as we have seen, every addition of a new member modifies the relation of all members to one another and that of all members to the totality. This modification may be profound or superficial, but never is it possible to have an insertion which leaves the existing order untouched.

It is likewise unthinkable that a member will be eliminated without a commutation. To show this we must first clarify the meaning of the term *"elimination"* (*Ausschaltung*). When, for instance, a member of the family grows old, he will integrate himself into the family life with increasingly more difficulties and less success. In the physiological, biological, psychological and social respects he less and less resembles the other members of the family. He dissimilates himself and literally becomes less like the others. He fulfills less frequently and less perfectly the function assigned to him within the framework of the family life. Death, properly speaking, is only the end of a long process of dissimilation. We will call this end *"disintegration."* Obviously, the death of a member modifies the total order of the family, in the sense explained above. So we arrive at the essential law: no elimination without commutation.

Why Does the Same Law Continue to Govern the Whole? In this connection spontaneously the following question arises. In elimination as well as in insertion the total order is disturbed. How then does it happen that notwithstanding these continuous changes and shifts in all internal relations the same inner law continues to govern the whole? Evidently, there is only one explanation—namely, that the modification called forth by the elimination is, at least in principle, compensated for by the opposite modification arising from an insertion. The family life which is disturbed by the death of a member can be restored by the expectation of a new arrival. On the other hand, the common life of a normal family under normal conditions is such that it favors the compensation of the loss suffered. This small community therefore is not governed by a rigid system of abstract norms, but by a living order, i.e. *an order which keeps itself intact by its own ordinating activity.* Nevertheless, even a living norm is an identical and identifiable norm. For this reason the family and its development in the course of centuries may not simply be compared with a stream. Something else than continuity can be observed in it —namely, an *inner law,* a proper nature, a "deeply impressed form which grows while living" (Goethe). Because of the special internal traditions and norms which live on in the family in question, we may speak of a royal House, a peasant's family, a working man's family, the spirit of *the* Bourbons, *the* Stuarts or *the* Hapsburgers.

Difference Between Family and Bodily Ego. All this is merely a comparison. For a human society is undoubtedly in the first place a *spiritual* whole and owes its origin to man's aspirations for complete development of his self. As a bodily ego, however, I am an existential unity. I exist in my quasi-objects. We would not have used this comparison if one of the greatest thinkers had not had recourse to a similar comparison. We mean St. Thomas, who wrote:

> We are to understand that the same thing happens in the parts of one man as in the whole population of a city, for each individual is cut off from the population by death, while others take their place: wherefore the parts of the people flow back and forth materially, but remain formally, since these others occupy the very same offices and positions from which the former were withdrawn, so

that the commonwealth is said to remain the selfsame. In like manner, while certain parts are on the ebb, others are being restored to the same shape and position, all the parts flow back and forth as to their matter, but remain as to their species; and nevertheless the selfsame man remains.[2]

Conclusions from this Comparison. Let us examine now to what extent the knowledge gained from the comparison with a community can be applied to the concept "my body." On the physiological level the matter is immediately clear. The reception of new elements takes place always in accordance with an inner rule. This seems so evident that I never even think of it. It does not occur to me to put a piece of bread into my ears or nostrils, but I eat with my mouth and I breathe through my nose. This instinctive activity and the automatic processes resulting from it take care that the elements received are assimilated and assimilate themselves. Here also the law holds that there is no insertion without commutation. The whole of my quasi-objective ego modifies itself as a result of the admission of new members into its vital structures. The process of elimination likewise obeys the same inner norms. What is being disintegrated by my body has already undergone a certain dissimilation. But my existence as a quasi-objective ego would be threatened if one wanted to cut out by force a perfect member from the ordered whole which is my bodily being. What is eliminated in conformity with my inner law is not "pieces" but inferior structural members whose presence disturbs and endangers the continuity of the flux.

The same situation occurs on the higher level, the one which is usually indicated as the "psychological" level. The realm of the psychical itself presents several stages. In our opinion, the laws of the fluid whole are valid for everything psychical insofar as it shows an actual differentiation. However, clear observation of these laws is possible only on the level of the conscious structure of lived experience. It is a well-known fact that a new content of consciousness is not simply taken into the whole of psychical structures. It is rather integrated into it, and the result of this internal insertion is so-called "apperception." According to L. C. T. Bigot, Ph. Kohnstamm and B. G. Palland, apperception is

an attentive perception and at the same time an understanding elaboration of the representations, an "apprehending as," an ad-

---

[2]*Summa theol.*, p. III, Suppl., q. 80, a. 4 c, as translated in *The Summa Theologica Literally Translated into English*, London, n. d., vol. 20, p. 180.

mission into a higher connection, an influencing of the new representation by the others that are already present.[3]

All this we indicate by the term "insertion." It is certain also that on the psychological level every insertion is connected with a commutation. In principle, *after* a certain experience the totality of the structures of consciousness differs from what it was before. This can be seen very clearly with respect to violent experiences. For instance, we can see that one who has personally experienced the horrors of war has become "another man." Finally, we find also in the psychological realm the process of slow dissimilation. A certain content of consciousness is forced back into the domain of the non-actual by another lived event. In the beginning I am still able to recall it at will, i.e. to restore to it its actual force. But later this member of the psychical structures obeys my free will less and less. It has become unlike the other structural members and therefore I do not easily find a way to rejoin it. Thus this content of experience slowly ceases to be a quasi-object of my free acts of remembering. In an incidental way the more or less automatic course of my associations may still bring this content back to the light of my awareness. But the various automatic processes characterize the realm where the quasi-objective ego borders on the non-ego. The content of memory is definitely eliminated when I have forgotten it. As soon as I do not know anything at all of a thing, I too have become internally modified. In our terminology we may say that the elimination is accompanied by a commutation.

Definition of the Fluid Ordered Whole. Perhaps it will be clear now what we mean by an ordered whole in a state of flux. The concept implies more than the Heraclitian flux. Identity resides here not merely in continuity, but in the inner law which renders this continuity possible. We therefore propose the following definition: *A fluid ordered whole is a whole which can exist only by ceaselessly assimilating elements into members and dissimilating members into elements.* From the dynamic viewpoint we may add to this that in a fluid totality the various member functions are fulfilled by always other members. This is possible only because of the inner law which harmonizes and rules the ceaseless renewal of functioning members, the rhythm of commutation by insertion, and that of commutation by elimination. Thus it can be explained that the total act of the whole remains essentially the same, not in spite of, but rather because of the ceaseless changing.

[3]*Leerboek der psychologie,* Groningen-Batavia, 1946, p. 73.

11. *Subjective Flux and Imperfect Immanence*

Connection of Subject with Good and Value. The vital flux is not merely a flow which refers back to itself, but is above all a subjective flow. It is by this that it is fundamentally different from all processes in inanimate nature. The question must be raised to what extent we may apply to this phenomenon the category of subjectivity. As we have tried to show elsewhere,[1] the concept of *subject* is inseparably connected with that of *good* and *values.* The reason is that there can be no question of a subject unless we have to do with a being that is directed to something, aims at something, tends to something. That to which it is directed, at which it aims and to which it tends is necessarily something which can complement, enrich and perfect the subject. With respect to the being in question such a thing is a good, i.e. a bearer of certain values. Briefly, we consider a subject to be a being which cannot be without knowing, desiring and seizing valuable reality.

Characteristics of Subjectivity. The specific character of subjectivity therefore does not lie in its closedness to the external, but in the fact that it is closed *to a certain extent* while being at the same time open *to a certain extent.* For the subject is essentially receptive with regard to the axiological aspect of reality—whence its accessibility and openness—, and it tries to retain in its inner self the goods it has acquired—and to this extent it is closed.

Another characteristic trait is connected with this. The subject is, as we have seen, a being that can exist only by ceaselessly taking something from its surroundings and attaching it to itself as intimately as possible. From this it follows that the subject must necessarily possess something which has relatively more value as compared with the world surrounding its life. For it has incorporated into itself, substantially united to itself, certain kinds of goods. In this respect we may speak of a *relative immanence,* although for the time being only in the very limited sense that the more refined, the more highly organized, the more differentiated "remains in" the subject.

Imperfect Immanence and Fluid Whole. This concept of imperfect immanence is no longer incompatible with that of the "fluid whole." For if the flux takes place in such a way that, on the one hand, the more valuable is ceaselessly taken in and retained as long and as intimately as possible, while on the other hand the useless

---

[1]*Objectiviteit en objectivisme,* pp. 7-10.

is not admitted or eliminated, then it seems to us that this flux originates from a *vital interiority*. In other words, if the flux and reflux has as its result that a being is able to enrich itself at the expense of its surroundings, to attach these riches to itself as intimately as possible, and to wash away everything which can impede and disturb the enriching stream, then we will not be able to doubt that we have to do with a vital phenomenon.

If we now apply these essential laws to our egological investigations, we see that the quasi-objective dynamism, including the automatic processes, is *my* dynamism insofar as everything naturally takes its course in such a way that the essential result remains in me (*"in-manet"*). As we have noted in our analyses of the execution of acts, something of my activity comes from the world, and something of the result of this activity returns to the world. But what has value in it, what because of its mode of being must be considered as superior, is retained by me. In this sense I am an imperfect interiority and at the same time a fluid whole. The apparent contradiction between these two metaphors can be solved by a reference to the immanent law of the whole. For the inner order, as it were, channels the stream, prescribes a definite course to it, and dominates it. Thus it forces the stream to leave behind in me the best it carries, to cede it to me as a relatively immanent "possession," as long as I exist as a quasi-objective ego.

12. *The Concept of Besouling*

It is time to ask ourselves what exactly it is that we have analyzed. What is the reality we have looked at from all kinds of angles? What is it that we have described successively as relatively self-subsistent, as the ordered whole formed by members exercising a function, as incomplete immanence and fluid interiority? The answer cannot be doubtful—what we have described is the phenomenon of my *besouled body*. As a besouled body, I am a multiplicity in a unity; as a besouled body, I have continually mutual relations to my vital surroundings; as a besouled body, I exist in a relative independence that is ceaselessly in flux.

Meaning of "Besouled." But, if this is so, innumerable new questions arise. What relations does the reality of my body have to the reality of my soul? How are my various members related to me-in-my-origin? How can I be at the same time quasi-object and subject and still only *one* person?

In the spirit of our preceding analyses we would like to answer that *to be besouled simply means to participate in my existence as ego.* My various members, structures and structural complexes are not in an original way "I," because they participate only to a limited extent in my existence as ego. Nevertheless, they are really "something of me," and I actually exist "in" each of them, although my being does not exhaust itself fully in the being of any of them. Something of me is hand; something of me is eye; something of me is sensation of pain; yet I am not simply hand, eye, or painful sensation. All members participate in a limited form in my existence as ego, and this partially in the same way and partially also in a different way. Briefly, the character of member is attributed to the various members in an analogous way.

Hierarchy of Besouling. Accordingly, the mode in which a besouled member participates in the besouling existence can be superior or inferior. This explains the *hierarchy of besouling,* which is so characteristic of my bodily being. In this hierarchy the temporal members and structures have a natural precedence. They channel my most intimate forces. If, for instance, I have hurt myself, the experience of pain will claim the lion's share of my life as ego. This is the reason why I call only temporal members "lived events" (*Erlebnisse*), although it is certain that I have also a lived experience of my spatially extended body. On the other hand, no matter how much these lived events "fill" me, they are not simply identical with me, for otherwise I would not have the *a priori* possibility to "get rid" of them. They belong to a privileged rank in the hierarchy of my besouled body. The precise character of this rank will have to be more closely described later.

However, also the level which usually is called psychological presents several ranks of besouling. It is, for example, a well-known fact that sensibility is not evenly distributed over the whole body. I can cut, for instance, my fingernails without feeling anything more than a slight pressure upon the underlying flesh. In contrast, the slightest speck of dirt touching my eyes causes sharp pain. In addition, it is remarkable how I am able to express what is going on in me by means of certain parts of my body—by some at will, by others involuntarily—, while other parts of the body hardly come into consideration as vehicles of expression. Several organs, e.g. my grasping hand, very faithfully obey all the impulses of my will; others, such as my eyes, have their own way of reacting which, however, I can influence in part by means of my will; the activity of others again, e.g. my heart, escapes from my control, although it is observable to me. Finally, my bodily life comprises also automatic processes which not only are beyond the control of my will, but also run their course without my direct knowledge; for instance, that I have kidneys or nerve cells is something which I know only from books. So we are justified in speaking of a hierarchy of besouling, a hierarchy which medieval psychologists endeavored to convey by means of their theory of levels of life.

On all these levels, in all these structures, in every one of these members, *I am present*. Whether they contribute to a phase of my "lived duration," put me into relation with my surroundings, maintain the vital flux, or are the expression and instrumental prolongation of my ego, they all are something of my reality. Even the structural members whose only function is to make it possible for me to exist in a space of a definite physical, chemical and biological nature participate in my concrete life as ego. Only, their share is infinitely more modest than that of the so-called "lived events." Perhaps matters may be clarified by this comparison: all my members "express something of me"; but they do not all say the same thing, they do not all speak the same language, and their communications are far from being equally important. Not one of them, however, fully expresses what I am.

Besouling and Flux. The phenomenon of flux makes the situation still more complex, although it does not change anything in our fundamental insights. Where above we said: "all my members participate in my existence as ego," we now complete the formula by adding "for a time." For none of them has a definite place in the hierarchy of participations. True, several vitally important functions remain essentially the same, but even these functions are fulfilled all the time by new structural members and ceaselessly renewed structures. This means that every member participates only for a time in the life of the ego.

Let us recall once more here our description of assimilation-integration and dissimilation-elimination. By means of these four terms we characterized the transformation of a foreign element into a member and that of a member into a foreign element. What then we considered principally within the framework of a theory of order we are now perhaps able to understand in its more profound causes. Assimilating insertion evidently means nothing else than a *"besouling"* which gradually gets a more and more superior character till it reaches the highest possible importance for my life as ego. The dissimilating elimination, on the other hand, must be considered as an increasing *degradation,* i.e. as a less and less participation in my life as ego, and finally as its total cessation.

Assimilation and Dissimilation. It is not difficult to provide some kind of illustration for these assertions. Suppose I have a piece of bread in my hand. This bread is still wholly foreign to me. As thousands of other objects, it belongs to my surroundings. But I am aware of the fact that this object possesses *ordinabilitas* with respect to my vital order. Then the assimilation begins. By a series of conscious, semi-conscious, and automatic processes the bread is "incorporated" into me; it becomes more and more intimately united with me; it becomes at a steadily increasing degree "important for me." A foreign object transforms itself into my flesh, my body heat, my strength, my life. But not forever. The moment will arrive when that which was first a piece of bread and then a "piece of me," ceases to be a piece of me and gradually transforms itself in me into a piece of "not-me." When this moment arrives, other series of automatic processes take care that that which no longer is part of me is removed from me. As soon as the object is wholly eliminated from me, I will face it again as a foreign object belonging to my surroundings.

Numerous processes which usually are studied by psychologists take place in essentially the same way. Let us take, for example, a perception. Perception also begins as a more or less accidental contact between me and something foreign to me. This non-ego, however, is not just any foreign reality. It has a certain *ordinabilitas* with respect to one or more of my senses. For this reason the automatic processes described in physiology and psychology can be put into motion. Non-ego energy is transformed into my energy; peripheral processes become central processes. Out of the domain of purely automatic dynamism sensations "grow" towards the realm of semi-conscious and conscious functions. Inflowing impressions are completed by contents already known, assembled into syntheses of identification, verified by "experience," etc. What originally was an accidental encounter with a foreign object of my surroundings becomes an "apprehension," a spiritual seizing and grasping. The "worldly" object has ceased to be purely "worldly"; it is now something of me; it participates to a certain extent in my life as ego; it effects in me a genuine knowledge. Again, however, we have to say: not forever. If a single cognitive synthesis were to maintain itself in the "focal point of consciousness," then the road to more extensive and richer knowledge would be blocked. For this reason my temporal life runs its course of necessity in such a way that in me interest is aroused in other data which complete and correct the first or have at least a meaningful connection with them.

"Sedimentation." The content of my former act of knowing then loses its force of actuality, i.e. it participates less and less in the besouling impulses of my ego. Here begins the process of dissimilation, which Husserl called "sedimentation." What he meant by it is easy to see. Just as movable elements carried along by a stream gradually sink to the bottom and build there motionless layers, so also certain contents of consciousness are no longer carried along; they remain behind, steadily lose their mobility, and change into an almost amorphous and lifeless mass. The process of sedimentation begins as soon as the datum in question is pushed outside the reach of conscious and free activity. First it is then incorporated into the structures that are not actually present in consciousness, although they still are subject to my will. Here it plays a role as the content of a memory which I can still actualize if I wish. But if I do not make any use of the content in question, if none of my vivifying impulses touches it or carries it along, then the dissimilation will take the course indicated above. From the realm of memory subject to free recall the temporal member will sink into the realm of associative memories, in which automatic processes play the important role. It still participates here in my life as ego, but in an infinitely more peripheral way. As soon as the object in question is definitely forgotten, it is also wholly "desouled," i.e. disintegrated. It is then exactly what it was originally—namely, a piece of the "world," a "worldly" object, with the sole difference that it has a greater *ordinabilitas* with respect to my cognitive dispositions, just as on the other hand my temporal structures show a greater aptitude to insert again the object in question.

13. *The Embodied Ego as Unqualified Unity and as Multiple Unity*

We may now devote our attention to answering the question with which we started at the beginning of this chapter—namely, how is it that I discover in me *two* realities while I am only *one* reality? How is it possible for me to be at the same time an irreducible subject and an ordered whole of quasi-objects? How can I exist as unqualified unity and as multiple unity and yet be only one person? In raising such questions one comes face to face with the problem of the unity of body and soul.

One could answer that soul and body are partial substances, and that it is only the one man who is composed of these partial substances who possesses complete being. However, in such an answer the terms "part," "whole" and "to compose" are given a fourth meaning which is entirely different; and if no attention is drawn to this fact, one cannot fail to give rise to false ideas.

I, Turned Toward the World. For this reason we ask ourselves whether it would not be better to present things in such a way as an analysis of my existence makes them appear. This analysis shows that I am a being among other beings, an ego in the midst of a universe of beings. No matter how different the interpretations are which various philosophers have given to this primordial situation, it is this situation which remains the starting point of every concrete metaphysics of being. Whoever reflects upon man and his existence cannot escape from taking into consideration two elementary truths, which are usually combined in a single statement: "I am, but not alone"; "I— open to the world"; "I—and you." In innumerable passages of his unpublished manuscripts Husserl speaks of an ego which by means of thought, feeling, sense of value, action, etc. inserts itself into the previously given world. Let us give the name of *existential movement* or *existential "turning toward"* to the act by which every subject, in virtue of an essential necessity, turns towards the world, the vital or social surroundings.

Care must be taken, however, not to lose sight of a fundamental fact—namely, that for man the world is primordially a material world. This does not mean that I am locked up in a world consisting of extended things. In my view of the world other egos, persons and their personal life play a decisive role. These other egos I understand immediately, without having to pierce through the armor of lifeless matter. I understand them immediately as *besouling spiritual acts, acts which besoul matter.* In an analogous way I grasp *immediately* also the products of social, cultural and artistic life as manifestations of spiritual persons in matter. Thus besouled matter is not at all a wall separating us, but rather a mediator between you and me; it is the support of personal animation and "spiritualization" (*"Begeistung,"* Husserl). I grasp the other immediately (and not by an analogous process of reasoning) as embodied person, because I myself am a body-soul unity. Notwithstanding the fact that its importance can hardly be overestimated, the relationship "I—you" is not the absolutely first datum of philosophical anthropology. Before being able to have a personal relation to other human persons, I myself must first exist as embodied person.[1] The primordial problem therefore is the problem of embodiment.

Embodiment. It is intentionally that we speak here of the *problem of embodiment*. My embodiment is not an event that occurred at a definite moment. It must not be explained as if God "infused" my soul into a body. Rather, my incarnation consists in this that I as spirit have been created in a transcendental relation to a situation in the material cosmos which demands a soul, and it is in this that consists the creation of the individual soul. Embodiment, therefore, is not an historical fact; it is a mode of being which, as long as I live, I do not cease to realize. Because I have been created with this transcendental relation, I can obtain my ontological fullness only as an ego which *embodies itself continually*.

In metaphysical terms, what is the meaning of this essential relation to the material cosmos? What is it to be embodied? Manifestly, it means that I make participate in my self-subsistent being, and this of necessity, things which are not " 'in themselves.' They are not persons but things, elements of the constant evolution of the universe," in which "the 'distinct from every other' is never found perfectly realized."[2] In other words, they are material relatively self-subsistent realities. By virtue of an essential necessity (*"per se"*) it belongs to me to raise "wordly" things and elements to a higher mode of being by forcing them to participate in my existential movement. For it belongs to the definition of my originating ego "to communicate to corporeal matter the 'to be' in which it itself subsists."[3] In order to reach the fullness of its being, my soul must be able to animate; it must penetrate the material world surrounding it; it must unite with itself in existential unity the material elements that possess sufficient *"ordinabilitas."* As St. Thomas expresses it, the soul "has a natural aptitude and inclination to be united with the body."[4]

---

[1]Obviously, this "before" must not be taken in a genetico-psychological sense, but ontologically.

[2]Louis de Raeymaeker, *The Philosophy of Being,* p. 243.

[3]St. Thomas, *Summa theol.,* p. I, q. 76, a. 1, ad 5.

[4]*Loc. cit.,* ad 6.

Accordingly, I am soul insofar as I have a respect to a material world; and I am body insofar as this respect is realized in me. As such, I am a single being.

Continuous Embodiment. We just spoke of "making things participate." This actively causing to participate manifests itself, for example, in the processes of integration and disintegration described in the preceding pages. We may even say that what we have called the "originating ego" is experienced by me primarily as the primordial driving force of my besouling and formative act. I am the constant source of the existential movement, and my body is its prolongation in the direction of the world. Maurice Merleau-Ponty is right when he writes:

> The union of body and soul is not sealed by an arbitrary decree between two external terms, of which one is object and the other subject. This union is brought about at every moment in the existential movement.[5]

This thought requires a more detailed explanation. In order to be able to exist as originating spiritual ego in a material world, I am obliged continually to bridge the gap separating me from the material world around me; and this means that I must continually embody myself. Between me as soul and the world of things there must always be an intermediary which is neither soul nor thing, but a besouled thing.

Moreover, I have to exist in a plurality of quasi-objects to find a passage to the unlimited plurality of "worldly" objects. I have to surround myself with concentric circles of members that are "outside" and "alongside" one another in order to obtain a foothold in a world of infinitely dispersed "parts outside parts." I have to live also in an orderly series of dynamic processes, which allow me to adapt myself to the ceaseless changes of cosmic formations. To maintain myself in the material world it is not sufficient for me to be "with myself"; I must also be "with" the material world, open and receptive to its values and non-values. From this it follows that in a material universe I can live only as an imperfect interiority.

Conclusion. All this is contained in the mystery of my embodiment, which is the ontological foundation of all forms of my human existence. In accordance with our analyses, we may summarize it

---

[5]*Phénomenologie de la perception,* 2nd ed., Paris, 1945, p. 105.

briefly as follows. I am spirit, but existentially I am not a self-sufficient spirit. This means that I am a besouling spirit which animates matter, a spirit-soul. As such, I am primordially oriented in my being towards a world of material (or materialized) realities. For I can reach the fullness of my being only if I exist in a way that corresponds with my natural lack of fullness. My mode of being therefore must be that of a *self-embodying spirit*. This means that I am spirit *and* bridge between spirit and matter. I exist *primordially* as spiritual ego and I exist *also* in my body. I am spirit-soul and I am also the matter which I besoul immediately. Thus, as an embodied person, I am a duality, a plurality, and at the same time a unity.

SIXTH STUDY

TOWARDS A PHENOMENOLOGY OF THE EGO AS INTERIORITY OF CONSCIOUSNESS

1. *The Problem of Quasi-Subjectivity*

To What Extent am I the Source of My Acts? At this stage of our investigations we encounter a difficulty which seems to raise a serious doubt regarding the usefulness of our whole method. We would like to call this difficulty the "problem of quasi-subjectivity." This problem flows from the provisional distinction made at the beginning of the second part of this book (pp. 79-108). We described there the real and possible object of retro-directed acts as besouled bodily being, and distinguished it from the egological reality from which these acts come forth. Evidently, this method was useful as long as it was a question of making it possible to define the concept "my soul." But is this method adequate to show from the viewpoint of the subject that the spiritual soul is the origin of all my acts? Certainly not. We simply took it for granted that all my retro-directed acts are performed solely by my spiritual ego. On closer inspection, however, this presupposition seems to be based upon an illicit simplication of anthropological problems. Have we ourselves not asserted in the course of our analyses that I am not the sole source of relatively immanent acts, but on the contrary "borrow" something from the "world" in these acts? Have we ourselves not concluded from this that I am not autonomously capable of performing vital acts, but only in union with quasi-objects and objects?

In the preceding chapter we indicated how we must conceive the existential union of the besouling act with a besouled plurality of members. But now that our problem is to distinguish what I am *primordially* from what I am *also,* entirely different questions arise. Now I want to know to what extent I am the source of my acts. To what extent does the surrounding world participate in the realization of retro-directed activity, and to what extent do I participate in it? How are we to distinguish in principle between the act that flows *immediately* from me and the quasi-objective occurrence which belongs to me *only indirectly?* How am I to know that anything at all depends on me and me alone? By what right do I speak of an originating ego when I cannot even prove in a philosophically exact way that a single action originates in me and in me alone?

I Do Not Find Myself as the Immediate Source of My Activities. As should be manifest, our difficulty is intimately connected with the problem of imperfect interiority. From the dynamic viewpoint relative immanence is based upon a collaboration of solidary members. One member turns to another or several other members, and thus there arises an active and passive collaboration which is to the advantage of the whole in a relatively permanent way. From this it follows that the immediate subject pole of retro-directed activity may very well be a member. Moreover, this conclusion is in complete harmony with our experience of life. Wherever we observe vital functions, we find a member that as a quasi-subject pole is directed to one or more others which function as quasi-object poles. Take, for example, the beating of my heart. What beats in me is I—but indirectly; that against which the beat takes place again is I—but again only in an indirect way. Everywhere I meet myself, but only as "existing in" or "acting in" my members. Nowhere do I find myself as the immediate source of my activities.

Is the Originating Ego Merely a Quasi-Subject? There is more to be added. We ourselves have taken into account the possibility that in a passing way I could live *exclusively* in the dynamism of my members. This could be the case, for instance, in the conditions of dream, sleep, hypnosis, or unconsciousness. But this possibility resuscitates immediately the old Cartesian motive of doubt. Who can assure me that I am not dreaming also *right now?* What guarantee do I have that what I consider to be my most personal life is not an automatic quasi-objective event? How can I know that what I consider to be *my* action is not the effect of very refined mechanisms? Is perhaps what we have called the originating ego in reality only a very perfect member of complex of members which functions as *quasi-subject?* Is perhaps "the anonymous center of my existence" nothing but a kind of "central organ"?

Necessity of Primordial Evidence for the Existence of the Ego-Source. One thing is certain. If we want to make philosophically justified statements regarding the ego-source, we will have to be capable of showing its existence by means of a primordial evidence. From a methodological viewpoint it may perhaps be justified to start from a *provisional* concept of the soul and to presuppose that the soul is spiritual. In doing so we make use of the same liberty as the geographer who in order not to have to face all difficulties at the same time at first describes the apparent motion of the sun around the earth. In the same way, for methodical reasons, we have characterized the soul as the principle of self-subsistence, unity, order, and active orientation to the world; briefly, as the principle of my existential movement. Now, however, it is no longer merely a question of the soul as the metaphysical foundation of a vital orientation, but, as was mentioned in the first part of this book, we are concerned with the spiritual soul as the source of genuine deeds.[1] If we want to reveal its permanent presence, we will have to show it as the egological reality which is no longer biologically conditioned by the world surrounding it, but based upon itself. Obviously, the method followed thus far is not suitable for this purpose. To reach it we will have to follow a different road.

2. *The Irreducible Subject and its Reducible Quasi-Subjects*

As has been pointed out above (p. 104), there exists an irreversible relationship between my originating ego and my body. This statement will now be clarified and completed by means of certain insights, gained in the course of our study of the order theory.

Member Relations are Reversible. In our besouled body there exists, as we have seen, a solidary collaboration of members. Every member is united with all the others, from both the static and the dynamic viewpoint.

It is not necessary that the functional relations of a to b be the same as those of b to a. Likewise, it does not matter whether or not the relation is immediate; a may be united with b by means of an intermediary member c, and vice versa. The only important thing is that the relation is *reciprocal*, i.e. that with respect to b, a can play the role now of a quasi-subject and then of a quasi-object, or that in one respect it functions as a quasi-subject pole and in another as a quasi-object pole. For, as Buytendijk expresses it, it is characteristic of organisms "that in every vital process the relations are *in two directions*, and that A determines B as well as B determines A."[2]

Irreversible Relation Indicates the Non-Member. This reversibility is implied in the very concept of "member." In the sense of our definition of the ordered whole we are to expect that in principle functional relations of a to b as well as of b to a are

---

[1] *Taten,* Cf. footnote 1 on p. 111.
[2] *Grondproblemen van het dierlijk leven,* Antwerp, 1938, p. 61.

possible. If we were to find an *a* which, not only in fact but as a matter of principle, cannot be the quasi-object of *b,* we would not consider it to be a member. Such an *a* could still be essentially united with a bodily whole, but not in the way of a member. In view of the fact that all members would have the mode of being of *b,* the whole body and all its parts would then be quasi-objects of *a,* or more simply, they would be *body for a.* Even those members which play the role of quasi-subjects would be quasi-objects with respect to *a.* For even if within the framework of the body they were the immediate source of quasi-subjective activity, they and their quasi-subjective functions would become at the same time quasi-objects of the actions of *a* which are of an essentially different nature. However, such a relation would no longer be reciprocal. For, all members of the ordered whole being included in the active and passive collaboration of the vital totality, all of them would likewise become object of the very special activity of *a;* on the other hand, *a* could never become the object of a biological directedness.

The Search for an Unqualified Subject. The question is whether it is possible to find in us such an element which is essentially different from everything having the character of an organ or member; an element which is neither quasi-object nor quasi-subject (for all quasi-subjects can become quasi-objects), but unqualifiedly subject. In other words, is there in us a subject pole which, although it is not separate from our body, nevertheless essentially differs from it?

To settle this question we will reverse our method. Everything that is a possible quasi-object has, as we have seen, the mode of being of a "member". Hence we have to ask ourselves whether or not it is possible to show in me an egological reality which in principle can never and in no respect become a quasi-object; a reality which, egologically speaking, possesses an irreducibly subjective character; a reality which I can consider as the ego pole of my whole concrete person.

3. *Reflective Reduction*

To isolate this reality by abstraction we will apply the method of reflective reduction, i.e. we will reduce our whole concrete being as persons till we arrive at something which we are forced to consider unconditionally as a subject. We eliminate everything that possesses the character of a thing in order to penetrate to the egological reality with respect to which the members are members.

Sense of the Term "Reduction". This reduction has a static as well as a dynamic aspect. What we eliminate is first of all any reality which has a quasi-objective mode of being; then also all activities which in running their course can become quasi-objective poles of intentional acts. Briefly, we "cross off" everything which can become the object of a directedness in order to lay bare at last the reality which ultimately is the origin of all orientation.

We think that we must make use of this term "reduction," although it has become, so to speak, hereditarily infected by the idealistic and immanentistic meaning attached to it by Edmund Husserl and other phenomenologists. This does not mean, however, that we intend to make ours the metaphysical framework of old-fashioned phenomenology. We do not intend to use the reductive method of transcendental phenomenology, but to give a new meaning to it. We engage in this hazardous undertaking only because we are convinced that our reduction is the only one possible. As we have suggested above (pp. 104 ff.), all "placing between brackets," every "reduction," every "epoche," is nothing else than abstaining by abstraction from making a judgment concerning "this" or "that." We are, moreover, well aware of the fact that even in the attitude of the strictest "epoche" there is no possibility of non-existence for that which in this way has been "put away by reduction," whether it be existence or existent appearance. In our consciousness it participates all the time in the absoluteness of being.[1] Only we do not want to make use of the knowledge we have of this, but suspend it. It should be noted, however, that such an abstaining from taking any position can be concerned only with a particular "this-here" or a particular ontological realm, but never with *the* world or the totality of being. On the contrary, it is our knowledge of being and the existents which constitutes the *a priori* condition for the possibility of any "epoche." Husserl himself seems to have felt this; for this reason he calls the world "an apodictic supposition," and in an unpublished manuscript he brands as "ridiculous" the attempt to eliminate "the world."[2] Hence there is no question of an "nihila-

---

[1] Concerning this point, cf. H. Robbers, *Wijsbegeerte en Openbaring,* Utrecht-Brussels, 1948, p. 27.

[2] "On the other hand, doubt concerning the existence of the world is ridiculous. It is manifest that the rank of the experience of the world . . . is of a higher evidential rank than that of the experience of the individual . . . The existence of the world has something of an apodictic character. It is not right that this existence would be doubtful for me who has experienced it." *Zur apodiktischen Präsumption der Welt,* B I 13/II, stenographed manuscript, 1933?, p. 18 in the transcription.

tion of the world." In addition, the existence of the ego which makes the "epoche" is not, as Husserl thinks, "the only thing that can be posited," but something which of necessity must be posited. "My existence in being"[3] therefore is a primordial, permanently pre-given situation, which in a general and necessary way must always accompany my thoughts. All abstractive efforts to suspend our judgment in this respect lead, as we have seen (cf. pp. 105 f.), to infinite regress, in which the same primordial data must all the time be reintroduced under new names.

Reduction and Abstraction. Thus we have already expressed our conviction that *the only genuine reduction is the reduction to that which is no longer abstractable.* Such a procedure of elimination can be used in a twofold way—namely, in general metaphysics and in philosophical anthropology. In general metaphysics it is used to justify the transition from beings to being; in anthropology it serves to distinguish the unconditional existential reality of the ego from the egological realities conditioned by it. In both cases the reduction is nothing else than the way to absolute concretion.

It is manifest that the regression to that which egologically is no longer abstractable can be effected only by means of methodically ordered, abstracted acts of thought. In this sense, the distinction which we want to establish is an abstract distinction. Accordingly, there is no question here of a kind of anthropological dualism. However, this abstract distinction is based upon an aspect of reality, a real "facet" of our personal human existence. It even seems to us that there is question here of an aspect which metaphysically is fundamental. Our intention is to try to fathom that which in the mass of egological data cannot be "left out of thought," generalized, "abstracted," or universalized. In this way we want to lay bare the existential foundation upon which my existence as ego is based.

Sense of the Term "Reflective." We consider here the concept "reflective," by which we qualify our reduction, as synonymous with "retro-directed," in the sense explained above on p. 82. Our reductive method, then, consists in this that I, i.e. everyone for himself, make my own concrete person the object of all possible acts, such as theoretical and practical acts, acts of knowing and of willing, of desire and of evaluation, etc. In this way we discover in our ego all possible members which play a partly quasi-subjective and partly quasi-objective role, but are wholly quasi-objective with respect to our act of dis-

---

[3]*Mein Sein in dem Sein.*

covering. In an analogous way, we find in ourselves all kinds of qualities, quantities, relations, situations, as well as diverse processes, functions and activities, all of which we can make the object of ego-directed acts. We eliminate everything which we discover in this way. By this we want to say neither more nor less than that *I exist in all these realities in a limited way,* and that therefore we cannot consider any one of them as the source of my existence as ego.

Reduction of the Body. Obviously, the first thing to fall victim to our reduction is our physiological body as well as all its phenomenological aspects. My body can be the object of retro-directed action insofar as it is the organ of perception as well as insofar as it is the instrument of practical activity. Evidently, in principle also all automatically functioning organs, structures and structural members can become objects of conscious acts. My body as organ of expression also is a possible quasi-object. For example, I make certain that this expression shows itself on my face, but try to conceal that one. Briefly, my body as the bearer of expression likewise is something in which I live to a certain extent, but which nevertheless can be consciously influenced. Therefore, it belongs to the realm of the reducible.

Reduction of the Temporal Level. Somewhat more difficult is the application of our method to the temporal level. Provisionally we are able to consider here only the various activities which are usually called "psychical." However, nothing prevents us from proceeding in this way. We will first examine the various functions and activities of the temporal level. According to the principle "action follows being," we may readily conclude: if the functions in question have a quasi-objective character, then the realities from which they flow immediately and upon which they act immediately must be quasi-subjects or quasi-objects; briefly, they must possess the mode of being proper to "members." For the time being this is all we need to know.

Reduction of Affective Life. It is manifest that the various functions and functional complexes can be examined separately only upon the basis of abstraction. But we have proved above (p. 94) that we have the right to proceed in this way. Accordingly, we may go on immediately and make the following assertions. In principle, all phenomena of affective life can be considered as quasi-objective. True, I can abandon myself without reserve to a feeling, an emotion and, above all, a passion. But, in principle, I have also the possibility to rise above them, to keep away from them and to get rid of them. For example, I am able "not to attach any importance" to my feelings, to dominate my emotions, to master my passions. This nowise means, as we have pointed out before, that I am always able effectively to do so. Nevertheless, this *a priori* possibility clearly reveals that my life as ego does not coincide with my affective movements. These movements are "something of me," they express something about me—perhaps even very much—, but they are not I myself.

Reduction of Perceptive Life. The same applies to my perceptive life. Of course, for some time I can be wholly, or at least almost wholly, absorbed in the contemplation of a landscape. But I have also the *a priori* possibility not to abandon myself to the naive absorption with and collection of impressions. While perceiving something I can judge, compare and correct the perception or reject it as an illusion. For instance, I am able to characterize as a sense deception the image of the stick that appears to be broken when the stick is put into water. We do not want to deny that as a matter of fact perceptive and intellectual activities are very intimately inter connected. The relevant point, however, is that in principle it is possible for me to place myself at a distance from every perceptive lived event and to dispose of it as a quasi-object.

Reduction of Imaginative Life. An investigation of our imaginative life, in the broadest sense of the term, leads to analogous results. Like Don Quixote, I am able to live in a world of fancies and imaginary adventures. This is possible for me, but it is not necessary. While building castles in the clouds, I can remain conscious that everything I imagine is based upon unreal suppositions. Therefore, my imaginations, my fancies, my dreams, my daydreams, my chains of associations are something in which I exist also, but they do not simply coincide with me myself.

Reduction of the No-Longer-Fully-Actual. In addition, all "lived events" which are not fully actual are possible quasi-objects. My former perceptions, imaginations, feelings, decisions, etc. constitute temporal structures of which I can still dispose to a certain extent, although they are ruled by their own laws. Likewise, what is given in my immediate memories, which, as Husserl expresses it, I "still hold in my grasp," functions as a quasi-object; for example, the terms I use in making comparisons, grasping relations, interconnecting and segregating. Whenever I perform conscious acts, I make use of my "historical ego." Thus it follows that the lived events which are no longer actual can play the role of quasi-objects, no matter the stage of sedimentation they have reached.

Reduction of the Not-Yet-Fully-Actual. With the necessary changes, the same applies also to all lived events which are not yet fully actual. I am able to suppress my incipient feelings, and replace representations by others before they have assumed a concrete form. I am able to "nip in the bud" a stirring of the will which I find evil, before it has taken the form of a volition in the proper sense. Above all, I am capable of rejecting as meaningless a judgment that is in the process of formation, before it has reached the stage of the convinced "It is so."

What is Left Untouched by Reduction? After all this we may ask ourselves: Is anything at all left? We have eliminated one by one the various aspects, regions and stages of concrete personal life. We have "crossed out" all members, structures and structural complexes, all processes, functions, and dynamisms. Everything that *a priori* belongs to the "disposable" part of my ego we have eliminated by reduction. All this evidently in some respect or other still belongs to my "determinable ego." But what is the "determining ego"? The determining ego, the irreducible subject, the ego with whose being my being fully coincides has been so closely circumscribed on all sides that we may consider it to have been negatively described. It is my intellectual life that manifestly has not been touched by the reductive procedure. *Will not my actual "I consider to be true" be that with respect to which I cannot place myself at a distance? Is not my actual willing for me something of which I cannot dispose at all?* Am I not obliged to identify myself essentially with my *"intelligo,"* my "I understand," and my *"volo,"* my "I will"? Are we not here at the most primordial source of my existence as ego?

But what is the meaning here of understanding and willing? Must these terms be understood as activities of thought and will in the sense of empirical psychology? This is what will have to be investigated in the following section.

4. *The Borderline of Objectivisability*

No Reflection to Infinity. Is there or is there not an absolute limit to our reflective thought or the chain of our reflective acts of thinking which are based upon one another? To determine this seems to us to be of decisive importance for the metaphysics of man. If, as Helmuth Plessner thinks, an unlimited possibility of the ego to reflect upon itself, an "infinite regress of self-consciousness" characterizes the human mode of existing, then we must conclude with him that man is essentially "without equilibrium, without place, without time, suspended in nothingness, and by his very nature without a 'fatherland.' "[1] However, we think that on the contrary the human tendency to reflect does not allow any infinite regress, that there is an absolute limit to it, an egological realm in which reflection becomes impossible and unnecessary. *The absolute limit will be reached when being present with myself I am present with being.*

Proof Inspired by Descartes and Husserl. First we must indicate how we do *not* want to prove our point. We do not want to take over the methodic procedure of Descartes and Husserl. Notwithstanding the fundamental divergence of our reduction, it would not be too difficult to proceed according to their method. We could simply reason as follows.

I, who make the reduction, am unable to eliminate myself by reduction. While abstracting from all possible egological functions, I am not able to abstract from my own abstracting ego. Briefly, I, who perform the reduction, cannot "place myself between brackets." In all retro-directed acts I am "also there." Hence it follows that there is an ultimate ego which is not a quasi-object at the disposal of my reflective power.

Continuing in the style of Descartes and Husserl, we could now try to determine the essential nature of this irreducible ego. We would then ask ourselves what is "necessarily true" with respect to this ego. Which properties, activities and powers must we *a priori* ascribe to it? What is this ego which performs the reduction? The answer cannot be doubtful. The ego of these reducing acts is I insofar as I *think* while performing them. Moreover, it is evident that the ego of the reduction is capable of making a voluntary effort. This is the only thing that I must in general and of necessity assert with respect to it. On the other hand, it is not at all an aprioristic condition that the ego of the reduction is a feeling, imagining, remembering or expecting ego. I alone, as understanding and willing, am an irreducible subject. As actually thinking and willing I cannot possibly be a quasi-object of my reflective power.

---

[1] *Stufen,* pp. 291, 310.

Critique of this Proof. We think that this proof as proof is valid. It is based upon the fact that, as we have pointed out before, a last observer must needs be co-present; I am not able to "cross out" this observer because I am not in a position to "go back far enough to raise the problem" of my own existence. To this extent the proof is correct. However, we have serious objections against this method of argumentation because it does not have the necessary metaphysical import. It says very little concerning me and my position in the universe of beings. It lays full emphasis upon my subjectivity in a way which gives rise to rationalistic and intellectualistic misunderstandings.

For this reason we prefer another method, which is far less "elegant" and more complicated. Notwithstanding these defects we give preference to it because it offers us the opportunity to acquire valuable metaphysical insights into the nature of the originating ego.

Method to be Followed. Our starting point may seem perhaps to be somewhat formalistic. The ego which resisted our reductive elimination was the understanding ego, the ego which knows by intellectual insights and wills deliberately. It was the ego of the Platonic "phronesis."[2] We must now try to seize this "fact" as an essential relation. However, in order not to go beyond the realm of the clearly and distinctly known, we choose as the object of our analysis an *act of judgment* as the prototype of intellectual understanding, and a decision as the exemplar of deliberate willing. We eliminate all psychological complications that can arise in them. Thus we assume that the intellectual or volitional act in question is performed after the manner of unqualified affirmation and that it is performed without any distraction, for any deviation from this "classical" case would make our analyses very complex without in the least altering their results. Phenomenologically, we can now make the following assertion: as long as we remain in the sphere of "phronesis" there is no possibility of a regress in reflective acts that are based upon one another. Evidently, *it is impossible to arrive by way of reflection "behind" our "being in the presence of being."* We will prove this statement by means of concrete analyses.

Concrete Analysis in the Speculative Order. Let us assume that I make the judgment *p* regarding one or the other objective state of

---

[2]Cf. *Phaedo,* 79d. This term will be used here in the Platonic sense and not in that of Aristotle. It means the inclination and ability to view the eternal and unchangeable ideas, or in modern terms, the capacity of grasping universal and necessary truths.

affairs. Obviously, it will then be impossible for me to formulate at the same time another judgment q whose object is the truth of p. What is striking here is that we are able to reflect immediately upon a judgment that has already been made, but not upon the judgment that is actually made now.

To illustrate this somewhat, let us assume that I want to know how much is two and three. Once I have understood that $2 + 3 = 5$ and have come to the conviction: "It is so; two and three is five," I will be able to confirm or correct, renew or reject this judgment in a subsequent act. But what cannot co-exist in me is, on the one hand, the conviction p "two and three is five" and, on the other, the thought q "my conviction that two and three is five is false." But where a negation is impossible there can likewise be no question of an affirmation. For, if my judgment q were positive, if it would be "Yes, it is true that two and three is five," and would coincide in time with p, then we would not have to do with two different judgments. There would be no mutual distinction between p and q, and therefore they would have to be considered as identical. Briefly, an explicit judgment evaluating the judgment I am *actually* making is impossible. I am able to make the *"pensée pensée,"* the "thought thought" the object of a retro-directed act, but the *"pensée pensante,"* the "thinking thought" is not an intentional object with respect to itself. A regress to infinity is impossible here, for the simple reason that the *first* retrogressive step is impossible.

Concrete Analysis in the Practical Order. The practical sphere allows analogous observations. I am not capable of making decision r and at the same time decision s whose object is the correctness of r. Again, we must say that, once the decision is made, I certainly am capable of confirming, completing, correcting, or reversing it in a subsequent act of will. But unthinkable is an actual decision r and a likewise actual resolution s having as its content: "I reverse r because it is not a fortunate decision." If, however, s and r would be simultaneous decisions having the same content, they would of necessity coincide in a single act of will, i.e. they would be identical. Briefly, our *"volonté voulue,"* our "willed will" is at our disposal as a quasi-object, but not our *"volonté voulante,"* our "willing will." Our actual conviction that something is really so or is really good is not a quasi-object of simultaneous ego-directed acts. We are faced here with ultimate, irreducible data, data which, no matter how paradoxical it may sound, are characterized by the fact that they are never "given" in the strict sense of the term, data that are never objective data for us.

An Objection. Objections are bound to arise here. Who guarantees that these analyses show anything else than interesting psychological observations without any aprioristic importance? Perhaps, what has been described here is characteristic of the special nature of the average human intellectual apparatus. But a superman would perhaps be able to make simultaneously judgment *p* and judgment *q* by which *p* is invalidated.

However, this objection is baseless, as a brief reflection can show.

When I judge that two and three is five, I do so on the basis of an insight, or what I consider an insight, into a situation. I allow myself to be ruled by that which is and the way it is. If now I must make a second judgment whose object is the truth of *p,* I will be obliged to go back to the same situation in order to check judgment *p*. To verify that my thought "two and three is five" is right, I have to investigate whether or not two and three really are five. Briefly, my judgment *concerning p* ultimately depends upon exactly the same premises that already determined my judgment *in accordance* with *p*. If I arrive in both simultaneous judgments at the same result, I can, properly speaking, say only that there is a single judgment, for what nowise differs from something else is identical with it. If, on the other hand, I arrived at another result, this would mean that I consider simultaneously as true that two and three is five and that two and three is not five. This, however, is impossible, and the reason again is not psychological but metaphysical. For, if I know something as evident, I have arrived in my procedure via the existents and beyond the existents in the presence of being itself.[3]

In an analogous way we may say that I make decision *r* because a definite state of affairs appears good to me. To verify whether my decision *r* is right, appropriate, and adequate, I cannot avoid investigating whether the objects or states of affairs intended by me are really valuable. If in both simultaneous acts I arrive at the same result, my decision *r* will be the same as my decision *s*. In that case there is only one act that is not distinct in itself. If, on the other hand, I would arrive at another result, this would mean that one and the same state of affairs appears to me simultaneously good and not good, valuable and not valuable, appropriate and not appropriate. But

---

[3] *Über die Seienden "beim Sein."*

this is *a priori* impossible, because as a being that strives according to intellectual insights I try to be in accordance with what *is* or *is good*. But being as being-true and being-good does not imply any internal contradiction.

A Misunderstanding. Care must be taken, however, to prevent a misunderstanding leading to grave consequences. When we assert that our strictly spiritual acts do not allow any simultaneous reflection upon themselves, this concept may seem to remind us of a kind of "unconscious spirit." As a matter of fact, the idea of unconscious though spiritual functions plays a very important role in the systems of certain analytic psychologists, especially that of Carl G. Jung.[4]
How it is possible for a psychologist and psychiatrist to adopt such a position is something we will see in the course of our subsequent discussions. But as of now we must emphasize that Frankl's concept of the "spiritual" needs to be critically examined. For, according to the view commonly accepted by the greatest thinkers of ancient times, the Middle Ages, and the modern period, one of the essential characteristics of the mind is to be present with itself in thinking and willing, to be "a source that thinks itself" (Karl Rahner). A mind which does not know anything of itself, which is blind for its own spiritual being, in other words, an "unconscious mind," is something wholly unspiritual.

In Spiritual Acts Self-Observation is Impossible. This shows itself clearly in the spiritual acts we have analyzed. In them "all self-observation and self-consideration" is actually impossible, but— and this is to be noted carefully—only because it is *unnecessary*. In other words, the spiritual cannot "come" to itself because it *is* already present with itself. So in our language the expressions "impossible," "incapable," "not able" do not indicate a limitation, deficiency or defect, but on the contrary are the negative aspect of a fullness, a power, a richness. Thus *an intentional reflection of my internal light upon itself is impossible because it is meaningless, and by virtue of my innermost nature I do not do what is meaningless*. In other words,

---

[4] While it is true that Jung does not explicitly use the term "unconscious spiritual" it will not escape the careful reader of his works that the unconscious, as described by Jung, possesses specifically spiritual qualities. A reality which is capable of producing "thoughts," discovering "objective truths," conceiving and communicating "ideas," including that of God, must be called spiritual in accordance with the universally recognized usage of this term. But according to Jung these abilities belong to the unconscious, namely the "collectively unconscious." Cf. Jung, *Über die Psychologie des Unbewussten*, 5th ed., Zürich, 1953, pp. 120, 122, 123.

the spiritual light shines in the darkness, but it does not throw a single ray upon itself. It is "unable" to do so because it is useless, meaningless, and therefore incompatible with the nature of spiritual light. In the spirit of this comparison we may say: as a being which thinks and acts according to evident understanding, I am fully present with myself and do not need to "reflect upon myself" in order to know that I am.

I am the Understanding of my Primordial Convictions. From this it follows, on the other hand, that I do not "have" my primordial convictions of truth and value in the same way as I have a lively imagination or a feeling of pain. I *am* my understanding of unconditioned values and ultimate truths. In my intimate aspiration to meaningful existence I am in an absolute way present to myself. I *am* the man who has taken this decision, who has freely chosen *this* and freely rejected *that,* the man who is "pervaded" by the truth of this and the falsity of that. There is nothing that is more myself than this my primordial being present with being. In scholastic terminology, it is the unfolding and ramification of my primary act of being in secondary acts of self-perfection. In my free search of meaning, and the taking of position regarding reality implied by this, in my free decisions, and the implied views of values which determine my decisions—considered not as a "system" or a "world view," but only insofar as they actually "live" in me—I am present with myself. No foreignness, exteriority or disposability is conceivable here; here I am alone in complete intimacy with myself, inescapably responsible for myself. For this reason it is in these acts of "considering to be true" and "holding to be valuable" that we have to see the specifically human feature, as well as the most personal essential characteristic, of my existential orientation.

5. *The Transcendental Character of My Existential Act*

Perhaps we are proceeding somewhat too hastily. After all, what has been proved thus far except that knowing and willing play a special role in our personal life? Granted that they probably are relatively the highest ranking operation of which we are capable, it follows that they cannot be the object of an activity belonging to a lower level. But who will say that our rational life also does not belong to the realm of relativity? In the domain of the relative there is no end to the number of conceivable grades and scales. Why then should these two kinds of acts occupy a privileged position?

The Transcendental Receptivity of the Ego with Respect to the True. To refute such objections, it will be sufficient to reflect upon the essential nature of "phronesis." In principle, we are convinced that we know an object when our mind is in agreement with the object to be known. To know an object means to let oneself be determined by the object, to submit oneself to the particular being and nature of the object. Thomas Aquinas calls this *"adaequatio"* or *"assimilatio,"* by which he understands primarily the passive submission of the knower to the norms of the thing known.[1] Thus it is manifest that the subject of universal knowledge must be fully "open" to all possible modes of being, for he must be receptive of the particular nature of all beings and things. If our mind had of itself definite material qualities or quantities, it would be unable to grasp cosmic reality. Just as we cannot judge the colors of a landscape if we look at it through blue or red spectacles, so also we would be blind to the infinite variety of modes in which reality appears if the source of our cognitive activity possessed this or that material property. Yet this would be inevitable if the primordial knowing ego were a member among other members. For, as we have seen, both statically and dynamically, a member has to let itself be determined by the inner law of the whole. Therefore, whatever is subjected to the order of besouled bodily being cannot be wholly receptive of the universal abundance of forms displayed by existing things. For similar reasons St. Thomas reached the conclusion:

> The intellectual principle itself, which is called "mind" or "intellect," has an operation proper to it, in which the body does not share.[2]

This Transcendental Receptivity is Not Yet Psychological Knowing. This transcendental receptivity, however, is not yet cognition in the psychological sense. To give rise to what is usually called "cognition," our "being present with being" must be referred to a particular object and interwoven with our bodily being, both of which take place by means of vital activities that are not fully open to clear understanding. For, on the one hand, our understanding must begin with the assimilation and integration of sense impressions, and, on the other, it must terminate with the insertion of the thing understood in the ordered whole of our previous experience. The first of these

---

[1]"Cognition takes place according to the assimilation of the knower to the thing known," *Summa theol.,* p. I, q. 76, a. 2, *ad* 4.
[2]*Summa theol.,* p. I, q. 75, a. 2c.

two points has been taught by traditional philosophy from ancient times; the second has been insisted upon with great emphasis, for instance, by Henri Delacroix: Consciousness "can neither perceive without apperceiving, nor apperceive without perceiving."[3] In other words, structures, already present, which are more or less in sedimentation must adapt themselves to every modification resulting from actual cognition. This means that under the influence of a new spiritual impulse the contents of consciousness which are no longer or not yet actual must be changed, rearranged and reorganized.

The Body is the Incarnation of My Understanding Ego. We see in this a new proof for the primacy of our spiritual ego in the above-indicated sense. If the structures of our besouled bodily being did not in principle adopt themselves to the original act of knowing, the "openness" of our ego to the world could not be realized. But, as a matter of fact, every new spiritual acquisition is immediately incorporated into the meaningful order of my earlier contents of consciousness, while these contents, in their turn, modify themselves, form new groups, alter their "form," etc. The so-called structures of consciousness are, as we will see, nothing else than ordered totalities of temporal members which make possible the incarnation of my *"cogito."* Accordingly, quasi-objective bodily being is at the disposal and service of actual spiritual operation. From this it follows that *my understanding of universally necessary truths is not an act of understanding exercised by my body, but my body is the embodiment of my understanding.*

The Transcendental Receptivity of the Ego to the Good. Being, insofar as it is true being, is the foundation of all my cognitive acts, and insofar as it is valuable being, it gives rise in me to acts of tending. In connection with this it is important to point out that in principle I value the good as such, no matter in what form it reveals itself. This, however, would not be possible if for me, who tend, only certain definite forms of goodness were valuable as such. On the level of bodily being I am definitely concerned with determined kinds of good. But I understand that these goods participate analogously in *the* good. This universal receptivity of my willing and tending ego is possible only upon the basis of a transcendental "being open to," which a member or structure of my body can never possess.

---

[3]*Les grandes formes de la vie mentale,* 2nd ed., Paris, 1937, hereafter quoted as *Les grandes formes,* p. 45.

This Transcendental Receptivity is Not Yet a Psychological Tendency. Again, the remark has to be added that this primordial receptivity with respect to values is not a "striving" or "tending" in the psychological sense. A psychological tendency does not arise before my universal "I will" is directed to a particular thing. In reality, all my lived events, experiences and contents of consciousness contribute their share in assigning a concrete goal to my transcendental willing. Reversely, the structures of my consciousness are modified under the influence of a new orientation of my tendency.

It is only in this way that the transcendental act of will becomes an act of my concrete person and the object of psychological judgments.

Accordingly, here again we must reverse the popular conceptions. The spiritual tendency is not a maximum performance or even a "super-structure" of the living organism; on the contrary, the living organism is *my* organism because it embodies my spiritual tendency. For I besoul my body by forcing it to participate in, and collaborate with my spiritual being and life. In this sense my body is the embodiment of my spiritual acts.

I am Autonomous in my Movement Towards Being. Precisely because my spiritual activity is not inserted as just another function in the bustle of biological processes and forces, I am capable of rising above this bustle by examining and judging it, dominating it and giving it its form. Because of this free activity—free in the sense that it depends on me alone—it is possible for me to oppose myself as subject to the body and to objectivize to a certain extent everything that is connected with it, as we have done in the course of our reflective reduction. But for the same reason I am not able —and therefore no one is—to make my primordial spiritual life a quasi-object or object. *In my movement towards being I am autonomous.* No finite being can snatch away from me or deprive me of anything here; no creature can prevent me from grasping the true as true and the valuable as valuable. In this respect I am subject only to the absolute and all-embracing laws of being itself.

Conclusion. From all this it follows that in me as a human being that which we have called the existential movement possesses a transcendental character. Insofar as my life is integrated into my vital and social surroundings, it does not ultimately aim at definite situations or the material cosmos. Through the relativity, the conditional character, and the limitation of my quasi-objects and objects I aim at the non-relative, the unconditional, the unlimited. Just as the magnetic needle points to the North, so the act which makes me a person is directed to real being and to valuable being. I exist absolutely and unconditionally in this orientation to truth and value. In everything else I exist *also,* i.e. in a limited, conditional, and analogous way. These are the conclusions which we have drawn from our reflective reduction. We may summarize them in the brief but eloquent statement that *my existential act is a transcendental act.*

6. *The Primacy of My Transcendental Mode of Being*

Experience and the Formula "I Besoul my Body." Our assertion that we live only in a limited and variable way in our psychophysical organism while we exist always and fully as spiritual beings is in flagrant contradiction with the empiristic and naturalistic views of man. At the same time our assertion seems to be out of harmony with our prescientific experience. Everyday experience painfully reminds us that nothing is as unstable, as ephemeral, as dependent as our intellectual and volitional life. It appears even to be the most vulnerable part of our personal life. The slightest fatigue, the smallest emotional or affective disturbance, the most trivial sickness quickly harms our intellectual capacity, weakens it, and hinders its normal operation. Often this can go so far as to give us the impression that we dwell fully in the sphere of impulses or automatisms. On the other hand, the participation of the biological processes in our life as ego seems to be much more secure. Certain instincts, drives, and vital functions constitute, as it were, the recurrent theme sung vigorously in the chorus of our egological activities. It is impossible to repress them completely or to ignore them in the long run. Sooner or later their constant massive presence will make itself felt. Is it therefore not exaggerated to assign them to the "disposable ego"? Did we not go too far when we asserted that I force my quasi-objects to participate in my existential act? Is it not pure nonsense to use such formulas as "I besoul my body"?

Meaning of "I" and "Besoul" in this Formula. Certainly, such a formula will sound strange if by "I" we understand "that man with brown hair, who is forty-three years old." And it certainly would be the utmost nonsense to conceive matters as if in addition to my regular tasks in public and domestic life I had all the time the additional duty of besouling my body. Evidently, such a view would be based upon a misunderstanding. The "I" of which there is question here is not the more or less familiar picture we have of our own person. On the contrary, it is the nameless ontological center that I am and was, even before I knew myself as a person among other persons. It is the absolutely elementary "self", Husserl's "primordial spring" (*Urquellpunkt*), Jaspers' "source of my thoughts and actions"; briefly, it is the anonymous reality of which we can say only that I am it primordially. On the other hand, we must emphasize that "to besoul" is not an accidental activity which I could just as well not exercise. "To besoul my body" is synonymous with "to exist in a material cosmos," "to exist as man." Accordingly, it is not an act performed by me in virtue of a voluntary decision. For what I will, desire, or tend to is of necessity *the other,* but what I besoul is *I.* It is in this sense that must be understood our thesis regarding the participation effected or imposed by me. For to make material realities participate in my existential movement means nothing else than to be in the "world," to be situated in a material cosmos, to insert myself in a "worldly" situation. In other words, it means to exist by virtue of one's essence as an embodied person. By asserting that I besoul my body we want to emphasize above all that that which besouls my body is *I,* just as correlatively everything which my body is, represents, or expresses is actually something of me.

Why the Spiritual Ego Does Not Always Reveal Itself. But now the question raised above becomes twice as imperative. Why is it that what we consider to be the most primordial element of the human person is so variable, so flighty, so unstable? On the other hand, why is it that something which does not immediately coincide with my being appears to me as relatively persistent, stable, and strong? Why does the servant behave as if he were the master of the house? Why does he who should really act as the host merely come and go as a distinguished but rare guest?

To answer this question we will have to add a complement to our explanations. We have previously pointed out that my soul is created in an essential relationship with a situation in the material world. However, till the present we have not sufficiently taken into account that this "worldly" situation changes all the time and is never exactly the same in two successive moments. A result of this is that the material elements which have to become the support of the existential movement reveal now a greater and then a smaller *ordinabilitas* with respect to this movement. They are not always equally suitable to participate in, and collaborate with my *"élan vital."* Therefore, the way in which the "worldly" objects and quasi-objects contribute to my existential orientation cannot be rigidly immutable. When the situation of my surroundings and quasi-objects is unfavorable for my spiritual bloom, it may happen that the whole strength of my spiritual act is spent solely in "making possible" my personal existence in this situation. The result will be that my spiritual nature as such does not at all show itself.

An Illustration from Sleeping and Dreaming. Let us take a daily experience, such as that of our sleeping and dreaming. What exactly is it to fall asleep? It is evident that every night I fall into a state of inner and outer powerlessness, although no force compels me. On the contrary, a kind of harmony arises between me and a definite situation. I lay myself down, close my eyes, and expect the situation—the quiet and darkness, my attitude of repose, my tiredness, etc.—to do its part in making the state of sleep take over. What is remarkable here from a phenomenological point of view is the fact that to a certain extent I "withdraw from the world." I retire as an inhabitant of the cosmos, insofar as I tend to a state in which I do no longer move around, make no motions at all or only very trivial ones, and no longer behave as a working and acting being with regard to persons and things. True, I still try to know "what is," to make decisions, and to behave rationally, but the data which should motivate my decisions escape me. The universe of beings with its inexorable laws is no longer distinctly present to me. My logic is very insufficient. Someone appears to me first as person A and then as person B. On the other hand, the quasi-objective processes play an incomparably more important role. Physiological operations, the dynamism of various instincts and drives, and associations play the leading role. They determine the level on which now I live.

Does this mean that I am now no longer directed towards being itself? Is my spiritual life stupified, sick, or dead? Am I now no longer a transcendental being? Not at all. What is true is only that I do no longer make much progress on the road to the transcendental horizons. And why? Because my quasi-objects are letting me down. They no longer insert me into the "worldly" situation in such a way that I can actively intervene. Reversely, the situation is of a nature to favor a decrease in the activity of certain quasi-objective structures. For this reason my "thought thought" and my "willed will" no longer put the necessary data at my disposal. True, even in my dreams I try to behave rationally, but the contents of consciousness needed for the formation of my motives do not come to my mind. Evidently, certain vital structures of my ego are exhausted. So long as they have not gathered the necessary energy for new impulses they will not insert me fully into the "worldly" situation. Till then I am not capable of rising by way of the concrete world to the recognition of truths and values. My spiritual act is still at work; even in this condition it still forces quasi-objects to participate in my primordial being. But so long as I am asleep its whole strength is needed to create the conditions for new spiritual actions. Its whole activity is oriented to make me again a being which is able to live spiritually in a material world. Briefly, the spiritual act is then only implicitly spiritual. It does not manifest itself in spiritual activity. For this reason, while sleeping, I live apparently "in" my vital functions.

The Role of Automatic Processes. Perhaps we can understand now why precisely the automatic operations constantly accompany all of our various activities. For it is these operations which connect me primordially with a material cosmos. They secure the fulfillment of the first and most elementary conditions of my embodiment. They take care that I can find a firm foothold in a surrounding world composed of material or materialized beings. If the automatic processes of my physical nature, if my vital instincts and my quasi-objective processes did not function, I would not be able to take even the first step on the road to my spiritual self-perfection. At the same time we understand also why this dynamism runs its course largely without my knowledge and consent. If they were not self-controlled, if every breath, every heart beat, every reflex, every instinctive action required special considerations and decisions on my part, then the very foundations of my existence as a bodily being would be endangered. My spiritual activity can display itself *as spiritual* because the biological basis of my being-in-the-world is rendered secure by a system of more or less automatic processes. When these vital functions are no longer performed "automatically," when because of illness, exhaustion, or tiredness they occupy a part of our spiritual energy, then I am forced to "withdraw" somewhat from the world. Then I am less involved in "worldly" affairs; I am also hardly able to reach the transcendental horizons by way of my surroundings and the world. The reason, however, lies not in a "spiritual illness," but must be sought rather in the fact that my spiritual ego is less perfectly embodied. I am and I remain a spiritual being, directed to being itself, even when I am less capable of displaying the spiritual forms of my existence.

Critique of the Cartesian Doubt of Consciousness. In this way we have also prepared the way for a critique of the Cartesian doubt regarding one's own consciousness, i.e. one's own being-conscious-in-knowing. For a more profound analysis shows that this doubt does not at all have the metaphysical importance which Descartes and Husserl ascribe to it. Obviously, the observation that I am dreaming while writing these lines would be very interesting, but only for the empirical psychologist. My ontological essential characteristics as an interiority of consciousness, as a self-subsistent free being, as a spirit, would not be put into question. For, as we have seen, even when I am asleep and dreaming, I am a being that is present with itself and directed to being itself. The same is true, evidently, with respect to hypnotic, hallucinatory, neurotic, and pathological states; in these states also my original spiritual being remains implicit and therefore hidden. Reversely, my "clear and distinct ideas" are nothing else than the highest unfoldings of the same original ontological situation, unfoldings which presuppose the "development" of whole series of acts that are not fully free, not fully understood.

As Delacroix remarks,

> It is not consciousness which is the first reality, but the activity of the subject, the dynamism of thought and action, the "I" and the ego, the person, all those forces of which consciousness is the achievement. But each of these forces is a movement and a degree of consciousness, an aspiration to consciousness.[1]

My existence as a spiritual being reveals itself essentially in this movement, this tendency, this laborious ascent towards the highest degree of consciousness, which runs its course through many stages and phases. Moreover, the level of consciousness varies from individual person to person, although this is merely a question of degree and not of essential differences. Even when I am dreaming, I struggle for the meaning of my existence; even if I were the wisest of all men, I would not be capable of interpreting my being-in-the-presence-of-being fully and under all its aspects. The question as to the level on

---

[1]*Les grandes formes . . .*, p. 16.

which I am between the two extremes with respect to other men is very important for psychologists, characterologists, and physicians. It is necessary and useful to design an empirical typology of the various specifically human ways and stages of arriving at consciousness. But there is nothing which gives us the right to construct a metaphysics of knowledge upon the basis of these empirical data. In the eyes of an infinitely profound spirit perhaps all my thinking is only an hallucination, all my activity only a somnambulism, and my whole life nothing but a dream. Nevertheless, even if this were so, it would not change anything in the essential character of my thinking. This thinking would still be an "aspiration to consciousness," a ceaseless effort to awaken, a perpetual struggle to arrive at clarity and truth.

7. Self-Consciousness as a Phenomenological and Metaphysical Problem

Primordial Self-Consciousness and Explicit Self-Knowledge. To prevent many misunderstandings which, as experience shows, often creep into an exchange of views regarding the problem of self-consciousness and thus make the discussion more difficult, we want to emphasize that we make a distinction between primordial self-consciousness and explicit self-knowledge. It is not necessary to indicate here the basis of this distinction. We know already that we owe explicit self-knowledge to intentional acts whose quasi-object is a part, aspect, state, or function of ourselves. Upon the basis of a synthetic combination of such cognitive acts we are able to form a picture of ourselves, our body structure, our external appearance, our characteristics, our relations with other persons, etc. This objective or objectivisable self-knowledge, as we have seen above, has the personal and social ego as its objects.

In this connection it is important to point out that the data of my self-knowledge are not a dead "ballast" of memory. Many of them play an important role in my personal life. I "know," for instance, that I look like *this* when I am doing *that*. I am aware of having a talent for one thing, but not for another, and this knowledge influences my behavior and my actions. Above all, my life is determined to a large extent by my familiarity with certain personal relationships. My awareness, for example, that in my family circle I am "at home," and that there are "strangers" outside this circle determines my actions to a high degree. Briefly, the "double" I have formed of myself, my conditions, my relations with other persons and communities constitutes a kind of psychical sounding board of my entire behavior; just as a sounding board, it vibrates in harmony with all my conscious acts.

Nevertheless, no form of objective self-knowledge would be conceivable without primordial self-consciousness. This can be proved in a convincing way. As is known, all explicit knowledge of ourselves is based upon intentional acts. So the question arises, What has forced me primordially to attribute certain object poles to my person as quasi-object poles? What makes me relate all data of my self-knowledge to this anonymous center of existence that is indicated as my elementary self-consciousness? We may answer briefly and succinctly in our accepted terminology: *the personal and the social ego presuppose the originating ego.* It is only the reality of my primordial self-being which makes possible all the various kinds of objective self-knowledge.

How to Know Primordial Self-Consciousness. We are faced again by the same enigma which we have encountered before. If elementary self-consciousness is the condition which renders all objective self-knowledge possible without itself ever functioning as the pole of retro-directed intentional acts, then how will we know that there is such a thing as an elementary self-consciousness? If "I think" accompanies all our acts, how can it itself become the object of any act? If the "determining ego" never changes into a "determinable ego," how will we be able to determine it? However, we have already indicated the direction in which the answer to this crucial problem must be sought. Till the present we have always started from the supposition that knowing is equivalent to knowing intentionally, that to grasp something spiritually we must be directed to an object, that every consciousness has to be of necessity a consciousness of "another as another." This view, however, of the essence of consciousness does not at all agree with the phenomenological data.

"To Know" and "to Know Intentionally." A first indication that matters are different is provided by the phenomenology of affective life. As Franz Brentano has pointed out correctly, there exist intentional sentiments. However, he goes too far when he claims that all sentiments present an intentional character. There cannot be any doubt that there exist also sentiments in which no internal reference to an object pole is contained, sentiments which are not a "consciousness of . . .," which cannot be considered as a "consciousness of a filling." We mean the "purely subjective" sentiments or, as they are usually called in ordinary language, *moods*. When I feel depressed,

lively, "empty," happy or melancholic, I am often able to indicate definite causes for these moods, but frequently also the opposite is true. In any case, the mood as mood does not refer me to an intentional object. My depression is not the "depression of something," as e.g. my perception is the perception of a room. Depression is exclusively a "depression of me," i.e. it is a "consciousness" of myself and of the state in which I am. The mood is something which is very close to me, very intimate, very personal. To this extent it really shows a certain relationship with self-consciousness. Probably as early a writer as Hermann Lotze held this opinion when he affirmed that

> all self-consciousness is based upon an immediate sentiment of oneself. This sentiment nowise can arise from the awareness of an opposition to the external world, but on its side is the cause why this opposition can be experienced as an unexampled opposition which cannot be compared with any distinction between two objects.[1]

Similar views may be found in C. Sigwart[2] and especially K. Oesterreich.[3]

Some time ago I have tried to complement these theories by drawing attention to the phenomenological distinction between intentional acts of affectivity and pure moods.[4]

We will not enter into the problem of the emotional implications of our immediate self-consciousness. They have been mentioned only to break the intellectualistic prejudice that by its very nature everything psychical has to be intentional. Actually the very existence of our non-intentional moods provides an argument against this view. On the other hand, unlike Oesterreich, we are in principle opposed to constructing the whole phenomenology of the self on the phenomena of affective life. As we have seen, my "affective life" belongs to the sphere of my ego in which I live *also*. But, as the process of our reflective reduction has shown, I do not simply exist in my emotional impulses. Sentiments, affections, moods, etc. are something I have and am. But our question is: How do we become conscious of the reality which I am absolutely?

---

[1]*Mikrokosmos. Ideen zur Naturgeschichte und Geschichte der Menschheit. Versuch einer Anthropologie.* 5th ed., Leipzig, 1896, 2nd part, p. 71.
[2]Cf. *Kleine Schriften,* Freiburg (Br.), 1881, 2nd part, pp. 226 and 237.
[3]*Die Phänomenologie des Ich,* pp. 1-26.
[4]"Personne et Sentiment," *Proceedings of the Tenth International Congress of Philosophy,* 11-18 August, 1948, Amsterdam, 1948-49, pp. 645-648. Cf. also *Das Gemüt. Grundgedanken zu einer phänomenologischen Philosophie und Theorie des menschlichen Gefühlslebens,* Utrecht-Freiburg (Br.), 1956.

Our objection here is not purely formal. There are many reasons against Oesterreich's view. The most important of these is that it is possible to have a doubt regarding the spiritual character of an affective state or mood. As a matter of fact, I become conscious of the fact that I am, say, depressed only by means of a retro-directed intentional act. I discover, so to speak, my own subjective condition. Then I usually ask myself: "Why am I so depressed or so full of vigor today?" Inevitably we meet here again the same old difficulty. We are face to face again with the same alternative. If we ascribe the act of discovering our affective state to our primordial ego, we will be unable to identify with our original ego that which we have discovered through this ego, at least not in the same sense. On the other hand, if we identify our ego with this barely awake pre-intentional consciousness, to whom will we have to attribute the act of discovering and asking? Does this act not suddenly appear like the intervention of a mysterious "deus ex machina"?

Purely Subjective Sentiment is Pre-Intentional. For this reason we think that the purely subjective sentiment is a pre-intentional condition. It is not yet differentiated; it has not yet any form or order; it does not contain any meaning. Only, from this vague and indistinct mood are born the various intentional acts, sometimes accompanied by sentiments, which are higher phenomena of consciousness, appropriate to the objective situation and bearers of meaning. *The pure mood, however, is not yet consciousness in the proper sense, because it does not have knowledge of itself.*

The Ego Does Not Simply Coincide with My Affective Life. Accordingly, we do not want to deny that I am the reality which "feels itself so mooded" (*"sich fühlen"*). But the opposite is not true. The reality which "feels itself so mooded" does not simply coincide with my ego. We may refer here to the innumerable egological states in which sentiment plays practically no role. Let us assume that I am adding a series of fifty numbers. In this moment it will be difficult for me to discover in me any kind of mood. My affectivity is, as it were, in a state of neutrality, and I observe no affective movements worth mentioning. Yet, I am no less conscious of myself. Primordial self-consciousness, therefore, cannot be reduced to affective states. Of course, the intimate "unity of the affective situation" contributes very much to my self-possession as a concrete person. Nevertheless the phenomena of primordial consciousness of my own self will still have to be explained in another and more profound way.

The Growth of "Tendency to Consciousness."   Previously already we have compared the "tendency to consciousness" with a process of development and growth. This comparison may now be expanded in several respects. Just as a seed hardly allows me to foresee the form of the future plant, so also the beginning act is formless, shapeless, hardly differentiated, and incompletely organized. Just as a seed, this act is still very vulnerable and sensitive to all kinds of influences. The slightest shift in the relationships of the complexes of acts that are already strong and powerful can cause its process of becoming to find a premature end. But just as the young shoot grows towards light, so also the nascent act pushes forward in the direction of the most actual life of the ego. The more the act develops, the better structured and organized it will become, the more delicately it will be tuned to its object. The more it approaches the anonymous center of my life as ego, the greater its actual and actualizing force will become. This shows itself above all in this that the act now groups around itself members or structures which are not yet or no longer actual. From an unimportant member of psychical dispositions that are not fully and clearly understood it becomes a point around which spiritual syntheses crystallize. For instance, in the sphere of practical activity a state of affairs that at first was barely noticed may become the motive determining a resolution or action. At the moment when this motive becomes *my* motive, I identify myself fully with it. Immediately after, the motive loses its actual and actualizing force, i.e. in this example, its force which motivates and attracts me to motivate. It is then a lived event, which I still possess, still have "under my control," of which I can still dispose as I like. In the further course of my life it may happen that the slowly dying act is again revitalized through another impulse that gives it meaning, e.g. through a memory, a comparison, or a contrast experience. If, however, no such thing happens, the act will slowly but steadily recede from the center of my fully conscious activity and sink back into the sphere of the "vital."[5] This process of increasing alienation, dissimilation, and sedimentation has been described above on several occasions. As we

---

[5]W. Stern expresses a similar thought in his thesis: "Lived experience grows from life and into life." *Allgemeine Psychologie auf personalistische Grundlage,* 2nd ed., The Hague, 1950, p. 100.

know, it ends with the absolute incapacity of reactualization, which we call absolute oblivion.

Directional Consciousness Leads to Primordial Self-Consciousness. For our problem the important fact is that because of the ceaseless succession of spiritual impulses which come and go in a meaningful interconnection a perspective of increasing or decreasing actuality will have to delineate itself. However, the comparison with a spatial perspective is not very appropriate. The intersection of parallel lines may be visible on the horizon, while the point at which all my egological processes converge is never given to me. Therefore, we prefer to compare this point and source of all that is "luminous" to us with the sun. As the sun makes me see without my being able to see the sun itself, so the spiritual focus of my ego is, as it were, invisible for me, not because it is dark but because it is too light. Nevertheless I know very well that the sun exists and where it is. To find out, I have only to follow the direction of the light rays or go in the direction opposite to that of the shadows. At the place where there is no darkness of any kind, the brilliance increases all the time, and I can no longer see because I am blinded by the intensity of the light, there, I "know," is the sun. In exactly the same way the numberless hues and shades of my more or less "meaningful" contents of consciousness point to a focus of meaning to which for me all sense and nonsense owe their validity or lack of validity. I *know* that this source of meaning-for-me exists, although I am unable to grasp it as an explicit object. I *am* this spiritual pole. I am the completion ("*Vollendung*"), the "entelechy" of all blind and half-blind processes of development. I am the secret goal of all egological functions, and at the same time I am the source from which issue all impulses that give meaning. Briefly, *I cannot conceive myself as an object, but I must conceive myself as a center*—the center from which radiate all my positive and negative "givings of meaning." It is upon this *consciousness of direction* that is based the primordial self-consciousness which is contained in all my acts.

Counterproof. It is easy to give the counterproof of this. In the same way as we have raised the problem of self-consciousness we may ask ourselves how we know the non-ego, the unconscious, the "it." For it is more than evident that we do "know" something of it. The proof lies in this that we constantly make use of this category, although usually only in an implicit way. We use it, for instance, when we say that we become acquainted with something, observe something, or understand something. On the other hand, we are also unable to avoid using such concepts as "to think of something else," "to pay attention to something else," or "to forget something." If we wanted to eliminate such concepts we would lapse into a kind of psychological immobilism, which is equivalent to the denial of all life of consciousness. By means of all these psychological concepts we implicitly give expression to the fact that something passes from the sphere of the unconscious to that of the conscious, or vice versa from the realm of consciousness to that of unconsciousness. Evidently we would not have any concepts to express these things if they were wholly unknown to us. But now we face the apparently paradoxical fact that something which by its very definition is not conscious nevertheless must be known in our consciousness as a content of consciousness. True, it must be admitted that if matters are conceived in this way, the concept of the unconscious will really imply a contradiction. In reality, however, it is obvious that we can have no more knowledge of an object called the unconscious than we are able to indicate an object that can be identified with our consciousness. But we do know the *direction* which leads away from the fully spiritual-presence-with-oneself to indefinite states of the ego which we no longer really possess and then further to what we have called the "non-ego in the ego." Our familiarity with the category of the "unconscious," which we display *in actu exercito,* therefore is likewise based upon an "internal reference to . . ."

Instances of Similar Situations in Metaphysics. However new our way of expressing the facts may seem, the matter itself is age-old, for other metaphysical concepts also are based upon non-intentional, nonobjective knowledge. We may restrict ourselves here to the two fundamental categories of "being" and "nothing." As the metaphysicist warns us explicitly, being is not "this" or "that"; it is not a possible pole of intentional and properly abstractive acts; it is not a collective noun. [6] We are able to grasp it only to some extent because of the hierarchical order of more or less limited beings, inasmuch as the perspective of steadily increasing ontological fullness or the opposite phenomenon of ever greater ontological limitation contains a reference to the infiniteness of *being itself.* As H. Robbers remarks,

_____
[6]Cf. Louis de Raeymaeker, *The Philosophy of Being,* pp. 33-38.

To know that there are limits and where they are means at the same time to have an idea of the direction to be taken if one wants to arrive at the *"terra incognita,"* the unknown region, beyond the limits. This is also the only way in which we can have knowledge of the unlimited.[7]

It is likewise impossible for us to "point out" "nothing" in an objective way. However, we possess a certain experience regarding relative non-being and its various modes, such as not-to-be-this, not-to-be-here, to-be-no-longer, or not-to-be-in-fact. The direction of this "less and less" refers us likewise to a certain pole, namely, absolute "nothing." Knowledge of this direction makes it possible for us to form the concept "nothing" and to make meaningful use of it.

It is in this sense also that P. Th. Hugenholtz writes:

> When we speak of the "ego," although one of its essential characteristics is to be always subject and not to be capable of ever becoming an object, we commit an error of thought which causes the idea formed of the ego to be nothing but an abstraction, nothing but a shadow of the true ego, projected on the level of representation. In reality, in its most proper active reality (*"Wirklichkeit"*), this ego cannot be represented. We do the same in a bona fide way when we speak about being *itself* (*des* Seins).[8]

In the present case there is no question of an error of thought, but of two phenomenologically quite different kinds of act, for not the objectivizing self-knowledge but only the primordial experience of the self is "at the same time . . . consciousness of being and of being the self."[9]

Our Concept of the Primordial Ego. Thus it should be clear that we possess also a concept of the originating ego and that we are able to make also this primordial ego the object of true affirmative and negative judgments without committing any error of thought. However, we should keep in mind that this concept is not based upon the intentional seizure of an object, upon the abstraction of an object which is stripped of its individual characteristics and universalized. In this respect the concept of the ego cannot be compared with such concepts as "red," "table," "man," or "state." It does not owe its origin to a consciousness of a datum but to the consciousness of a di-

---

[7]*Wijsbegeerte en Openbaring,* Utrecht-Brussels, 1948, p. 50.

[8]"Over het Ik en de Psychismen," *Nederlands Tijdschrift v. d. Psychologie,* vol. 1 (1946), pp. 126, 127.

[9]Louis de Raeymaeker, *op. cit.,* pp. 14 f.

rection. It is not so much based upon an abstracting apprehension as upon the exercise of a certain movement of the mind whose aim is glimpsed somehow but never really reached. Nevertheless our knowledge regarding the possible terminus of this movement is so firmly founded and so far removed from the possibility of error that we unhesitatingly use a conceptual symbol for this terminus, which is never really seized or encompassed. This notional symbol may be compared with the unfinished sketch map of an explorer who has met with an accident and put an arrow on his map with the remark: "By continuing in this direction I would have reached my goal." Accordingly, the concept of the originating ego is nowise purely formal, meaningless, or empty. The consciousness of direction, for example, which is the basis of the concept of the primordial ego differs from that which gives rise to the concept of being. We execute a different spiritual movement according as we want to think of the unconscious, of the absurd, or of nothing. Such concepts are not empty, but insufficient, improper, inadequate. Thus it is not correct to assert that we are wholly unable to conceive the ego-source. What is true is only that we cannot conceive it absolutely.

Here lies the source of all the above-mentioned difficulties, paradoxes, and "errors of thought." They find their explanation in the fact that the originating ego is a genuinely metaphysical concept, which, although it is presupposed by innumerable non-metaphysical judgments, nevertheless can be completely inserted only in genuinely metaphysical statements. In the following study we will draw the epistemological consequences of this situation.

8. *The Spiritual Ego as Interiority of Consciousness*

FIRST CHARACTERISTIC

Spiritual Ego is Unqualifiedly Subsistent. We are finally in a position to prove that the major theses of Thomistic anthropology are fully justified. They apply integrally once we have laid bare the reality to which they should be applied, viz., as soon as we are no longer concerned with the besouled body, but with the spiritual soul. The question here is to establish first of all that our spiritual ego is not merely relatively self-subsistent but *unqualifiedly self-subsistent.* By this we mean that in order to be able to exist the soul does not need any material surrounding world as its support. For its existence it does not need the help of objects or quasi-objects. True, the spiritual soul is essentially related to a material world. To realize its full perfection the soul is obliged by its very nature to become embodied and to impose the law of its essence upon relatively self-subsistent material elements. But it is the spiritual reality which gives the form that raises the mode of being to a higher level. This reality is the "entelechy" of all organic functions, the beginning and end of all vital developments. Thus in opposition to material realities we must consider this soul as unqualifiedly subsistent.

SECOND CHARACTERISTIC

The Spiritual Soul is a Simple Unity. Our spiritual soul is a *simple unity.* It is not a complex, an ordered whole consisting of parts, elements, or members which are connected in one respect but not in another. In my spiritual life I am myself in an undivided and indivisible way, no matter what I do or what is done to me. From this it follows that I can metaphysically interpret my spiritual being and activities only as a transcendental relation between my self-subsistence and my accidents. For in every moment of my existence I am one and the same ego, and in every moment of my existence I am another ego. For instance, I am now convinced of "this" and then of "that"; now I want this and then I want that. My tendency to knowing and my desire for values fill me fully; yet at the same time they vary ceaselessly. They exclude the simultaneous occurrence of any divergent conviction or opposite tendency.

I am My Spiritual Soul. It is important to emphasize that all this is valid with respect to the domain of "phronesis." As soon as we fasten our attention on the sphere of the besouled body, on the sphere of the not-wholly-understood and the not-really-willed, we notice immediately the inner tensions described at the beginning of this book. Then, for instance, I can "see" a stick half immersed in water as broken, yet "know" that it is not broken. I can also consciously tend to something, and at the same time struggle against it in my "subconscious." I am then convinced *somewhere* that S is p, i.e. that S is good, but at the same time I think *elsewhere* that S is not p, i.e. that S is not good. In my transcendental life there is no room for such a "somewhere" and "elsewhere" which can be explained physiologically or psychologically.[1] Here I am an ego which in an undivided

---

[1]Thomas Aquinas remarks "the fact that man wants not to covet and yet covets occurs because of the disposition of the body by which the sense appetite is prevented from totally following the command of reason." *Summa theol.,* I-II, q. 17, a. 7, *ad* 1.

way every time makes a decision with respect to a truth or a value. As a transcendental being, I coincide always and fully with myself, and yet am always another. This situation can be described neither within the framework of a positive science nor in an aprioristic theory of order. A purely metaphysical explanation has to be sought. To interpret these phenomenological data we have to admit the metaphenomenal relationship of a principle of subsistence with a principle of becoming. It is only the mutual penetration of these two principles which makes possible the reality of the soul as one and subsistent. Accordingly, there is no question here of a hypothetical substance which would be the unknown support of its known accidents. I am my spiritual soul as a self-subsistent reality, and at the same time as an accidental reality. I am this soul in a primordial way—for this soul is the source of my existence.

THIRD CHARACTERISTIC

Authentic Interiority. In this way we arrive at a third and very important essential characteristic. We are now in a position to show that my existence as an ego has its foundation in an authentic interiority.

To clarify this difficult concept we may perhaps make use of our theory of order. In describing the higher forms of order we were able to conclude that there exists in them a certain solidarity between the members of an ordered whole. Each member is to a certain extent present with respect to the other; each member, as it were, "feels" what the other is and does; each member collaborates in a definite way with the others. This is the reason why the organic whole is relatively more closed and independent with respect to its vital surroundings. On the other hand, notwithstanding the remarkable collaboration of structure and organs, there is in the biological sphere a spatio-temporal or purely temporal dispersion, a fragmentation of the total act in different functions, a division of energy over several centers.

Let us now pass over from the besouled body to the spiritual ego as such. In this spiritual reality we find no absence at all of the one with respect to the other, no mutual foreignness, no inner tension. Perfect unity rules here, in the sense of perfect presence of the whole relative to the whole. This unity therefore does not have the characteristics of primitivity, such as that of a lump, or of poverty, as that of a point. This spiritual unity is infinitely more rich and at the same time more intimate than that of the most differentiated organism. In the realm of the spiritual there is evidently no limited solidarity of one member with one or more others, but a complete availability of the whole for the whole. Everything is comprised here in a single act which refers to itself and is its own foundation. This mode of being can be characterized only as an *active presence of the spirit with itself*. This follows from our preceding analyses, for if in my inner self I would face myself as a stranger, an unknown reality, a being with its own will, I would here also be subject to the law of dispersion, i.e. to the law of matter. Evidently, this is not the case. On the contrary, as a spiritual ego, I am not "outside" myself, not "alongside" myself, not "opposite to" myself, but in myself, *present* with myself, *grasping* myself.

"Perfect Reflection." All these expressions, of course, are based upon metaphors borrowed from imperfect immanence. The very idea of immanence itself in its absolute meaning is likewise essentially inadequate and therefore linguistically and conceptually capable only of improper expression. This use of metaphors may give rise to serious misunderstandings. Therefore, it is important to emphasize that when interiority of consciousness is described as "perfect reflection," or as *"reditio completa,"* complete return, one should carefully avoid imagining this reflection as a retro-directed or ego-directed act. There is no question here either of a subject pole which "bends backwards" or of an object pole over which the subject pole "bends"; likewise, there is no question of either a subject ego which "returns" or of an object ego to which the subject ego "returns."[2] The very terms "subject" and "object" are even no longer quite suitable here. For the *"reditio completa"* is not a mirrored reflection of oneself, nor is interiority of consciousness a "mirroring consciousness." It is important to note this, for spiritual immanence is often described as follows: "I think and insofar as thinking I think myself." Even in Thomas Aquinas we find expressions echoing this idea. He says, for instance, that "perceiving its act, the soul understands itself whenever it understands something."[3] However, it should not be forgotten that for St. Thomas "to understand" has another meaning with respect to "itself" than as directed to "something." The act of presence with itself is the basis of every form of

---

[2]When Thomas Aquinas characterizes the spiritual presence with oneself as a "returning to one's essence by a complete return," he emphasizes at the same time that "to return to one's essence is nothing else than that a being subsists in itself." *Summa theol.,* I, q. 14, a. 2, *ad* 1.

[3]*Summa theol.,* I, q. 93, a. 7, *ad* 4.

consciousness. But this spiritual self-possession is no objective self-knowledge, no "introspection" in the sense of psychology. As Maurice Pradines remarks very correctly, "A conscious being is not a being that looks at itself in a mirror, but a being that possesses itself."[4] Moreover, the empirical sciences offer a wealth of arguments for the correctness of this view. It is very well possible to be a "rational animal" without possessing objective self-knowledge. It may be sufficient to point here to the case of consciousness in children and primitive men. Ethnologists tell us that primitive men are not conscious of themselves, that they do not conceive of themselves as subjects, and that their own existence appears to them as that of a thing among things. It would, however, be more correct to say that they do not possess any *explicit* self-knowledge. They are so fascinated by the spectacle of their surrounding world that they never arrive at the idea of making a quasi-object pole of the content of their lived events. Nevertheless, they possess the primordial spiritual presence with themselves which makes it possible for them to grasp themselves as identical self-subsistent beings among other beings, and these other beings as others. This proves that we must not conceive "understanding oneself" as a retro-directed act, as a reflecting upon oneself, but as an existential presence with the self which, even when it is not conceptually explicated, makes it possible for the subject to affirm himself throughout the inexhaustible multiplicity of lived experiences.[5]

"To Understand Something." In "understanding something," on the other hand, I am directed as a subject to an object. Here rules the typical subject-object tension; here we find that relation which nowadays goes by the name of "intentional." "Understanding something" therefore is a "tending to," a conscious grasping and spiritual embrace of a "worldly" object or a quasi-object. However, even this understanding owes its clarity and "illuminating" character to the interiority conscious of itself from which it comes forth. But primordial self-consciousnes is not a second act based upon a preceding act. With Fernand Van Steenberghen we would prefer to characterize it as follows.

> Self-consciousness is not, at least at first, a distinct act in opposition to the knowledge of the object. Rather it is the same act in so far as it is transparent to itself.[6]

[4]*Traité de Psychologie générale,* 2nd ed., Paris, 1946, vol. I, p. 7.
[5]Cf. A. Dondeyne, "Idealisme of Realisme?", *Tijdschrift* v. *Philosophie,* vol. 3 (1941), pp. 607 f.
[6]*Epistemology,* New York, 1949, p. 103.

So we must interpret the above-quoted text of Thomas Aquinas in this way. I am originally in a cognitive relation to myself, and this primordial knowing is the foundation of all my particular acts of knowledge. As a spiritual ego, I am with myself, and this spiritual presence with myself makes it possible for me to be present with the other in a knowing and understanding way, in an act of spiritual directedness (an intentional act).

Psychological Self-Knowledge. We may complete these considerations with the remark that psychological self-knowledge does not have the "thinking thought" as its object but the "thought thought." This self-knowledge therefore can begin only when acts of consciousness have passed from the stage of actuality to that of quasi-objectivity. Accordingly, psychological self-knowledge requires a special theoretical act which is based upon a preceding act that is no longer fully actual. When as psychologists we revert intentionally to our own temporal members, we succeed within limits in explicating our implicit presence with ourselves in true judgments, which, however, are necessarily inadequate. It is in this sense that Thomas Aquinas remarks regarding self-knowledge:

> The act by which the intellect understands a stone is different from the act by which it understands that it understands the stone.[7]

This view of St. Thomas is fully in accordance with the phenomenological data. Edmund Husserl, for instance, describes objective self-knowledge as follows:

> First of all, one must realize that every "reflection" has the character of a modification of consciousness, and this modification is of such a nature that in principle every consciousness can experience it. One may speak here of modification insofar as every reflection essentially proceeds from certain changes in attitude which cause a certain change in a pre-given lived event or datum of lived experience hitherto possessed unreflectingly. This modification affects the very mode of the consciousness or object of consciousness reflected upon.[8]

---

[7]*Summa theol.,* I, q. 88, a. 4, *ad* 2. Cf. the very profound and extensive study of P. H. J. Walgrave regarding the problem of "Zelfkennis en innerlijke ervaring by St. Thomas," *Tijdschrift v. Philosophie,* vol. 9 (1947), pp. 1-62.

[8]*Ideen zu einer reinen Phänomenologie . . .,* p. 458.

Merleau-Ponty likewise asserts:

> No particular thought reaches us in the heart of our thinking; such a thought is not conceivable without another thought as its witness.[9]

He complements this idea as follows:

> What is considered to be the thought of the thought, as pure self-perception, is not yet thought and needs to be revealed."[10]

Thus Merleau-Ponty also admits a primordial self-consciousness, a "confused grasp of originating subjectivity on itself,"[11] which, however, is contained only implicitly in every particular act of consciousness. To make this self-consciousness explicit and grasp it in an objective synthetic judgment a second act is required which testifies regarding the first act that is no longer fully actual.

"I Will My Willing." It is in this sense also that we must interpret the formula "I will my willing." For if the first and second willing did not have a very different meaning, this sentence would be meaningless. The best way to show this is by means of a fully concrete situation. Let us assume that we are in a restaurant and answer the waiter's question as to what we desire by saying "We desire our desire." If the waiter were very intelligent, he would reply: "You desire your desire; therefore you desire nothing." This conclusion would be wholly valid, because the subject desire and the object desire effectively neutralize each other. For this reason we prefer to express the profound thought which does not receive justice in the above-mentioned formula in the following way. All our particular acts of will are grounded in a primordial willing. This primordial willing, however, is not a conscious tendency to "this" or a desire of "that." On the contrary, it represents my original self-affirmation as a "striving" spirit, which in all my intentional acts of willing is particularized and directed to special poles. In other words, as a striving spirit I am present with myself, and this makes it possible for me to strive in an act of interior directedness after the other as other, knowing it, valuing it, and loving it.

---

[9]*Phénoménologie de la Perception,* 2nd ed., Paris, 1945, p. 458.
[10]*Op. cit.,* p. 462.
[11]*Op. cit.,* p. 463.

FOURTH CHARACTERISTIC

Transcendence of the "World." Finally, we would like to indicate a fourth fundamental difference between genuine and imperfect interiority. We have characterized relative immanence by saying that something of the being comes from the surrounding world, and something of it returns to the surrounding world. Hence the flux which is the characteristic phenomenon of vital interiority. The flux and reflux takes place in such a way that what at a given moment is more valuable, higher ranking, more finely differentiated, more forceful remains in the being. For the organism derives all the valuable elements which it needs for its formation and conservation from its surroundings. For this reason it lives fully turned to the external. Even the primitive man and the little child appear wholly absorbed in the spectacle of the world; they are, so to speak, magnetically attracted by all these moving, multicolored, sonorous, desirable, or frightening things. But with respect to man the situation is different. Because as a transcendental being he is directed to being itself, he has by his very nature a firm and lasting anchorage, so that he is more than just a ripple on the stream of life, more than a "worldly" situation, more than a nodal point of vital connections. He does, therefore, not have to expect all his values from the world and his surroundings. He is able to reflect upon his spiritual nature and to discover in himself spiritual values. Of course, it is another question whether he does it in the form of explicit and conceptual reflection. Thanks to his interiority of consciousness man is primordially a bearer of values in the material world. He does not receive all his values from his surroundings, and especially not those values which are decisive with respect to his full self-development. Not everything and certainly not the best of what he needs for his self-development comes from the cosmos. Therefore, we may conclude that not everything, and especially not the best of him will return to the cosmos.

To possess a spiritual interiority therefore means to have within oneself one's own foundation as a being that grasps values and realizes them. It means to be a primordially knowing and primordially willing being in an existential unity. These are the essential characteristics which make man a self-subsistent being endowed with a spirit or, in the words of perennial philosophy, a person.

SEVENTH STUDY

THE CONCEPT OF THE SOUL IN METAPHYSICAL AND EMPIRICAL PSYCHOLOGY

1. *The Explanation of Spiritual Self-Experience as the Task of Philosophical Psychology*

After the preceding series of purely philosophical studies we may now return to our starting point. We are now better prepared to overcome our original epistemological problems, because we have successfully worked our way to a genuine metaphysical distinction between the soul and the besouled body. However, there remains one question to be settled. In the light of the essential insights acquired in the preceding studies we must ask again: Does the object investigated by the empirical psychologist belong to the extension of our philosophical concept of the spiritual soul? In other words, is the psychology of man still a study of the soul? Does this term retain any valid meaning? Is the object of empirical and experimental research really our originating ego?

Empirical Psychology is a Positive Science. Let us begin with the simple statement that empirical psychology, as it is practised nowadays, is a positive science. By a positive science we mean a science which is exclusively concerned with data that can be grasped objectively. "Positive," according to André Lalande, means "from the viewpoint of knowledge, that which is given, presented as a fact by experience, even when its reason for being so is not known."[1] That this description applies to empirical psychology follows from the very fact that it is a science of experience. Empirical psychology is a science of *"empeiria,"* i.e. systematized knowledge of something concrete that is known through "familiar intercourse." This, however, does not mean that the facts studied by the psychologist have necessarily to be perceptible, measurable, or numerable. Even a mental disease, a religious experience, a work of art are "facts" in this sense. They are concrete realities with which I am directly or indirectly in contact, and which therefore I can describe, analyze, or compare. Above all, I can make every fact the object of an abstract-

---

[1] *Vocabulaire technique et critique de la Philosophie,* 5th ed., Paris, 1947, p. 771.

ing and universalizing act; therefore, I am able to insert them in a system of concepts, use them in theories and hypotheses, connect them with a prediction, etc.

Regarding the question as to *which* objects psychology should investigate there exist, as is known, different opinions. Should psychologists take into consideration in their research the objects of internal experience or exclusively consider the physical and chemical changes? Ought they to emphasize the physiological data or the phenomena of immanence? Are they to investigate only conscious processes or also the unconscious? All these questions have been and still are the subject of heated disputes. However, regardless of the answer, there is always question of *data*. Whether the psychologist studies a diary or the behavior of an animal, the chronographic picture of human motion or his own sensation, the material investigated will always consist of facts. Of course, this does not mean that empirical psychology is merely an accumulation of scientific facts, but it does mean that as a science of facts it is concerned only with objective and quasi-objective data.

The Spiritual Soul is Not the Object of Empirical Psychology. Thus it follows that empirical psychology can never take the spiritual soul *as such* as the true and proper object of its research. For, as has been proved, we think, conclusively (cf. pp. 103 ff.), the spiritual reality with which my existence begins is in principle unable ever to appear to me as a fact among other facts. Accordingly, the question regarding the existence and nature of the intellectual soul *qua* intellectual cannot be raised in a meaningful way within the framework of a science which is concerned merely with objects and quasi-objects, objective and quasi-objective situations, objective structures of thought or theories. It can make sense only in a science which starts from the immediately given and then investigates the conditions that must be fulfilled in order that objective reality can exist at all. This science is metaphysics. By its very nature metaphysics is concerned with the structures of reality that are no longer structures of objects, structures that cannot be seized adequately in an abstractive act of thought. My spiritual ego is one of these transobjective realities. We may assert this, for in the preceding studies we have become convinced that this ego is always and of necessity the subject pole of all my real and possible acts and never the object pole of any intentional experience; that we are not able to grasp this ego in an adequate concept because it resists abstraction as well as universalization; and that we never possess it in the form of a consciousness of a "content," but only in the form of a consciousness of direction. Hence it is correct to say that we have a primordial experience of our spiritual ego, and it is true also that we are able to explicate, to "unfold," this experience in phenomenological judgments. However, what is unfolded in this way is not the experience of "this" or "that"; it is not at all an "experience of facts." Precisely because this experience is at the same time a consciousness of the self and of being (cf. p. 182), it cannot be put on a par with the "observation" of any fact whatsoever. Thus the *"empeiria"* of the human mind is neither the "familiar intercourse" with phenomena that follow one another in a definite way nor the knowledge of a condition or situation, but its ultimate basis lies in the spiritual presence with oneself of the living spirit. This spiritual presence may be approached and conceived in metaphysical study, but can never be shown in experiments, discovered in observation, "proved" by induction. No more than being itself can the consciousness of being become the object of a positive scientific investigation; it transcends the limits of all psychological concepts and categories, even though each one of these concepts and categories presupposes it. Briefly, *the spiritual soul is not the object investigated by empirical psychology.* The correctness of this thesis has been proved in the course of our preceding analyses.

The Difference Between Empirical and Metaphysical Psychology. Accordingly, the difference between empirical and metaphysical psychology is not simply a question of method. The two sciences are distinct not only with respect to the question of the *how* but also regarding that of the *what.* The opposite also is true: the methods are different because the objects differ. The roads followed in both lead in different directions because the goal is not the same. The philosophical psychologist endeavors to solve the enigma of the transcendental and immanent mode of being in the light of a metaphysical "view of man." He tries to penetrate into the actual consciousness of being and the self, and to describe it in philosophical concepts, although these concepts are never fully satisfatory and adequate. True, the various forms under which the transcendental act is embodied and objectivized also hold interest for the philosopher, but mostly insofar as they are manifestations, objectivizations, and indications of the non-objectivizable act.

The empirical psychologist, on the other hand, is exclusively concerned with these objectivizations. For they manifest themselves in the form of facts, which are capable of being the object of empirical, experimental, and partly even of more or less exact investigations. It is for this reason that in the course of the last hundred years the empirical psychologist has become more and more emancipated from philosophy and is determined to examine whatever interests him by his own means and according to his own lights.

Philosophical Psychology Examines the Foundations, Methods, and Theories of Empirical Psychology. We do not want to say that the philosophical psychologist should show only scant interest in the results of positive psychology. On the contrary, for it is his special task to bring the facts discovered by the positive science of his time into harmony with the strictly essential concepts of philosophy in a constantly renewed synthesis. This is what at all times has been the goal of all great thinkers in the realm of anthropology.

It is true that the development of modern sciences in the last three hundred years has made this task much more difficult. It has become impossible to dominate the mass of objective data which numerous scientists have gathered in the most divergent realms. Moreover, the hypotheses and theories built upon these groups of facts are not immediately accessible to everyone. A certain familiarity with the subject matter in question is required to be capable of judging the importance and bearing of these theories. This situation demands that one pay the necessary attention not only to the fundamental theory of being but also to the special metaphysical disciplines. For the philosopher has the right and the duty to investigate and criticize the foundations, methods, and theories of the positive sciences *in the light of his eidetic knowledge.*

An Important Restriction. The restriction expressed in the italics is important. The philosopher is neither entitled nor in a position to verify the usefulness of the result obtained by the positive scientist, of the method used by him, or of the hypothesis he formulates to explain the facts harmoniously. The task of the philosopher consists exclusively in surveying the facts, theses, and theories, and assigning them a place in the universal theory of reality which is called metaphysics. In doing this he cannot avoid pointing out possible internal contradictions, obscurities, logical mistakes, etc. On the other hand, he will have to determine in a critical way the contents of the fundamental concepts and categories which the various empirical scientists use all the time without justifying them philosophically. Accordingly, there is—as there was in the past—a special metaphysics of material nature, of life, and of society, a philosophy of language, of law, of history, etc. In the same sense we speak also of a *philosophical psychology*. Such a psychology is not necessarily based upon a Thomistic, Catholic, Christian, or other world view. Wherever man endeavors to give a philosophical interpretation of the data of psychological experience and to lay bare in a critical analysis the metaphysical foundations upon which the psychologist constructs his science, he engages in philosophical psychology. Evidently, nowadays there are many non-Catholic and anti-scholastic thinkers who philosophize about the soul. As a result, a need is felt for a special philosophical discipline in which the metaphysical presuppositions of empirical psychology are investigated. The philosophical psychologist has as his task to lay bare the metaphysical content of concepts that are used in a vague and naive way, such as body and soul, matter and spirit, sensing and thinking, conscious and unconscious, structural and summative, and give them a better foundation on the basis of his essential insights.

What is the Object of Introspective Psychology? Thus we have adopted a definite viewpoint with respect to metaphysical psychology, but not regarding its empirical sister science. On the contrary, the nature of this science appears now twice as enigmatic. If it is certain that the empirical psychologist cannot make the spiritual soul as such the object of his research, one may ask with what, then, is he concerned.

In the framework of our investigation we have to answer this question especially with respect to introspective psychology. Hence it is perhaps most appropriate to ascertain first about what the introspective psychologist speaks. What is the object of his scientific judgments? Which realm of reality, concretely speaking, does he investigate? If we open any textbook written in the spirit of introspective psychology, we will find that the objects considered are called "sensations," "perceptions," "elementary affections," "representations," "associations," "cognitive activities," etc. All these are bundled together by the introspective psychologist under the title "phenomena of consciousness" or "psychical facts." Often he will consider them also as actions or states of "the soul." Above, we have already proved that from a metaphysical point of view this summarization must be branded as illicit. But now we face a new difficulty. The facts, actions, situations, and laws of which the introspective psychologist speaks are undoubtedly not simply nothing. Even if he detaches them in an abstract way from the whole of personal life, it remains true that this abstraction has an ontological basis; it is an "abstraction with a foundation in reality." Whether an experimental science can profit from such an abstraction is a question which the empirical psychologists themselves must decide. In any case, as philosophers, we must try to clarify the question to which ontological realm the facts belong which the psychologist discovers introspectively. We have already determined that they are not accidents of the intellectual soul. However, this negative statement needs to be complemented. If "psychical facts" are not accidents of the soul, what, then, are they "in reality"? Especially within the framework of a metaphysics of being we may not try to avoid this question.

2. *Organized Time as Material A Priori of Psychical Being*

Messer's Position. The idea that the psychical is somehow connected with temporality is not new. Often, however, the matter has not been taken too seriously. It was thought that a purely negative statement was all that is needed in this respect. August Messer, for example, declares:

> What, then, is the difference between the corporeal and the psychical? Everything corporeal fills real space, while the psychical does not fill any space. . . . Who has ever heard anyone saying "I have to build a bigger house, for I do not have enough room for my thoughts"? Or has anyone ever constructed a closet in which to keep his affections and decisions?[1]

Critique. This way of presenting things seems to be somewhat *too* popular. We would like to append the following critical remarks to this quotation. What is the basis of the assertion that the psychical does not fill any real space? First of all, it is beyond doubt that every "psyche" is related to a spatially extended body. Moreover, it is a fact that certain psychical functions are conditioned by definite spatio-temporal processes. Thus they are dependent on organs, structures, or structural members which are spatially determined or at least determinable in principle. Where, then, does Messer find a basis for his assertion? We may express this basis in the same popular terms in which we have heard it hundred of times. "No one has ever yet been able to perceive psychical reality in space. No biologist, physiologist, or anatomist has ever found a trace of psychical reality

---

[1] *Einführung in die Psychologie und die psychologischen Richtungen der Gengenwart,* 2nd ed., Leipzig, 1931, p. 4.

under his scalpel in dissecting a living body. Moreover, the psychical is not a phenomenon that is intersubjectively perceptible.[2] Spatially extended realities, on the contrary, are perceptible by means of our senses. In both pre-scientific and scientific experience they can be identified and defined by different subjects at the same time. Therefore, the psychical does not belong to spatially extended reality."

These are the usual popular arguments. We could raise here such questions as: Is it quite certain that the psychical processes occurring in another ego are not at all perceptible? Am I not capable, for instance, of localizing somewhat a sensation of pain in my own body? However, we prefer to abstract from the problem whether or not the premises of this conclusion are wholly valid in their generality. Our objection to the argument is concerned with a much more essential point. This point is that the premises of this argument are exclusively based upon induction. If matters are presented in this way, it will not be inconceivable that some day an anatomist or physiologist will "discover the psychical"; that with the aid of a technical discovery the "psyche" can be made directly or indirectly visible, as has been done with micro-organisms and very distant stars; and that in this way we will discover that the psychical also has the mode of being that is proper to spatial things. Thus the above-mentioned popluar distinction between the physiological body and the "psyche" will have merely the provisional character proper to inductive hypotheses.

Moreover, there is question here of a negative judgment. Hence, according to this view, the psychical has a temporal mode of being, because we have not yet succeeded in showing, determining, and measuring it spatially.

The Task of the Phenomenologist. As philosophers and phenomenologists, we cannot be satisfied with such inductive conjectures. Our task, evidently, is to determine the essential characteristics of psychical being. We will have to examine whether the temporal mode or being belongs to the material *a priori* of the psychical, while the spatio-temporal mode of being is not to be considered as such an *a priori*. Obvisously, this would not exclude that *de facto* much that is psychical appears also in space. What, however, is the meaning of "to be temporal"? This concept needs to be given a positive content. Our task would be to show how the psychical fills time. Thus

---

[2] Cf. Messer, *op. cit.,* pp. 4 and 5.

we would have something more concrete to offer in contrast with the purely negative notion of non-spatiality presented by positive science.

For a long time already the need, pointed out here, has been felt as such by many modern thinkers. Psychologists as well as philosophers have zealously endeavored to clarify the concept of the "duration" of our psychical functions and activities. Since the end of the nineteenth century a striking change has made itself felt in this respect. This change reveals itself in the fact that psychology has emancipated itself more and more from the tendency to take the exact sciences of nature as its ideal and thus has learned to distinguish between the abstract time of the mathematician and the concrete time of our lived events. Three generations of philosophers, phenomenologists, psychologists, and to some extent also physiologists have made strenuous efforts to indicate and describe the phenomenon "time." In this connection mention is deserved, on the one hand, by Bergson, Husserl, Heidegger, Merleau-Ponty, Lavelle, Nogué, von Weiszäcker, Buytendijk and Plessner, and on the other, by William James, Stern, Hönigswald, Pradines, Koffka and other Gestalt psychologists. Taking into account the works of these thinkers, let us now indicate exactly what we mean by "organized time."

Physical Time. It is commonplace nowadays to assert that the being-in-time of lifeless reality differs from that of living beings. Nevertheless it is perhaps not superfluous to recall in what this difference consists. The spatial thing is, according to a profound expression of Leibniz, a *"mens momentanea,"* i.e. the continuation of its independent existence in the dimension of time is secured by this that it is, as it were, transmitted by one "now" to the succeeding "now." Evidently, this is possible only because the whole reality of the physical thing is contained in one and the same "now." It *is* fully at the instant t_n. It is neither the thing of instant t_{n+1} nor of instant t_{n-1}. Its duration may be compared with a line. Just as one may represent the genesis of a concrete line by a joined series of infinitesimally small but mutually independent things, so the physical thing endures in moments which in their succession constitute a continuity while in other respects they are strangers to one another. If we consider two successive points of "now," we can say that the thing at the moment t_{n+1} is exclusively the result of the thing at the moment t_n. If, then, we know the condition of the thing as well as that of its surroundings at the moment t_n, we will be able to predict with the highest degree of probability the condition it will be in at the moment t_{n+1}. For what was before t_n and what is expected after t_{n+1}, does not influence the transition from t_n to t_{n+1}. Briefly, the thing transmits itself from one moment to the next, but it does not possess and dominate time; no part of time is *its* time. For this reason it is possible to consider physical time abstractly as a homogeneous continuum which is subject to infinitesimal division. More accurately, physical time permits such an abstractive way of consideration. It is not, as Bergson thought, "quantified time" but "quantifiable time."

Psychical Time. If we try to apply this concept of temporal existence to our concrete life, we will be continually faced with enigmas, as can be proved by a very simple phenomenological analysis. I see, for example, an object from all sides; while I consider its back, I still know how the front looked. It is only because of this that I am capable of uniting the various aspects of the thing into a synthesis of identity. Or I hear a melody; while I listen to the fourth bar, I am still well aware of the first. Higher intellectual activities, such as adding, comparing, and selecting, likewise could not be explained if we always lived merely from one point of time to another. Our practical activities are based upon the same phenomenological presuppositions. Let us take first a case of so-called instinctive action, that of eating. Our eating "grows" somehow from a "feeling" of "dissatisfaction" and tends to a "feeling" of "satisfaction." Hunger is *still* in us, and the feeling of being satiated is *already* present. The whole instinctive action is a leveling of these internal oppositions by means of a series of partial functions, such as the search for food, taking it, and tasting it. Here again we must speak of an ordered whole, in which "earlier," "simultaneous," and "later" are determined by the place and function of the partial effort in question with respect to the whole action. The function of one member calls for that of the next; the instinctive action runs its ordered course, which comes to an end only when the inner tension is dissolved and the opposites are leveled. For this reason instinctive action is also called an "everything or nothing reaction." On a higher level this order is to a greater or lesser extent deliberately created. For instance, I cross a street. I foresee that I will be safely across before the car which has just sounded its horn will be here. Note that "has just sounded" refers to the past, and "will be here" to the future. Apparently I can perform so simple an action as crossing the street only by synthetically joining together my past and my future. My present behavior is an adaptation to the very recent past and the immediately expected future. Accordingly, I do not live in an infinitesimally small moment and still less in an infinitely homogeneous continuum of time. My concrete life as a person runs its course in a definite and limited duration, which I experience as a whole and dominate as a whole.

This situation will have to be examined more closely. If we assume that my crossing of the street takes place at the moment t_n, it will be manifest that my behavior is not only the result of the condition at moment t_{n-1} which is just passed. This follows from the very fact that an event that has not yet taken place but is expected by me at t_{n+1}—the actual presence of the car at this spot—co-determines my action.

An Objection. Many are inclined to object against this argument that the future motion of the car is already present as a determining factor at the moment t_{n-1}—namely, insofar as I represent to myself the expected event. However, this objection assumes what has to be proved. We may appropriately counter it by asking: Why is this representation a representation of a *future* event? How does it distinguish itself from an act of consciousness which has as its object a simultaneous or past situation? How can I be directed to something that does not yet exist in the physical world? The answer evidently is that the future somehow is present in me before it is realized in the world of things. Of course, being internally present is not equivalent to being explicitly expected, as we have shown in our analysis of instinctive action. It is the task of the phenomenologist or psychologist to characterize the mode of inner presence more precisely. Meanwhile it is certain that my personal actions are co-determined by events and situations which have a place in the time of my lived events, but not or not yet in the space-time of physical nature.

Contemporary Psychologists and Psychical Time. Numerous thinkers and empirical psychologists have come to the same conclusion.[3] Among psychologists, especially M. Pradines has clearly understood the principle that is at stake in the matter. He remarks:

> Matter does not "travel" through time, but life "lives" through
> it. For matter time is an "environment"; for life it is a form

---

[3]The reproach has been made that not a single psychologist shares our view. For this reason we adduce here the testimony of contemporary psychologists and physiologists.

of being. In life the moments of time that were hitherto dispersed are joined together.[4]

According to Pradines, this shows itself most clearly in the phenomenon of attention.

> Attention is essentially a function of thought. It is a synthetizing activity, and this synthesis consists at first in bringing the whole experience of the past to bear upon the present. . . . It follows that one can hardly be attentive without *awaiting (expecting)*.[5] . . . To be attentive is to look out in the present for the expected signs of the future . . ., but it is also to anticipate in it a *future*.[6]

L. Van der Horst emphasizes that if we want to understand psychologically the process of an act of perception of time,

> We must take into consideration the anticipation, which is of fundamental importance in becoming conscious and in all perception. By means of anticipation we seize beforehand what is still going to come.[7]

In opposition to physico-mathematical integration, V. von Weiszäcker calls "the biological integration of space . . . a representation."[8] In a study of figurative motions A. Derwordt observes:

> In an isolated cross section of the motion the effect is not necessarily determined in function of the components, but the actual process is governed *in advance* by the effect.[9]

Buytendijk expresses himself analogously:

> Moreover, every motion takes place from a "here" to a "there"; what is later or "expected" is already implied in the "here."[10]

He appeals in this connection to the concept of the "present as bridging time" proposed by Prince Auersperg.[11] William Stern ascribes an anticipating character especially to affective life. In the "preliminary level of affection" he sees:

---

[4]*Traité de Psychologie générale,* Paris, 1946, vol. I, p. 122.
[5]*attendre (s'attendre à).*
[6]*Op. cit.,* p. 58.
[7]"Tijd onder psychologisch aspect," *Ned. Tijdschrift v. Psychologie,* vol. 3 (1948), p. 348.
[8]*Der Gestaltkreis,* 3rd. ed., Stuttgart, 1947, p. 11.
[9]"Untersuchungen über den Zeitverlauf figurierter Bewegungen beim Menschen," *Pflügers Archiv f.d. ges. Physiologie,* vol. 240 (1938), pp. 661 f.
[10]*Algemene theorie der menselijke houding . . .,* p. 97.
[11]*Ibid.*

A pregnant reference [*Sinnbezug*] to that which is to come, an indication, a preparation, even an anticipation of future volitional or intellectual processes.[12]

Perhaps the suspicion will arise that the above-mentioned psychologists are influenced by a definite philosophical setting of the problems, while scientists of a "positive" orientation are generally opposed to such views. However, this is not the case. To become convinced of this it will be sufficient to take a look at the collection of studies in animal psychology entitled CONDUITE, SENTIMENTS, PENSÉES DES ANIMAUX, in which e.g. Paul Guillaume and André Tilquin have collaborated, and which is introduced by a violent attack of E. Rabaud on the "finalists" Buytendijk and Claparède. The collaborators of this collection cannot be suspected of being *a priori* inclined to metaphysical speculations. Yet one will notice that one of them, W. Fischel, in his study concerning "emotion and memory in animals" is unable to explain a certain type of animal behavior in any other way than by means of "the causes in the past and in the future."[13] Leaving aside the question whether or not the concept of cause is appropriate here, we limit ourselves to the remark that the phenomena of life and especially of psychical life are co-conditioned by events, conditions, and situations which, physically speaking, are not or not yet real.

Organized Duration. Let us consider the structure of my original experience of time somewhat more precisely. This structure consists first of all in a limited duration which in a continuous way runs its course in accordance with the law: the condition at moment t_n results from that at moment t_{n-1}; the condition at moment t_{n-1} is the result of the condition at t_n; etc. Briefly, the duration consists in a *temporal homogeneous coupling.* The segment of time, moreover, owes its relief to the various "detached" actual, no longer actual, or not yet actual moments which I possess internally, and which have a definite place and a definite function with respect to the duration. Finally, these different moments of time are related to one another as "before," "simultaneous," and "after," and this relation is determined by the functions of the moments within the framework of the "lived duration." In this way the various events obtain the "mean-

[12]*Allgemeine Psychologie auf personalistischer Grundlage,* 2nd ed., The Hague, 1950, p. 768.
[13]p. 76. The study goes from p. 72 to 120. The collection was published by Alcan, Paris, 1938.

ingfulness" and "datability" required by Martin Heidegger.[14] Briefly, Bergson's "lived duration," Stern's "psychical time of presence," or Husserl's "original sphere" is nothing else than *a temporally ordered whole*. The definition of a "whole" which was given above in another context (p. 120), fully applies to the temporal whole. Accordingly, the duration of my lived events cannot at all be compared with the flux of Heraclitus. It consists in organized wholes or in a whole hierarchy of temporal wholes. To avoid awkward circumlocutions we will from now on call such a temporal totality an *organized duration*.

Hierarchy of Temporal Wholes. What is to be understood here by the term "a hierarchy of temporal wholes"? Perhaps the best way to clarify this concept is by means of a phenomenological analysis. As we have seen, in crossing the street, I build, as it were, a bridge between a past which I still have under my control and a future which I already possess. To the extent that my action constitutes the organizing principle of a definite limited duration we may consider this action as a unity from the temporal point of view. Let us assume now that I have crossed the street to buy stamps at the Post Office. This more inclusive action evidently also is the connection of something earlier with something later. I am *still* aware of not having stamps at home and I consider *already* that I will have some letters to mail tonight. Thus the purchase of stamps is an action by which a reality that is no longer is connected with a reality that is not yet actual. If we consider the matter in this temporal perspective, everything which lies between the realization that I have no stamps and the final mailing of the letter will constitute a single organized duration; the various partial activities, such as leaving the house, crossing the street, entering the Post Office, etc., will not have a duration but have the character of a "now," which may be "earlier," "simultaneous," or "later." However, I do not invariably adhere to this temporal viewpoint. For instance, when I cross the street, my over-all plan disappears, as it were, at the temporal horizon, and what previously was a "now," say, the crossing the street, becomes a duration. In reality innumerable perspectives cross and displace one another. These complicated situations could be made the object of numerous interesting phenomenological analyses. Here, however, it is sufficient to have pointed out

---

[14]Cf. "Sein und Zeit," *Jahrbuch für Philos. und phänomen. Forschung, Buch* VIII, Halle a. d. S., 1927, p. 442.

that it is essentially possible for a single organized duration to dominate several others. Our psychical life consists of such a hierarchy of temporally organized wholes.

3. *Organized Time as Besouled Time*

Characteristics of Organized Time. Investigating the characteristics of organized time, we arrive at the conclusion that we have to do with three kinds of data:

1. A limited segment of time, in which the perduring subject transmits himself from moment to moment.

2. Meaningful moments of "now" in this segment of time, which are partly actual and partly not yet or no longer actual and therefore interconnected by a primordial "simultaneous," "earlier," or "later."

3. The definite place, the definite position, the definite function which these meaningful moments possess with respect to the organized duration.

"Presentification." Regarding the second of these characteristics, it is to be noted that the moments of "now" owe their importance to a certain activity of the ego, which with Husserl we will call *"presentification."* The meaning of this term appears from our analyses. The car in itself would not have interested me, but the car which because of my "presentification" is "already" in the place where I stand leads me to behave in a determined way. Even the sounding of the horn would probably have escaped me; however, in connection with a representation of danger I "presentify" the sound and bring it into relation with the car, likewise "presentified," that is now here. It is here that we must seek the explanation of the fact that past and future events can be actual for me, although I am well aware of their temporal distance—they owe their privileged position in the relief of psychical actuality to my presentification. It must not be overlooked here that not only objectively earlier or later events but also simultaneous events and situations must be made present by me to acquire meaning for me. From the hundreds of noises in the street I selected only the warning sound of the horn, while the others "did not even exist for me."

Temporal Quasi-Objects of Presentification. Perhaps we have made enough progress now to make a first contribution to the clarification of the problem of psychical being. In accordance with our original intention—insofar as this is abstractively possible—we will leave the entire non-intentional substructure of psychical life out of consideration and limit ourselves to objectivizing psychical contents, i.e. those psychical facts which directly or indirectly somehow refer to an objective reality and are "at my disposal" in the way described in the preceding chapter. We may now say that the act by which I effect this "disposability" is always one or the other form of pre-sentification. In this sense all objectivizing psychical realities are possible quasi-objects of a presentifying internal experience. Whether we have to do with abstract contents of memory or with representations, with expectations or remembrances, with a "thought thought" or a "willed will" makes no difference: all these members of psychical structures are able to become quasi-objects of my spiritual activity. Even what we call *inner perception* is nothing else than the *actualization and presentification of psychical realities that are no longer fully actual*. Just as in perceiving a stone in space-time I call forth the real presence of the object "stone," so in my internal perception I effect the reactualization of my lived experience "perception of a stone." When I do this there is at my disposal a segment of organized time, i.e. time which I have "lived" and "shaped," e.g. as a remembrance. In this sense we call the psychical contents temporal quasi-objects-for-me. They are data which acquire importance for my spiritual ego or have the real possibility[1] of acquiring importance to the extent that I call forth their presence. In the relief of actuality they have a closer or a more distant place in accordance with the meaning I attribute to them. Thus the relief of actuality is to a great extent the work of my orientating activity; it is primarily the result of the spiritual domination I exercise, in principle, over all my lived moments of "now."

Temporal Quasi-Objects as Structural Members. However, this statement needs to be complemented by another. We do not mean that *"one* content of memory," *"one* representation," or *"one* decision" is an entity by itself, a "psychical element" or a psychical building block ready for use. On the contrary, real and possible temporal quasi-object poles are conceivable only as members of the whole "psyche." The order reigning among them, therefore, is not the result of a kind of associative mechanism or of a random influence of the surrounding world. It is just as little the effect of a sovereign creative

---

[1]In the following we will carefully distinguish real possibility from pure or logical possibility.

spirit. The truth lies in between. It is that I am able to attribute a definite meaning to a temporal quasi-object only in function of the other quasi-objects, theoretically speaking, of *all* the others. The lived event of one moment owes its meaning to the living of numerous other "members and moments" and that of the whole organized duration. The same applies, with due changes, in reference to more extensive temporal structures. A system of subordinate temporal totalities has its definite value because of the place it occupies within the framework of the hierarchy of time structures that determine my personal life. To use again the example analyzed above, the sounding of the horn was important only in connection with my crossing of the street and the proximity of the car. On the other hand, my crossing had meaning only with respect to my intention of buying stamps. A single action "grows" from past actions by active adaptation, differentiation, and ramifying specialization of a will directed to a purpose. Important resolutions, plans, and decisions affecting my whole life also have their roots, as positive or negative takings of position, in the totality of the organized mass of lived events. For this reason the members of my historical ego cannot at all exist by themselves; they are conceivable only as connections in the whole of my temporal organization.

Besouled Time. This conclusion follows from our description of ordered duration. For what is ultimately the meaning of the statement "I live in an organized time"? Evidently, it can be understood only in the sense that somehow I take a position with respect to my diffusion and dispersion in time. I "try" to bridge the temporal dispersion, to connect the temporal "parts outside parts," and to interrelate them in a meaningful connection. I do not at all run my course mechanically through a temporal continuum; on the contrary, *I make time a dimension of my existence*—namely, by assigning to each lived "now" a definite meaning in connection with other lived moments and ultimately in relation to my whole existence. I live in a time in which every moment is "knotted together" (Hönigswald) with all others; in which every moment has its meaning with respect to all others; in which every "now" has its own value in function of its relation to all other "nows" of my concrete life. But all this is possible only because of a vital principle which allows me to dominate spatio-temporal and purely temporal situations by a meaningful adaptation. All this is included in our statement that I live in a *besouled time*.

4. *The Psyche as "Organ"*

Imperfect Interiority. Let us call the ordered whole of my temporal members *my psyche* and try to characterize this temporal organism somewhat. In the spirit of our theory of order we have to consider it as an imperfect interiority. It shows a certain closedness and impenetrability and at the same time a characteristic openness for values in the surrounding world. The psyche gathers impressions, knowledge, experiences; it unites them as intimately as possible with itself and retains them as long as possible. Useless knowledge, i.e. knowledge which it does not use, is eliminated by it as "ballast of memory." Thus the psyche shows all the essential characteristics of relative immanence.

Multiplicity in the Psyche. This indicates that the psyche contains an aspect of multiplicity. One content of consciousness is not the other; one meaningful connection has nothing to do with the other; one does not simply coincide with the other.

The Psyche is Governed by its Own Laws. The psyche, moreover, is governed by its own laws, which do not always and perfectly allow it to adapt itself to my free thinking and willing. True, automatic functions play a lesser role here than on the physiological level of my bodily being; nevertheless, even here much occurs without my consent and against my will, and this not only in the case of a "psychological illness."

The Psyche is Not Transcendental. Finally, the psyche does not possess a transcendental character. From the metaphysical point of view it is something which allows me to assert myself in the material cosmos. Accordingly, just as my body itself, the psyche belongs to the *category of what is appropriate for life.* This purposive character of psychical functions can hardly be subject to doubt. It reveals itself, for instance, in the fact that my actions as a psychical being are not reactions to isolated stimuli, but always determined by my past and my future. As a psychical being I am able to "receive" impressions, gather experiences, foster certain expectations because of definite events I have "lived," etc. Briefly, what we have called temporal structures are very refined and delicate organs. They are, so to speak, antennas directed to the future; they are blood vessels through which I pump my past; they are finely tuned "sense" organs which acquaint me with many things that coexist with me in time without being near me in a spatio-temporal way. Because of my psyche I have knowledge also of objects which are spatially far away; thus I am able to get hold even of goods that are difficult to obtain, such as to avoid dangers before they arise here and now.

The Psychical Belongs to the Realm of the Besouled Body. Accordingly, the psychical activities favor, secure, enrich, and raise my "worldly" life. Because of my psychical organization I am capable of inserting myself in very complex vital and social situations, but this organization does not enable me to attain through these limited situations to genuine insights into being. My psyche allows me to acquire "intelligently" this or that good, but not to arrive at knowledge and love of *the* Good through the world of goods. Briefly, the psychical is not identical with the spiritual; on the contrary, it is something which acquires its more profound meaning only insofar as it is an organ of my spiritual ego. The temporal structures are very closely united with my spiritual life; they have a much more immediate relation to my willing and understanding than my physiological organs; they serve my spiritual life much more intimately. However, ultimately it is not the temporal structures that give meaning; on the contrary, whatever importance they possess beyond the purely vital level they have received through supra-temporal insights. *In this sense the psychical belongs metaphysically to the realm of the besouled body,* the domain of animality, the sphere of sense life.

Relationship of Psyche and Body. What is the connection between my physiological body and my psyche? How is the spatio-temporal organization of my existential movement related to its temporal organization? Our theory of order allows us to give a brief and accurate answer. *They are related as a substructure to its superstructure.* More specifically, my temporal organization is related to my physiological organization as an *"adjunction."* This means that, although the psychical and the physiological are in themselves ordered wholes, they are not wholly self-sufficient, not wholly autonomous. They are interrelated, "joined." Thus, on the part of both, "joining" members are at work which take care of the well-ordered collaboration of both structures within the framework of the besouled body. So we see that our essential insights are perfectly in agreement with the data of experience gathered by the physiologist and the psychologist. For, the physiologist proves that certain spatio-temporal processes, such as those of the central nervous system, are incomparably much more directly concerned with the psychical than others; and the psychologist, on the other hand, observes that many "lower" functions can be connected in an easy and relatively accurate way with physiological processes, while the same is not readily possible with respect to "higher" psychical phenomena. Metaphysically speaking, the psychical as well as the physiological are two mutually dependent order systems of members, which both lack autonomy and are at the service of the embodiment of my spiritual act. Moreover, it should not be forgotten that it is very well possible for the logically and ontologically prior (the superstructure) to be genetically posterior in development.

Not Two Besouled Bodies. Accordingly, there is no question here of a twofold body—one spatio-temporal and the other purely temporal. On the contrary, we have to do here with two levels of one and the same besouled body—the level of the spatio-temporally ordered whole, on which spatially and temporally dispersed parts are "informed," and the level of ordered duration, on which temporally dispersed "parts outside parts" are joined together into lower or higher unities.

Not Two Besouling Acts. On the other hand, there is likewise no question of a twofold besouling, but of a *single besouling spiritual act* which stagewise rises from self-alienation to complete presence with itself. For, ultimately what is the meaning of the term "to besoul"? To besoul means to rouse from the rigor and inertia of matter and to raise to a state of higher activity. To besoul signifies to unite mutually foreign and dispersed parts at least into the relative closedness of an interiority. To besoul means also the conquest of the spatio-temporal dispersion of matter. Now it is very well possible that on a lower level of "information" a certain solidarity of spatial parts is reached, while on a higher level of besouling spatial dispersion is overcome fully and temporal dispersion to a certain extent. Thus there is question only of a single spiritual act, which appears as spiritual on neither the physiological nor the psychical level, but nevertheless *creates on each level the necessary conditions for its further unfolding,* and finally as "phronesis" becomes *what is was all the time implicitly.* For, as Henri Delacroix expressed it:

> In its formation consciousness leaves behind the means which have enabled it to constitute itself; but at the same time it absorbs them and goes beyond them.[1]

---

[1]*Les grandes formes de la vie mentale,* p. 48.

This constitution of the self by the self can be seen in the development of the human individual, as is shown to us by the phenomenology and psychology of the various stages of ontogenesis. But it is contained also in the genesis of every single spiritual act. Every volition, every intellection has its obscure origin in the implicitly spiritual; it organizes itself, grows, and enriches itself in the organico-psychial sphere, till it finally illuminates and elevates our whole being as a kind of "participation in the Uncreated Light."

Maurice Blondel has given us a masterly description of this inner genesis with respect to a special case, that of motivation.

> Impenetrable remains the birth of what is most worthy of admiration, yet often least admired—internal light. Just as those plants which during the course of a hundred years gather the perfumes and costly juices with which to feed the single flower that exhausts them in a single day, so an obscure labor drains all the forces of life to feed the source of active consciousness. No water comes to swell this spring unless it passes through the subterraneous passages that are impervious to distinct knowledge. . . . The motive is nothing but the echo and synthesis of a thousand silent activities; this is the reason which renders it naturally efficacious. The motive does not appear all of a sudden, so to speak, by a kind of spontaneous generation; it is the representative of a host of elementary tendencies that support and urge it; it is the conclusion of a whole internal system and serves as an intermediary between habitual dispositions and particular circumstances.[2]

5. *The Theoretical Foundations of Introspective Psychology*

THE ERROR OF INTROSPECTIVE PSYCHOLOGY

The great error of introspective psychologists is to believe that "consciousness" is the object of their research. All their other errors flow from this fundamental mistake—and all evidence indicates that this is no mere coincidence. Whoever is familiar with the history of introspective psychology will confess that there is hardly any realm of science in which more serious efforts have been made to arrive at clarity and unity of convictions regarding theoretical foundations, but also that only rarely such vast endeavors have yielded such meager results. This proves that the lack of success is not to be ascribed to some matter of detail, but to the very theoretical foundations themselves of this psychological trend and especially that

---

[2]*L'Action,* Paris, 1936, vol. 2, pp. 139 f.

of its supposedly most central concept—the concept of consciousness. For this reason it will be necessary to subject this concept to a critical examination.

If we ask what consciousness is we meet at once the difficulty that the concept to be explained has many meanings. Fortunately we are able to make use of the penetrating analyses made by Edmund Husserl,[1] Alexander Pfänder,[2] Joseph Geyser,[3] and August Messer.[4] Because the studies of Husserl and Geyser are in the main concerned with, respectively, phenomenological and metaphysical problems, we will generally follow the explanations offered by Pfänder.[5]

The Meanings of "Consciousness" According to Introspective Psychologists. According to Pfänder, we must distinguish four different meanings of the term "consciousness."

1. *Consciousness is self-consciousness* in the sense of objective knowledge of oneself. "Conscious," then, is he who thinks about (reflects upon) his own being and nature or makes himself the object of an intentional act. The opposite is sometimes expressed by the term "unconscious," used to designate that reflection on oneself, one's state or one's physical and psychical activities has become difficult, reduced, or wholly eliminated. In this sense it is said, for instance, that a somnambulist reacts and acts "unconsciously."[6]

2. *Consciousness is knowledge of something.* In this sense consciousness means the same as "objectivizing consciousness" or "consciousness of an object," i.e. the clear or confused grasping of real or possible objects, real or possible relationships. Abstracting from more subtle distinctions, we may say that there is question here of an "intentional consciousness." Thus as contents of consciousness are considered all objects (or all parts, aspects, and non-autonomous moments of objects) to which a consciousness is intentionally directed. Hence the expression "a thing is conscious"[7] means "it is intentionally grasped by a consciousness." Reversely, as "unconscious" is considered everything which is not the pole of any

---

[1]*Logische Untersuchungen,* bk. II, sect. I, pp. 343-425.
[2]*Einführung in die Psychologie,* Leipzig, 1904, pp. 373-397.
[3]*Lehrbuch der allgemeinen Psychologie,* vol. I, pp. 1-28.
[4]*Empfindung und Denken,* 3rd ed., Leipzig, 1928, pp. 81-89.
[5]We have to do here with an explanation of the concept of consciousness as it is used by the empirical psychologist. So we consider it quite natural that Pfänder does not speak here of primordial interiority of consciousness.
[6]Cf. Geyser, *op. cit.,* vol. I, p. 96.
[7]*"Ein Ding ist bewusst."*

inner directedness. Because "knowledge of . . ." can go through all imaginable modal variations—from vague, empty, and obscure presentiments to clear, sharply defined, and wholly understood insights—"consciousness" in this sense has many different degrees. Note that from this point of view all psychical acts oriented to the "world" are "unconscious." For, if we do not reflect, we are psychically directed to the world of persons, things, and situations, and thus our own psyche is not a "content of consciousness."

3. *Consciousness is psychical being.* "Something is conscious" does not mean here that something is received in consciousness, but on the contrary that a psychical reality exists. Accordingly, thoughts, representations, sentiments, volitions, perceptions, etc. are conscious in this third sense. On the other hand, if they are performed in an unreflected way they are unconscious in the second sense. Reversely, colors, sounds, and odors are conscious in the second sense and unconscious in the third sense of the term. Evidently, consciousness in this third sense does not admit of any degrees, for a reality either has or does not have the ontological status of the psychical. Thus as "conscious" in the third sense is considered everything which really belongs to a psyche.

4. *Consciousness is the psychical subject,* insofar as it is the real or possible support of consciousness in the second sense of the term. Many introspective psychologists identify "the soul" with consciousness in this sense.[8]

CRITIQUE OF THIS VIEW

It does not seem difficult to simplify Pfänder's summarized view somewhat. First of all, it should be clear that objective self-consciousness is a particular case of intentional consciousness in general. Next, we think that there is a necessary metaphysical connection between the second and the fourth meaning. At least implicitly, we must conceive "consciousness of something" as the consciousness of a conscious being.

Is Conscious Being Identical with the Soul? May we simply identify conscious being with the soul? As we will show presently, this is not permissible. However, provisionally we will limit ourselves to the following reflection. If we understand the implication of this question clearly and take into account the second concept of conscious-

---

[8]Pfänder also makes this identification. Cf. *op. cit.,* pp. 381-385.

ness, we will have to reformulate it as follows: Is that which reveals an "intentional orientation to . . ." exclusively the soul? When, for example, I "see" something, am I not directed to the visual object as a whole man? Is the assertion that the entire psycho-physical ego participates in the visual act not proved by my whole behavior, such as the rotating of my eyes, the turning of my head, and the kinesthetic motion of my body? Hence, should I not conclude that in principle all my organs, members, and structures somehow participate in my seeing and therefore also in my "knowing of . . ."? If we do not wish to lapse into a kind of dualism akin to that of Descartes, we will have to answer these questions in the affirmative.

From this we draw the important conclusion that there is no consciousness without an existing being which in its existential totality is conscious of an object. There is no life of consciousness without a living subject which consciously lives in its surrounding world or simply in "the" world. There are no acts of consciousness without the conscious behavior of an existing totality that is endowed with consciousness. These statements are a first step connecting a richer and more concrete content with the abstract schema of introspective psychology.

Necessity of a Criterion of Psychical Being. It is much more difficult to give a more precise description of the third meaning. It is a fact that this meaning plays an important role in the language of scientific thought. Nevertheless the theoretical justification of this concept is very weak. Usually the question: "What exactly do you mean by psychical being?" fails to get an answer from the positive scientist or the empirical psychologist—and justly so. His instinct tells him that the definitions proposed, for instance, by Wilhelm Wundt, Carl Stumpf, Franz Brentano, Edmund Husserl, Paul Natorp, Theodor Lipps and Joseph Geyser are of little use in his concrete work of research. The criteria usually given do not harmonize with the facts. First of all, the psychical is not the purely subjective, for it is made the object of objective research. Secondly, it does not belong to the realities which can be observed only by a single subject. Modern research in the realm of the relationship "I-You" has revealed how erroneous this axiom is. Likewise, the definitions given by Husserl in his junior years describing consciousness, in the sense of psychical being, as "the real-phenomenological unity of the lived experience of the ego"[9] must be considered as unsatisfactory. For wher-

---

[9] *Op cit.,* bk. II, sect. 1, p. 347.

ever a phenomenon appears to us as a unity, it stands in a definite relationship to another unity appearing as such. Therefore, if Husserl emphasizes the unitary aspect in his definition of the psychical, he will not be absolved from the duty of indicating a positive mark which distinguishes this unity from another.[10]

Criterion Proposed by Introspective Psychologists. Many theorists see this positive criterion in the fact that the psychical is accompanied by a "representation" (*"Vorgestellt-werden,"* Brentano), a "lived experience" (*"Erlebt-werden,"* Lipps), or a kind of "knowledge" (*"Gewusst-werden,"* Geyser). However, this assertion is wholly un-phenomenological, at least in this form. When we are directed to the world by our acts, for example, when we are absorbed in the reading of a fairy tale, the observation of an event, or a mathematical demonstration, it is not possible to observe any parallel experience in the form of an accompanying representation, lived experience, or kind of knowledge.[11]

Their Basic Error. It does not seem difficult to indicate the basis of the error committed by Brentano, Lipps, and Geyser. These theorists are right in thinking that the essence of the spiritual ego must be described as a primordial being-present-with-oneself. However, they are empiricists, and therefore believe it possible to discover this spiritual self-possession as a fact (or as an aspect, a component part, or an element of facts) among other facts. They are objectivists, and therefore they start from the tacit assumption that all consciousness is consciousness of an object, i.e. that it must consist in a "representation of *something*," "the experience of *something*," "the knowledge of *something*." Finally, they adopt a one-sided empiristic viewpoint insofar as they consider it possible to demonstrate the self-presence of the human spirit on the level of positive psychological experience. In the preceding studies, however, it has been sufficiently demonstrated, we think, that genuine interiority of consciousness cannot be grasped as a datum or as an element discovered in the analysis of data, but can be approached only by means of an inner reference to a source from which all "giving of meaning" originates; that we can never conceive it as an object but only as a direction; that it is not a psychological datum but the material *a priori* which precisely makes all conceivable psychological data in general possible.

---

[10]Similar arguments may be brought to bear against the explanations of Natorp in his *Allgemeine Psychologie nach critischer Methode,* Tübingen, 1912, pp. 1-38.

[11]Cf. Husserl's critique, *op. cit.,* bk. II, sect. 1, p. 376.

Absurd Consequences of Their View. Thus it is not surprising that the view of Lipps, Brentano, and Geyser leads to absurd consequences. For it is evident that the representation by which a psychical act is represented would itself demand to be represented, just as also a lived experience would have to be lived all over again before it could be considered as "conscious." Likewise, the "simple knowledge" of processes of consciousness would have to become the object of another act of knowledge, and so on to infinity. Moreover, the term "simple knowledge," used by Geyser, is misleading. Knowledge of a definite event taking place in me is essentially a reflective act; in *this* respect it does not essentially differ from the "higher acts" of self-knowledge. Briefly, whoever accepts the postulate of continuous, objective and explicit reflection cannot escape from infinite regress.[12]

Moreover, this conception excludes the notion of unconscious psychical being—a notion which, as we have seen, cannot be dispensed with by the empirical psychologist.[13] The "unconscious" is a category which he uses continually, at least in an implicit way. So Geyser does not agree with the facts when he indicates "awareness" (*"Bewusstheit"*) as "the general distinctive characteristic of the psychical insofar as it is given in experience,"[14] "awareness" being understood here as "the original consciousness of contents."[15] If this were true, the activity of the psychologist would be limited to making as complete an inventory as possible of all contents that are known by a subject in the form of simple or higher acts of knowledge. But it is evident that our experience of the psychical nowise coincides with the knowledge of the sum total or ordered whole of contents.

Similar contradictions between theory and concrete research may be found in other introspective psychologists. For instance, Lindworsky emphasizes that "all those phenomena which by their very nature are immanent" constitute "the object of experimental psychology," while "the unconscious . . . [does not belong] to the proper object of psychology."[16] However, this does not prevent Lindworsky the experimenter from investigating forgetting,[17] disturbances of atten-

---

[12]Cf. S. Strasser, "Het Ikbewustzijn," *Annalen v. h. Thijmgenootschap,* vol. 38 (1950), pp. 1 f.
[13]Cf. p. 179.
[14]*Op. cit.,* p. 117.
[15]*Op. cit.,* p. 110.
[16]*Experimentelle Psychologie,* 5th ed., München, 1931, p. 6 f.
[17]*Op. cit.,* p. 158.

tion,[18] sleep, [19] etc. In this investigation he emphasizes, for example, that falling asleep is not an instinctive action, for "instinctive actions are conscious activities. Sleep, however, appears to us wholly as a state and not as a conscious activity."[20] Thus we face here the curious fact that unconscious states are "by their very nature immanent to consciousness."

OUR OWN POSITION

To clarify our own position, let us return to Pfänder's summarization. For we have not yet fully examined whether and how, after the elimination of the first concept of consciousness, the three other concepts are connected—namely, consciousness as *knowledge of something* (the second meaning), as *psychical being* (the third meaning), and as *conscious subject* (the fourth meaning). The solution offered by Brentano, Lipps, and Geyser consists, as we see now clearly, in postulating the identity of all four kinds of consciousness named by Pfänder. On the one hand, everything psychical is supposed to be by its very nature object also of objective self-consciousness; and on the other hand, the subject of the "representation," the "lived experience," or the "knowledge of . . ." is assumed to be also its object. With these thinkers we are willing to admit that there is an intimate connection between the various meanings of consciousness, reduced by us to three. But the connection, we think, must be sought within the framework of our dynamic view. In this sense we would like to summarize the connection of the concepts in question in the concise but eloquent statement that *the conscious being is conscious of an object by means of that of which it is not* (not yet or no longer) *conscious.* The meaning of this assertion should be clear from our preceding analyses. We are convinced that in principle we have to see in the really existing conscious subject (the fourth meaning of the term) the concept of consciousness that is most fundamental from the ontological point of view. Next, the conscious being is conscious (in the second meaning) of an object that exists, whether really or possibly. It is conscious of this object *by means of its psyche,* i.e. by means of the ordered whole constituted by its contents that tend to consciousness or unconsciousness and by all its functions which render possible and regulate this process of appearance and disappear-

---

[18]*Op. cit., p.* 237 f.
[19]*Op. cit.,* p. 266 f.
[20]*Op. cit.,* p. 268.

ance of consciousness (in the third sense). These considerations are in harmony with our philosophical view of man. For the spiritual-material nature of man reveals itself precisely in this that his life of consciousness in the proper sense can unfold itself only upon the basis of animal and vital processes which are not wholly conscious, not wholly free, not wholly interiorized.

6. *Consciousness in the Strict Sense of the Term*

Our assertion that the psychical is the sphere of what is not, not yet, or no longer fully conscious squarely contradicts the ideas of many generations of philosophers and psychologists. This contradiction has its basis partly in matters of principle and partly in terminological differences. Thus it appears indispensable to clarify both these points.

"Conscious" is an Analogous Term. The difficulties begin already with the apparently very simple statement that a being is conscious of an object. Evidently the term "conscious" is used in a very different sense with respect to diverse kinds of beings. If, for example, the question is asked whether or not plants have consciousness, we attribute to "being conscious" a meaning that is partly the same with respect to plants and ourselves, but partly also different. We are not referring here to a mere hierarchy of gradual distinctions, but to essential differences in the mode of being conscious. Briefly, "conscious" as predicable of a subject (consciousness in the second sense) is an analogous concept. It is formally predicated of different subjects and quasi-subjects in such a way that it remains partly the same and becomes partly different.

In its Primary Meaning Consciousness is Thetic, i.e. Takes Explicitly Position with Respect to Being. The meaning of an analogy becomes clear only when the primary analogate has been defined. So we must ask, When are we *"conscious of an object"* in the most proper sense of the term? For even in ourselves we distinguish, for instance, between vague and clear consciousness, semi-consciousness and full consciousness, consciousness of an horizon and consciousness of an object. On the basis of our metaphysical insights into the transcendental character of all our spiritual activity (cf. pp. 159-169), the strict meaning of the term "conscious" should be described, we think, as follows—*we are conscious of an object if we are able to make it, as an existing or possibly existing thing, the object of explicit thetic acts.* Insofar as we try to seize as existent that which is and to reject as non-existent that which is not, we tend consciously to knowledge. In objectively comparing what is good with what is less good or evil, we make a conscious choice. In setting ourselves a goal in accordance with the situation as it really is, we act consciously. If by virtue of similar real or supposedly real ontological insights we arouse corresponding sentiments in us, these sentiments will be "conscious sentiments." For this reason we are in full agreement with H. Robbers when he remarks:

> [The] orientation to being necessarily pervades always the conscious level of human life. . . . [For] to know of something that it *is* . . . is at the same time to know also about the whole framework of the realm of being. . . . Every action implies an orientation to the totality of reality.[1]

In our abbreviated terminology we may say also that *"conscious" in the strict sense of the term is he who takes a position with respect to reality explicitly under the "aspect" of being.*

It is not necessary that the position taken with respect to reality be correct and still less that it be perfect. Because consciousness of being is, as we have seen, a consciousness of direction, it is very well possible for the knower to be in an erroneous way present with being. Likewise, one who acts stupidly or sinfully can be aiming in the direction of the good. Insofar as in both cases they express this orientation in thetic acts, they act in full consciousness, even if they utterly fail in the choice of their object.

On the other hand, our definitions require that an interpretation or taking of position be not merely possible but real. In this point age-old wisdom and the latest findings of phenomenology and psychology go hand in hand. The thesis, the explicit taking of position, the "express" making of the interpretation of being is, as is realized nowadays, not a secondary act of "communication" which could perhaps be dispensed with. On the contrary, every "phronesis" tends to expression as to its ultimate completion. For example, the final taking of position expressed in the words "It is so" belongs to the judgment; if it does not take place, the judgment will not be fully completed.

Reversely, the fact that a being behaves positively or negatively with respect to goods does not suffice to make us certain that it is

---

[1] *Wijsbegeerte en Openbaring,* Utrecht-Brussels, 1948, p. 27.

acting consciously in the strict sense of the term. A behavior which implies a kind of choice does not yet prove that the being in question takes a position based upon a genuine *insight* into value. No implicit "feeling" for what is valuable can be considered equivalent to the operation by which a being is considered *being good*. The active interpretation, based upon insight of "what is," does not necessarily have to culminate in verbal formulas, although it is true that language must be considered as a manifestation of it which occupies the highest rank, is most unambiguous, and possesses the greatest value for the development of personality.[2] However, by its very nature the fully conscious act must come to completion in a *verbum mentis,* a mental word, which, according to Thomas Aquinas, "is nothing else than something conceived by the mind in which man expresses the things of which he thinks."[3] In this sense whenever a subject explicitly takes a position with respect to the existent, whether it be by way of judgment, question, doubt, evaluation, aspiration, desire, or love, he offers a proof that the subject in being present with himself is present with being.

Animals are Secondary Analogates with Respect to Consciousness. Thus far we have been speaking concerning the primary analogate. If, however, we say that an animal has consciousness, we mean that it takes spontaneously a position with respect to certain realities. The animal behaves *as if* it has recognized certain realities as existent. This is the case with all beings which we call "conscious." Yet what we do not ascribe to these secondary analogates is the grasping of being as *being.* An animal which seeks food and avoids dangers takes a position with respect to the good and evil of definite things and situations. But it does this in an implicit way and exclusively within the framework of a vital situation, a situation to which it itself belongs. Here a relatively self-subsistent subject faces a relatively self-subsistent object. If the subject behaves meaningfully ("intelligently") and consequently with respect to the good or evil of the things, it does so not because the things as such *are* good or evil, but because they function as members in a typical, biologically meaningful structure of its surrounding world. This surrounding world itself is not present as such so far as the animal is concerned, but constitutes

---

[2]Concerning the last-named aspect of our problem, cf. P. J. A. Calon, *Over de persoonlijkheidsontwikkeling by kinderen met aangeboren of vroeg verworven doofheid,* Nymegen, 1950.

[3]*Summa theol.,* I-II, q. 103, a. 1, *ad* 2.

merely an area of possible forms of behavior. For this reason, unlike Leibniz, we prefer not to speak here ot an *"analogon rationis,"* an analogous kind of reason; on the contrary, there is question here of an *"analogon conscientiae,"* an analogous kind of consciousness, i.e. a *"cum"* + *"scire"* of realities whose interconnection is not discovered by virtue of an insight into their being.[4] The difference between these two ways of taking a position relative to objects is not merely a question of degree but essential.

Our Besouled Body has Consciousness as a Secondary Analogate. With respect to the philosophical explanation of the besouled body we are, of course, forced to similar observations. Our besouled members and organs also behave in an implicit way with respect to the existent; otherwise the automatic course of many physiological and psychological functions would be unexplainable. Only our spiritual soul has the possibility of "phronesis"; only the soul is capable of turning to being with clear understanding. However, our spiritual ego can attain to explicit insight only by means of implicit knowledge, just as reversely the implicitly conscious "participates" in the explicit understanding of the spiritual soul.[5] Thus it seems useful and necessary to interpret the traditional "sensing," in the widest sense of the term, as a *knowing without explicit insight into being,* for only in this way will it be possible to overcome the innumerable difficulties of which an example has been given at the beginning of this book (p. 11).

The Twofold Meaning of Consciousness. In this way it is immediately seen that the concept of consciousness has a twofold meaning which has escaped even such outstanding analysts as Geyser, Messer, Husserl, and Pfänder. If "understanding" is considered as a "consciousness of . . . ," *"sensing" is not a "consciousness of . . . ," but a medium to become conscious of an object* (becoming "unconscious of . . ." must also be considered as such a medium). On the other hand, if "sensing" is considered as a "consciousness," i.e. as a predicate attributable to a subject or consciousness in the second sense, as is done by most theoretical psychologists, one will have to take into account the possibility that temporarily or partially no taking of a

---

[4]"Consciousness" is derived from the Latin *cum scire,* to know together or at the same time. Thus "conscious" does not necessarily refer to the universe of being, but also to a limited number of realities which constitute a biologically important structure or "Gestalt." In this case we should like to speak of an *analogon conscientiae.*

[5]Cf. Thomas Aquinas, "The body participates in the being of the soul, but not as nobly as the soul itself." *De anima,* 1, *ad* 17.

position relative to reality can be observed in a subject, e.g. in the state of somnambulism. For there is question here of implicit behavior, and in the sphere of the implicit there is an unlimited possibility of degrees and stages which gradually approach the zero point where objects no longer appear. As a matter of fact, this zero point is reached in the state of deep sleep or syncope. In other words, to remain consequent the theorist in question will have to introduce the notion of "unconscious consciousness" and show that it does not imply any contradiction.

We prefer, however, to speak on the one hand of *consciousness in the strict sense* and on the other of an *analogon conscientiae,* an analogous kind of consciousness. Accordingly, we see the whole body, but especially its intimate psychical organization as the bearer of implicit consciousness and the medium of becoming fully conscious.

7. *Phenomenology of Psychological Research*

Which of the two types of consciousness described above consti- tutes the object of research in introspective psychology? Our answer is a persistent neither one nor the other. True, the psychical plays an important role in psychological research, but—no matter how strange it may seem—only as an indication and a reference, and not as its proper object.

Consciousness is Not the Object of Introspective Psychology. We would like to show this by means of a phenomenological analysis. Let us assume that as the subject of an experiment I am given the task of calculating the volume of my room. The director of the experiment expects of me that I measure, count and calculate in order to arrive at an explicit knowledge of my room and its spatial dimensions. What interests the empirical psychologist in this ex- periment? Does he want to know whether or not I am a psychical subject possessing self-consciousness? If I were not such a subject, the whole experiment would be unthinkable. Does he want to know the object of which I am conscious, the volume of my room? This piece of information may be of interest to an architect, but not to a psychologist. Does he want to take an inventory of the thoughts, representations, feeling, etc. I "have" while I am conscious of the result of my calculation? But these psychical realities do not reveal themselves better but rather less clearly in the judgment which I then make than they do in numerous other judgments. If this is the item that interests him, it will be hard to understand the purpose and usefulness of the whole experiment. So we see that none of the four concepts of consciousness enumerated by Pfänder is the object to be more accurately determined by introspective psychological research.

The "How" Interests the Introspective Psychologist. In reality the psychologist will ask the following type of questions relative to my acts of thought: How did you measure? In what way did you use the measuring device? What method of calculation did you use? What was the progress of your thinking: did you find the correct answer at once or did you first make a mistake? What is to be noted here is the constant recurrence of the interrogatives: how? in what way? what method? etc. What interests the psychologist evidently is not the contents of consciousness as such nor the psyche as such, but the course of a definite process of becoming conscious. The way in which my intellectual labor was prepared, organized, and accomplished by me, the dispositions, abilities, and habits which played a role in it, these are what arouses his interest. Not the consciousness that this room has a volume of sixty cubic yards, but the way in which this has become part of my knowledge, appears to be important from the viewpoint of his *"theoria."* "Understanding is a part of knowing *how*," affirms Ryle as a faithful follower of the empirical method in psychology.[1]

Of course, the psychologist may ask me also, How much is 5x4x3 yards? But even then he is not interested in the fact that I *know* the correct answer—I could have learned it from someone else—but in the fact that I have obtained this answer *in this or that determined way.* The contents of my knowledge as such does not interest the psychologist, although these contents may perhaps arouse the curiosity of my teachers, examiners, colleagues, collaborators, and on occasion that of a prosecuting attorney. But the fact that I, this man, have arrived at a determined notion under determined conditions and in a determined way constitutes a specifically psychological fact and as such concerns the psychologist, while the others are interested only insofar as perhaps they also like to know something about psychology.

The States Between Full Consciousness and Unconsciousness Hold the Interest of the Psychologist. To become thoroughly acquainted with a road one usually travels it in both directions. This

---

[1] *The Concept of Mind,* 2nd impr., London, 1949, p. 54.

is true also for the psychologist. To become wholly familiar with the trail leading to the confrontation with being, he endeavors to reconnoiter also the road that leads away from clear and distinct understanding. In other words, his domain extends not only to becoming conscious but also to becoming unconscious. For this reason the psychologist investigates not only attention, learning, striving, etc., but also the disturbances of attention, forgetting, the renunciation of a goal, etc. States that are characteristic of the transition from the fully conscious "I will" and "I understand" to semi-conscious functions, such as falling asleep, dreaming, hypnosis, daydreaming, and purely associative trains of images, are carefully examined by the psychologist. Likewise, the state of not yet or not yet fully being conscious in higher animals, small children, and abnormal adults can be instructive for him. In general, what arouses the attention of the psychologist is that which occurs in *between* the taking of a position in the strict sense of the term and fully automatic processes. This is no pure coincidence. What the psychologist investigates is, as we have seen, our subjective effort to interpret being. The start of this endeavor is necessarily shrouded in darkness; the terminus, on the other hand—this would seem to be now beyond any doubt—can no longer be the object of *"empeiria"*; but the intermediary stages and the provisional aims of our progress to transcendental heights is all the more interesting. To explore these intermediary stations the experimenter often tries to arouse artificially transitional states between full consciousness and unconsciousness, between the "I" and the "it." This procedure would be absurd if the science of psychology had really the facts of consciousness as its object.

Conclusion. Accordingly, the theory of introspective psychology is unsatisfactory and out of harmony with concrete psychological research, including that of the introspective psychologist himself. Introspective psychologists do not investigate consciousness but becoming conscious and becoming unconscious; they do not examine the contents of consciousness, but the genesis and disappearance of these contents; they are not concerned with acts of consciousness, but with the roots and effects of these acts. Briefly, they investigate the implicitly spiritual conditions of our spiritual existence.

8. *Psychology as the Science of Existential Orientation*

The judgments of empirical psychology have as their object neither the spiritual soul nor consciousness. These are the two negative conclusions to which our long and difficult inquiries have led us thus far. However, we cannot be satisfied with such a negative result and want to arrive at a positive solution of our problem. For these studies had as their purpose to express in philosophical terms what is being done by the psychologists, at least by the introspective psychologists. At first sight the answer does not seem to be any longer difficult. Should not the psyche, as it has been characterized above, be the proper object of psychological research?

The Psyche is Not the Proper Object of Psychology. We have already rejected this purely apparent solution, which, moreover, would be out of harmony with psychology as it really is. The primary interest of psychologists lies in "reactions," "lived experiences," "actions," "functions," etc. True, in all these functions and activities the psyche plays an important role. But this does not take away from the fact that, for example, an action is always and of necessity the action of the whole being. I cannot answer the question, Who acts? by saying, My soul acts, but only by replying, *I* act. The same, of course, applies not only with respect to actions of a "worldly" orientation but also to my imperfectly immanent activities. It would be just as false to assert that my psyche learns as that my cortex has understood something. Here also the only way of stating the matter correctly is to say that I learn. I, this unity of body and soul, learn. This means that I learn also "in" my besouled psyche, in my besouled cortex and in many other besouled members and structures—the term "to learn" being used here not in the univocal sense but analogously relatively to these egological realities. If, for instance, I learn a new gymnastic exercise, my muscles "somehow" participate in the learning. For this reason we have stressed that in principle we see in the whole body a bearer of implicit consciousness. Once this is clearly understood, there will be no danger that one will think of limiting the object of empirical psychology to the psyche, psychical functions, psychical contents, etc.

The train of though developed in the preceding section contains perhaps a slight indication that can guide us in our further inquiry. Assuredly, it cannot be a pure coincidence that we arrived at the conclusion that not consciousness itself but becoming conscious is what interests the psychologist. Will it not be possible to enlarge this notion somewhat? For the transition from not fully conscious psychical functions to thetic consciousness is only the final phase of an extremely complex relatively immanent development. This final phase has decisive importance in many respects, so that it is understandable that introspective psychologists have paid attention to it in an almost exclusive way. Nevertheless, this phase is after all only the culminating point of a whole "history of sense." As Delacroix remarks correctly, "consciousness is the supreme degree of self-realization."[1] Would not the task of empirical psychology consist in giving an objective description of the process of this self-realization?

The Task of Psychology. In our opinion it is in this direction that the solution of our problem must be sought. True, the introspective psychologist investigates primarily the psychical, but in doing so he has a special purpose in mind. He does not restrict himself to a kind of descriptive anatomy of temporal structures, but for him there is question also of activity and passivity, of acting and being acted upon, of abilities and functions. We may say even that the functional[2] viewpoint predominates in his considerations. But what is the function of the psyche? Its whole function is but a partial function of the besouled body. As such it aims at inserting us in our vital surroundings, in our social environment, briefly, in "the" world. Especially the psychical functions make it possible for us, for instance, to enter into relation with other persons and things, even if they are far away from us in space-time. They contribute in the highest degree to our capacity of behaving meaningfully as spiritual dwellers in a material world with respect to material and embodied realities. They allow us "to insert ourselves into the pre-existing world with our life, our judgments, our feelings, our evaluations, our actions, etc." (Husserl).

We ask now: Would there be no science which is concerned with this "vital insertion"? Are there no men of research who show interest in our existential orientation to our biological surroundings, our social world, and our world of culture? Does no branch of science speak of man's insertion into family life, school life, sexual life, business life, religious life? Is no study concerned with the development of the existential movement, both normal and disturbed, deviating and pathological? And if the answer is affirmative, what would we call this study? What other name could be given it if not *psychology?*

Is Psychology a "Science of the Soul"? The question may be asked how this view harmonizes with our previous affirmations? Evidently, the proposed solution will have to take into account that

---

[1]*Les grandes formes de la vie*, p. 47.
[2]The term is not used here in the sense of Koffka but in that of Buytendijk. Cf. his *Algemene theorie der menselijke houding* . . .

man's existential act does not stop at the limits of natural and social surroundings. This act constantly transcends limited situations and endeavors to seize being in its absolute aspects. This act, the "transcendental act," which constitutes the essence of our spiritual ego obviously cannot become the object of objective empirical research, as we ourselves have repeatedly pointed out with much emphasis. So it would seem that psychology is a natural science alongside many other sciences of nature. Thus, in principle, Kant would have been correct in characterizing psychology as a "physiology of the inner sense." From this point of view, therefore, empirical psychology could not claim to be a "science of the soul."

However, this viewpoint is wholly onesided—because it is completely abstract. For our spiritual act does not appear on the stage of this world as a sudden *"deus ex machina,"* but explicates itself, gradually unfolds itself, and arrives at full self-realization only after a long and difficult process which reveals its typical stages and transitional phases. The transcendental act grows from its involvement in the organic to actual spirituality, from its implication in the vital to the conscious self-possession of the spirit (cf. pp. 178 f.). This development consists in a succession of indispensable necessary preparatory stages which are precisely the conditions that make possible our actual spiritual life in a material cosmos. If, then, interiority of consciousness is to manifest itself as such, certain conditions have to be fulfilled—conditions which are concerned with the sphere of the "world," such as vital surroundings, social environment, cultural, moral and religious situation; also conditions that are connected with the besouled body, such as hereditary traits, the physiological body and the psychical organism. All these conditions which must be fulfilled in the world of objects and quasi-objects, and especially the connection between these conditions and the spiritual act belong to the—sole—competency of empirical psychology. These conditions can be studied in an objective way because there is question here of relations, conditions, and properties of objects and quasi-objects. Thus the psychologist investigates the real possibilities offered by the besouled body, in the broad sense we give to this term, and also by its surroundings, by society and social institutions for the development of genuine interiority of consciousness. However, he does not investigate them as such, but only insofar as they constitute *real possibilities for the unfolding of our spiritual act.*

Is Psychology a Positive Science? But, one may object, how can the psychologist study the relations of objective conditions with the spiritual act without going beyond the limits of *"empeiria"?* Assuredly, the transcendental act does not give rise to positive observations. How, then, concretely speaking, will the psychologist be able to observe, perform experiments, and make statistical surveys? Will he not have to leave the realm of science concerned with positive facts?

The answer is an emphatic no, for every impulse coming from our transcendental life is a besouling act which somehow embodies itself. True, the spiritual act is originally "present with itself," but it does not remain with itself; it objectivizes itself and thus gives rise to changes in the world of quasi-objects and usually also in that of objects. Hence the results of our spiritual activities are positively observable facts. They reveal themselves as definite changes, although these changes are only modifications of the most refined organs of the mind, the temporal structures of the psyche. Thus the empirical psychologist is in a position to compare real conditions with actually attained results, or the condition from which the spiritual act has grown with the results achieved by it. In many respects he will observe the regular succession of certain "if . . . then" relations; so he has the necessary basis to proceed by way of induction to the formulation of empirical laws. Where he has to do with the person as such, he will, for example, be able systematically to observe, gather, compare, and organize its typical possibilities and forms of expression, and construct an objective characterology. Such a typological theory implies, philosophically speaking, a survey of the characteristic modes in which the transcendental act of man embodies itself under given conditions, such as in a man of *this* temperament, *this* sex, *this* age, and *this* cultural status. True, typology and characterology are not empirical sciences of the spirit—there are no such sciences— but they are *objective sciences of spiritualized reality.* The representatives of these sciences actually investigate the most immediate objectivations, the most intimate forms of expression and concretization of our spiritual being. Similar remarks apply to other branches of psychology. In this restricted sense empirical psychology may be quite correctly considered as a "science of the soul."

Metaphysical and Empirical Psychology. On the other hand, we must not forget that these men of research can describe human interiority only insofar as it "exteriorizes" itself, i.e. insofar as it is no longer genuine interiority. They endeavor to grasp this interiority by means of its real possibilities and its actual realizations. But because all realizations here are at the same time new possibilities for further personal unfolding of the self, we may say also that *the empirical psychologist considers the soul through the medium of objectivations and quasi-objectivations.* He grasps the spirit to the extent that it is more or less alien to itself. Thus it becomes clear that he obtains a negative picture of the spirit. The experimental psychologist will find typical probabilities, although the essence of our transcendental act is freedom; he will be faced with a complex multiple unity notwithstanding the fact that our interiority is a simple unity; he will speak of a relative self-subsistence, although our "intellectual soul" is simply self-subsistent. However, this situation cannot lead us into error, because we know now that the empirical psychologist and his metaphysical colleague, at least in part, do not describe the same object. Their judgments do not contradict each other but are complementary. The metaphysicist speaks about the *soul,* the empirical psychologist about the *besouled being;* the former tells us what *spiritual being* means, the latter *under what forms* it embodies and objectivizes itself; the former investigates the *transcendental act,* the latter the *transcendental act insofar as it is existential.* Moreover, there is a difference of formal viewpoint. The metaphysicist ascertains what belongs to the material *a priori* of living being, psychical being, conscious being, while the experimental scientist describes the facts that actually occur in these realms. The metaphysicist must not seek to find a basis for his philosophical thought in the data of positive research. The empirical psychologist, on the other hand, in principle is forced to take into account all the results and data of the experimental sciences. Thus the living totalities will be described by these two types of thinkers in entirely different ways.

To characterize the relation between empirical and philosophical research in psychology we may once more have recourse to a comparison. What the empirical psychologist gives us is, as it were, the negative cast of our freedom, of our interiority of consciousness, and of our spiritual independence. This negative cast is very valuable because it is concretely perceptible, very accurate, and rich in interesting details. But the material of which it is made is "worldly" matter. Hence the cast in itself would not have anything to tell us if the metaphysicist were not able to indicate what really fills the cast and what in general and necessarily must be its contents.

Accordingly, the representatives of both types of psychological study are not called to combat but to complement each other. It is only from an intimate collaboration of the philosopher and the psychologist that can be born a scientifically justified modern anthropology which stays close to life and describes concrete man in his organico-spiritual unity. But such a collaboration demands that both explorers of human reality learn to know, understand, and appreciate their different viewpoints, scopes and methods *in their very diversity*. It is my fervent hope that these studies may have contributed something to a new and better mutual understanding between empirical and metaphysical psychologists.

APPENDIX

THE PHILOSOPHY OF BEHAVIOR

1. *Introduction*

The Nature of Scientific Concepts. Many, though not all, be-havioral psychologists[1] are convinced that in their science they do not have to make use of any philosophical thesis. This conviction is fully justified so long as they limit themselves to using the complex of concepts proper to their special science without ever reflecting on them. For in this case their considerations remain wholly within the confines of a definite *"univers de discours,"* a self-contained system of thought, whose terms are sufficiently defined by their mutual rela-tionships. However, such a "universe of thought," e.g. the one of the behavioral psychologist, is an artificial universe and does not at all agree with the real world in which the man of research lives, thinks and works.

We may illustrate this peculiar situation of scientific theory by means of a comparison borrowed from Arthur S. Eddington. A zoologist is told to find out how many fishes are contained in a pond. He has at his disposal only nets with a two inch mesh. Our zoologist begins his investigation by formulating a definition of fish more or less as follows: a fish is an animal whose diameter is more than two inches. He then starts his work without any further hesitation.[2] Thus in the "universe of thought" of our zoologist the object of research is determined by its relation to the means of research. In an analogous way, his basic concepts are defined through their relationship to other presupposed concepts. Undoubtedly, this method of defining will sim-plify and facilitate his research, but it is quite a different question whether it brings the researcher closer to the *"adequatio intellectus et rei,"* the conformity of intellect and reality. What actually happens

---

[1] We distinguish here between behavioral psychology and behaviorism. Behavioral psychologists are those who realize that in their experiments they do not have to do with souls, contents of consciousness, or drive mechanisms, but with the behavior of men and animals. In the terminology adopted here the scope of the term "behaviorism" is less extensive, because the behaviorist sees behavior only as a reaction to a complex of stimuli. As behaviorists we may consider, for instance, Watson, Holt, Weiss, Hull, Kantor, and Lashley. The group of behavioral psychologists, on the other hand, contains, in addition to the extreme behaviorists, all those experimental psychologists who have achieved emancipation from introspection, no matter how much their opinions differ in other respects.

[2] I have intentionally modified somewhat the example given by Eddington in *The Philosophy of the Physical Sciences,* Cambridge, 1949, pp. 16 ff.

is that such conventional definitions more closely resemble the rules of a game than true judgments.

For the insider it is evident that in psychology also use is made of such "fishy" definitions. Even first rate psychologists sometimes cannot do without them. It will be sufficient to refer here to Alfred Binet, who answered the question as to what intelligence really is by saying: "Intelligence is what is measured by my tests." Binet's attitude finds a startling counterpart in that of James Mc.K. Cattell, who, invited to define the science of psychology, replied: "Psychology is what psychologists do." The similarity of these two replies is not a pure coincidence. Both men refused to go beyond the boundaries of their charmed circle and say what things *really* are, because they were unable to provide the answer.

A Danger for the Intelligibility of Psychology. There is a serious danger here, against which Edmund Husserl has sounded emphatic and repeated warnings[3]—namely, the danger that *experimental psychology suffers a loss in its character of intelligibility.* As a result of such an attitude, the relation of experimental psychology to other forms of scientific research, as well as to other sectors of human activity, gradually becomes less and less open to understanding. In this way, what psychologists do tends to become as puzzling for an outsider as the activity of chess plays is to one who knows nothing about the game. The men of science lock themselves up, as it were, in the "world of their game" and its rules. They are no longer able to explain to non-players what their game really means. Worst of all, they themselves no longer know it exactly. Thus the result is that "enigmatic, insoluble unintelligibility" for which Husserl blames modern science in general and psychology in particular.[4] There is only one way to escape from this danger—namely, to investigate thoroughly and systematically the fundamental notions of the psychological "universe of thought." In this investigation the basic theoretical concepts must be viewed within a framework that is broader than that of a single positive science. For, no matter how justifiable, for instance, the question is as to the "proper nature" of psychology, it cannot be answered in psychological terms. In this sense one can understand the attitude of Binet and Cattell. If we want to do justice to this question, we must appeal to a more fundamental science—to philosophy.

---

[3]The last time in his important work, *Die Krisis der europaischen Wissenschaften und die transzendentale Phänomenologie,* The Hague, 1954.

[4]*Op. cit.,* p. 4.

Necessity of a Philosophical Investigation of Behavior. Thus it is clear that the philosophical discussion of the fundamental presuppositions of the positive sciences is useful and necessary. It is the means to prevent a crisis in the intelligibility of the psychological sciences. It was on the basis of this conviction that we have analyzed the most important notion of introspective psychology, that of the soul. By way of supplement, we want to clarify the concept of behavior, because this concept is central in the research of most modern psychologists.[5] We will arrive at the conviction that fundamental problems of the philosophy of nature confront us in the critical discussion of this basic concept. On the other hand, perhaps certain results of our preceding studies will show themselves useful for this discussion.

2. *Definitions of Behavior*

Greene, Carnap, Hollingworth. It would be unfair to complain that modern men of science and especially the psychologists have not made any effort to clarify their central concept. The opposite is true. Numerous attempts have been made to determine this important notion as clearly as possible. Edward B. Greene, for instance, defines behavior in this way:

> The term "behavior" refers to any series of acts of any individual which occur in a particular place during a particular time. The individual may be an object, a person or a hypothetical entity such as an electron. The acts may be thought as purely physical or as involving mental phenomena.[1]

Starting with this definition, one could speak of "behavior" even when a lump of sugar is dissolved in water or when a hypothetical Indo-German verbal root supposedly changed among a certain people in a certain period of time. If this definition were true, it would be possible to fuse all positive sciences together into a single science. Under the same title of "behaviorism" one would be able to study the reaction of an atom or a kidney, just as well as that of a famous character in history. Nevertheless, such ideas are seriously considered by positivistic thinkers. Rudolf Carnap, for example, would like to unify psychology, physiology, the humanities, social sciences

---

[5]Thus our study differs in scope from Maurice Merleau-Ponty's significant work *La Structure du Comportement,* Paris, 1942. While Merleau-Ponty endeavors to correct misconceptions in psychological theory, we want to aid psychology in understanding itself.

[1]*Measurement of Human Behavior,* New York, 1941, p. 3.

and history under the name of "behavioristics."[2] Harry Hollingworth goes even farther and openly declares that "all sciences are studies of behavior."[3] However, to such a theory of the sciences one may apply the principle: *"dictum de omni, dictum de nullo."* For, if all sciences are behavioristic, the question arises as to what constitutes the typical character of psychology. By what right does this science call itself the science of behavior?

Maier and Schneierla. N. R. F. Maier and T. C. Schneierla describe behavior as follows:

> The environment furnishes energy which acts upon a *receptor* in the animal, and sets into effect an excitation which is conducted by a *nervous system* or some other transmissive system to parts capable of action, the effectors.[4]

With respect to this definition, it must be pointed out that these authors do not determine what they mean by "animal." If this concept is left out of consideration, their description can be applied to a machine. A motorcar, for instance, has parts upon which energy can act; it has transmissive mechanisms (*i.a.* electric ones), and also parts which act as effective "organs" of the transmitted energy.

Holt. E. B. Holt appeals to two separate characteristics. According to him, behavior can be recognized 1) by the "genuine 'objective reference' to the environment which is not found, so far as I can learn, in the inorganic, or in the world prior to integrated reflex response"; and 2) by the fact that it corresponds to a higher level of phylogenesis: "here if anywhere, evolution turned a corner."[5] The first part of this description raises serious doubts. Is it really true that in inorganic nature there is no objective reference to a definite environment? When, for instance, a certain substance undergoes a chemical change only in the presence of definite other substances and catalyzers, at a definite pressure and a definite temperature, one surely must speak of an objective reference to a definite environment. With regard to the second part of his definition, it seems far from fitting to us that the definition is made dependent on the evolutionary hypothesis which unfortunately is still so vulnerable. Moreover, Holt moves in a

---

[2]*International Encyclopedia of Unified Science,* vol. I, no. 1, Chicago, 1938, "Logical Foundations of the Unity of Science," pp. 45-49.

[3]"The Psychophysical Continuum," *Journal of Philosophy, Psychology and Scientific Methods,* vol. 13 (1916), p. 187.

[4]*Principles of Animal Psychology,* New York-London, 1935, p. 8.

[5]*The Freudian Wish,* pp. 50 ff., 154, 161, 169, quoted by A. A. Roback, *Behaviorism and Psychology,* Cambridge, Mass., 1955, pp. 76, 77.

circle. On the one hand, he considers the behavior of certain kinds of animals as one of the marks that characterize a higher level of evolution; on the other, he uses this higher phylogenetic level thus characterized to define the concept of behavior. Evidently, such a train of thought does not lead anywhere.

Tilquin. Far more prudence is shown by André Tilquin, who writes:

> Beyond the divergences of factions, there is a definition to which every behaviorist subscribes: behavior is the whole of adaptive, objectively observable reactions which an organism, generally provided with a nervous system, executes in response to stimuli that likewise are objectively observable and come from the environment in which it lives.[6]

Nevertheless, it is doubtful whether this definition is satisfactory. Let us take a simple case. Someone consumes something undigestible and in consequence has to vomit violently. Note that the attack engages the whole individual in question. More muscles, vessels and glands take part in it than in activities which one would unhestitatingly qualify as behavior. Certainly, the spasmodic vomiting is a "concrete whole activity" in the sense of John B. Watson.[7] Tilquin's term, a "whole of adaptive, objectively observable reactions," fully applies to it. Although a physiologist and a physician may be able to draw scientific conclusions from these reactions, for the psychologist the observation of the spasm will not provide an occasion to arrive at psychological laws.

A Difficulty in Principle. Our example clearly reveals that in principle there is a difficulty here. A. Robinson puts his finger on it when he writes: "If digestion turned out to be a process in which the whole organism was active instead of a process performed by the stomach, it would not therefore pass from the physiologist's to the psychologist's domain."[8] In other words, physiological reactions of the whole organism may be psychologically of little importance. On the other hand, the psychologist will have to take into account that a simple smile or gesture may give expression to an existential decision.

---

[6]*Behaviorisme,* Paris, 1942, p. 18.
[7]*Psychology from the Standpoint of a Behaviorist,* Philadelphia-London, 1919, pp. 13 ff.
[8]"Behavior as a Psychological Concept," *Proceedings of the Aristotelian Society,* vol. 18 (1918), p. 276.

If it is admitted that the difference between physiology and psychology is still of any importance, we will have to try to discover this difference by means of another approach.

3. *Behavior and Value*

First Evidence: There are Specifically Psychological Judgments. Our method is based on an elementary phenomenology of the psychological research in behavior as it is actually performed in Europe and America. We start from the evidence that there exist both specifically psychological judgments and others which are not specifically psychological. Till the present only the most extreme behaviorists, such as Lashley[1] and Zing Yang Kuo[2] have doubted this evidence. We call judgments specifically psychological if they can be scientifically justified only by means of typically psychological methods. For instance, the statement of Maier and Schneierla that " 'growth responses' are observable in all seed plants and are brought about by effects which alter the physiology of the tissue"[3] is not a psychological judgment, notwithstanding the fact that the authors mimic psychology by using its specialized terminology as much as possible. The reason is that this statement is based on observations of botanists, biologists and physiologists using *their own* observational methods. On the other hand, the statement that in a certain region the children of unskilled laborers have an average I.Q. of 84, while those of skilled laborers show one of 90[4] must be considered as a specifically psychological judgment. It would be recognized as psychological even if it were encountered in a medical, pedagogical, juridical, or criminological context.

Second Evidence: Not All Beings "Behave." The phenomenology of psychological research supplies us with a second evidence, which is as elementary as the first—namely, that psychologists cannot experiment with just any kind of beings. No matter what the extreme behaviorists say in their theoretical writings, in their laboratories they proceed with more discrimination. There they are in-

---

[1]"The Behavioristic Interpretation of Consciousness," *Psychological Review,* vol. 30 (1923), pp. 237 ff., 329 ff.

[2]"Prolegomena to Praxiology," *Journal of Psychology,* vol. 4 (1937), pp. 1 ff.

[3]*Op. cit.,* p. 10.

[4]A. J. Swaak, "Gezinsgrootte, geboortenummer en intelligentie," *Tijdschrift voor Opvoedkunde,* vol. I (1955-56), p. 291.

terested only in the reactions of certain *well-defined* beings. Since they call "behavior" those reactions which do interest them, we may conclude that not all but only certain beings behave. Perhaps we can make a first, provisional contribution to the solution of our problem by asking ourselves: *Of what* (of which categories of beings) *can we meaningfully say that it behaves?*

This question seems to be very clear. Yet from a philosophical standpoint, it is still too vague and too general. Because there is no behavior independently of a self-subsistent being that behaves, we should, first of all, determine the ontological support, the *"suppositum"* or *"hypokeimenon"* of this kind of dynamism. A second question should be concerned with that which occasions or elicits this peculiar activity. In other words, we have to ask:

1. What behaves?

2. What causes a being to behave?

Only a Besouled Being Can be Meaningfully Said to Behave. The answer to the first question is relatively simple. That which behaves is in any case the self-subsistent being as such. By "being as such" we mean *the being in its ontological totality.* This point is of special importance for Thomistic philosophers. In speaking of a living being, they should carefully avoid any phrases which seem to suggest that the soul alone behaves, while it uses the body as an instrument. In fact, neither the soul nor a faculty or bodily organ behaves. If Thomas Aquinas were alive today, he would make with respect to *"se gerere"* behaving, the same statement which he made concerning *"sentire,"* sensing: *"est operatio conjuncti,"* it is an activity of the composite.[5] In other words, behavior can be attributed in a meaningful way only to besouled being.

Modern psychologists belonging to different schools of thought express almost the same idea, although in a different language, when they stress that behavior is "neutral in psycho-physical respect." What they mean by this formula is, negatively speaking, the fact that behavior does not originate from a being behind the behaving being. B. F. Skinner, for instance, makes the following typical remark:

> In more advanced systems of behavior ultimate controls have been assigned to entities placed within the organism and called psychic or mental. Nothing is gained by this stratagem because most, if not

---

[5]*Summa theol.*, p. I, q. 75, a. 3.

all, the determinative properties of the original behavior must be assigned to the inner entity, which becomes, as it were, an organism in its own right.[6]

Neo-Thomistic philosophers can agree, I think, with the psychologists' postulate that behavior must be ascribed to the living being in its entirety.

The Behaving Being is Necessarily a Subject. One may ask whether this statement does not imply a *petitio principii.* Did we not first explain the concept of "subject" through that of "behavior," and then the idea of "behavior" by means of the notion of "subject"? We would, indeed, lay ourselves open to this charge if we were incapable of characterizing the mode of being a subject along other lines. However, we are able to do so. For it is evident that a subject must be a finite, imperfect being which needs other beings to become more perfect. These other beings are called its objects. Necessarily and universally, *the subject is directed towards its objects,* because they are for it supports of positive and negative values. In the language of traditional philosophy we could also say that the object is a good insofar as it can contribute to the perfection of the subject, and that it is an evil whenever it hampers, endangers or annihilates its perfection. Something that is neither a good nor an evil for the subject (the "adiaphoron" of the Greek philosophers) does not give rise to any form of directedness. On the purely sensitive level this is evident, for what is entirely neutral with respect to an animal does not cause any behavior; most of the time it is not even perceived.

On the other hand, it is obvious that, if there exists a perfect being, this being will not behave—for the simple reason that there is nothing which could oblige it to assume an attitude of directedness. To ascribe behavior to a being which in a meaningful way could be called God would simply be a contradiction. Only a finite, precarious and indigent being is, for its very existence, dependent on the aid and support of other finite beings. Only such a being behaves.

Meaning of the Term "Value." The introduction of the term "value" should not be misunderstood. We do not claim that experimental psychology as such, i.e. if abstraction is made of its applications, is a science which determines value in the sense in which literature

---

[6]*The Behavior of Organisms,* New York-London, 1938, p. 3.

or the history of art is determinant of value.[7] For the values with which we are concerned here are values with respect to the subject of the psychological investigation. So far as the experimenter or observer is concerned, they are not values but phenomena of value. What the psychologist himself thinks of these phenomena is wholly irrelevant for the theoretical investigation. In this respect he is a "disinterested spectator" in the sense of Edmund Husserl.

Nevertheless, in our view, one cannot deny that phenomena of value play a role in the research of the behavioral psychologist. The proof lies in the phenomenology of his experimental procedure. If, for example, the director of an experiment want to provoke a certain behavior, he will look for something which to the subject in question is a good or an evil. He knows, for instance, that generally speaking for higher types of animals food, sexual companionship, and freedom are goods, while hunger, emprisonment and pain are evils, and he acts accordingly. In the case of an experiment on man the human subject will consider it a positive value to be able to contribute somewhat to the solution of a scientific problem. Even for a patient in an asylum the person of the clinical psychologist is usually a pole to which he is positively or negatively directed. When such a directedness is not present, as in conditions of apathy or stupor, then there is, psychologically speaking, very little that can be done with such a patient. Thus we arrive at the general judgment that a psychological experiment is unthinkable without the presence of objects which for the subject of the experiment are either valuable or value-threatening. Hence it appears that it is either a good or an evil that causes the subject to behave.

Value and End. It is to be noted that we speak of goods as bearers of values and not as ends. Thus there is a difference between our standpoint and that of Roback and the representatives of so-called "hormic psychology," as it is conceived by William McDougall. In our opinion, whoever speaks about "end" in psychology calls forth the idea of a "purpose" and an awareness of it. McDougall himself explicitly states that "this guidance [of hormic activity] is effected through a cognitive activity, an awareness."[8] McDougall, the phil-

---

[7]That *applied* psychology, at least implicitly, determines value does not appear to be to doubt. For every clinical psychologist starts from the axiom that sanity of mind is better than being insane; every social psychologist considers social adaptation as a good; every industrial psychologist calls a conflict in industry an evil. For this reason the awareness of value constitutes the guiding principle of success for a practical psychologist.

[8]*An Introduction to Social Psychology*, 29th impr., London, 1948, p. 461.

osopher, seems to interfere here with McDougall, the psychologist. The psychologist has to investigate separately for each species and situation the way in which a good incites the subject to activity. But this is a task which can be accomplished only by means of empirical methods. It will be easy for an experimentalist to show that in numerous instances of behavior there is no question of a purpose flowing from one or the other form of awareness of a purpose. For instance, it is true that air is a good for me, and that to breathe is an activity which serves to obtain this good. Nevertheless, it is only exceptionally that my respiration will be accompanied by my awareness of it. On the other hand, so far as philosophical arguments are concerned, they likewise do not support the claims of the hormic psychologists. The axiom *"omne agens agit propter finem,"* every agent acts for an end, expresses only that whatever is active, is active for the sake of an end. There is no question in it of a directedness that is either conscious or immediate. Obviously, this axiom is not the same as the claim that "every being is active because of a consciousness of an end." The classical formula contains a general metaphysical thesis, while its faulty interpretation expresses a psychological assertion, which, moreover, is untenable.

For all these reasons we have no intention of identifying "behavior" with "purposive behavior." We limit ourselves to the statement that only subjects behave, and that they do so with respect to goods or evils. Whether and how the valuable or value-threatening character of objects "appears" to various subjects is something that must be determined by the sciences of experience.

4. *A Difficulty Flowing from the Philosophy of Nature*

It may appear that the conclusion of the preceding section indicates the solution of our problem. As a matter of fact, a certain amount of progress has been made, thanks to the fact that we have raised the problem in the light of a genuine metaphysics of being, free from all kinds of prejudices stemming from the influence of Cartesians and introspective psychology. Thus we were able to find at once the correct starting point. However, it is no more than just a starting point. As soon as we want to apply our general ontological insights to reality, there arise new and unexpected difficulties to remind us that, strictly speaking, we have not yet proved anything.

Does a Falling Rock Behave? If we start from the concrete, the new setting of the problem is felt immediately. Why, for instance, do we not speak of behavior with respect to a falling rock? One would be inclined to reply: because a rock is not a subject; by falling it does not realize any value. However, on what is such an assertion based? Aristotle, as everyone knows, was convinced of the opposite. The least we can say is that we do not possess any clear evidence of it. As phenomenological philosophers, we do not want to take a single step which is not based on direct or indirect evidence.

Do Atoms Behave? Moreover, our problem is very actual. There are, for example, microphysicists who speak of a "chemical behavior of the atom." They point out that an atom with a neutral outermost shell is less open to chemical influences; thus by keeping its outermost shell occupied with the full number of electrons the atom "protects" its existence.[1] Thus we must ask ourselves whether in such a case one can avoid speaking of value.

Do Plants Behave? We have to go even further. In certain cases where there is not the slightest doubt that values are realized, the phenomenon of "behavior" does not occur. Let us consider a plant. We do not hesitate to affirm that its roots "tend" to the soil, its stalks and leaves to light. Vital values correspond to its geotropism and heliotropism. A plan inserts itself appropriately into its vital surroundings, yet it does not "behave." Apparently, not every "turning towards" deserves to be called behavior. Thus it is not a pure coincidence that the psychologists gets nowhere with a plant, even if he is convinced that it is a besouled being. A plant does not provide him with any opportunity to pronounce specifically psychological judgments; it cannot be used as a subject of psychological experiments. What is the reason? As long as we do not know the answer to this question, we cannot flatter ourselves that we have solved our problem.

How to Establish the Distinction Between Behaving and Non-Behaving Living Beings? We are faced here with a great difficulty. Evidently, we have to draw first a philosophical dividing line between living and non-living, and then in the realm of the organic separate again life which behaves from non-behaving life. In doing this, we may perhaps be guided by our preceding considerations in the realm

---

[1] Cf., e.g. the article "Atoom" by Zwikker in the *Lexicon van Winkler-Prins,* 5th ed., Amsterdam, 1933, vol. II, pp. 291 f.; D. F. Comstock and L. I. Troland, *The Nature of Matter and Electricity,* pp. 2, 21, quoted by Roback, *op. cit.,* p. 75.

of the philosophy of nature. As we noted there, the various typical modes of being-in-time constitute a criterion which may be used to characterize the different modes of being proper to existent reality.[2] However, we want to stress that we do not consider this method as the only one suitable for the purpose. Perhaps an analysis of the concept of space would lead to the same goal. Such outstanding psychologists as Viktor von Weiszäcker,[3] Erwin Straus,[4] F. J. J. Buytendijk[5] and Maurice Merleau-Ponty[6] have shown that space as experienced by a subject is not the geometric space on which the physicist bases his thought. Moreover, the self-motion of the animal subject, undoubtedly, is not simply to be compared with the mechanical motion of lifeless objects.[7] Nevertheless, we prefer to take our arguments from an analysis of the concept of time, because in this way we hope to reach results which are in agreement with the phenomenology of psychological research as it is actually carried out.

5. *Besouled Time as the Characteristic of Life*

Organized Duration. We will start here with the concept of organized time, as it was developed above in study Seven.[1] It was shown there that in organized time three principles of order can be distinguished in such a way that the higher principle always presupposes the presence of the lower principle:

1. A limited duration which arises because that which endures continues to exist for one moment and another moment and another moment, etc.

2. The second form of order presupposes the presence of the first. But something is added—namely, primordial "earlier," "simultaneous," and "later." The relation of t_n to t_{n+1} differs from that of t_{n+1} to t_n. It is an asymmetric relationship. The road from t_n to t_{n+1} is other than that of t_{n+1} to t_n; it is even conceivable that one cannot go back over the same road. When this is the case, duration assumes

---

[2]Cf. Study VII, Sections 2, 3, and 4, pp. 195 ff.

[3]*Der Gestaltkreis*, Leipzig, 1940.

[4]*Vom Sinn der Sinne*, Berlin, 1935.

[5]*Algemene theorie der menselijke houding en beweging*, Utrecht-Antwerp, 1948.

[6]*La phénoménologie de la perception*, 2nd impr., Paris, 1945, Part I, ch. 3, pp. 114 ff.

[7]Cf. H. Pleszner, *Die Stufen des Organischen und der Mensch*, Berlin, 1928; F. J. J. Buytendijk, *op. cit.*

[1]Sect. 4, pp. 206 ff.

an irreversible character. One is faced with what Eddington has called "the arrow of time." "Earlier," "simultaneously," and "later," in addition to their purely numerical value, assume also a qualitative meaning.

3. The third principle of order is unthinkable without the existence of moments of "now," as chacterized under 2. What is new here is the fact that the various moments of "now" are not only interconnected by a definite asymetric relationship, but in addition have a certain function with respect to the whole of the limited duration. This new characteristic induced us to speak of a temporally ordered duration.

Every Living Body Has a Temporally Ordered Duration. It is easy to show that the life of every living being is temporally an organized duration. For in the life of every organism there are "critical" moments of "now" which play an irreplaceable role within the framework of the life in question; for instance, the moments of nuclear division and separation, birth, sexual maturity, death. However, this statement is still too succinct. We have to add that the organized duration of life is subdivided and differentiated into subordinate temporal wholes. For example, in the development of a simple phanerogamic plant the terms "to germinate," "to bloom," "to bear fruit," and "to wither" indicate meaningful moments which mark the beginning or end of typical phases of its vegetative life. In its turn, the phase, for instance, of "bearing fruit" may be subdivided into a number of briefer but important and typical periods which all together belong to the vital process of bearing fruit. Analogous statements could be made with respect to the other phases, such as that of nuclear division. For this reason it seems more correct to say that *in its temporal respect organic life may be considered as built of hierarchically ordered wholes of time.*[2]

Life is Characterized by Immanent Temporal Laws. Thus we meet here a palpable difference between organic and inorganic nature. Organic life possesses *its own* rhythm. The way in which it is built of temporal wholes corresponds with an *immanent* law. True, this vital rhythm is somewhat subject to modification. Light, heat (or more generally, the influence of certain rays), and the presence of certain substances can accelerate or retard it. However, these influ-

[2]Cf. Study VII, Sect. 3, pp. 203 ff.

ences do not modify the typical succession of the phases. They merely change the duration of these various phases in a purely accidental way. Once awakened, life runs its course in accordance with its own immanent temporal laws, which are essentially unchangeable.

The same cannot be asserted with respect to inorganic processes. Of course, such processes also may reveal a rhythm and obey temporal laws. However, this rhythm does not correspond with an inherited immanent law, but rather depends on a constellation of external causes. To illustrate the point, when a tree is planted or a seed is sown, one can ask about the duration of the vegetable life that will awaken from it. The question is meaningful and, within certain limits of accuracy, can be answered with great probability. No answer, however, is possible with respect to the duration of an atom, a crystal, or a piece of furniture. Their relative self-subsistence and unity will be maintained till one or more occasional causes destroy them, for their duration is totally dependent on extrinsic causes.

It is to be noted that occasional influences may play a role also in the development of organisms. Yet, in such a case these influences are in sharp contrast to the whole of factors which together constitute the "environment" of the living being. Such an occasional influence is considered as an "accident" in both the philosophical and the ordinary sense of the term. For these reasons we think that the fact of referring to itself, which is so typical of the living being manifests itself nowhere with more clarity than in its adherence to the immanent temporal laws which govern all its functions.[3]

A Further Difficulty. Are we now ready to determine the concept of "behavior"? Not yet. With due changes, everything we have said thus far applies to the whole realm of life. Whatever lives, lives in a besouled time. Not only does every organism, whether sick or healthy, possess its own rhythm, but even relatively independent organs are characterized by their own temporal laws. Nevertheless, no one would think of speaking, for instance, of the behavior of a human ovary.

To overcome this difficulty, we see no other alternative than to analyze still more profoundly the being-in-time of the various realities. Evidently, the distinction between the temporality of the physical thing and that of the living being is insufficient. Other essential differences can be pointed out, or rather could be pointed out, if they had not been obscured by an inaccurate scientific terminology. Thus it becomes important for us to disclose this inaccuracy.

---

[3]Cf. Study V, Sect. 10, pp. 134 ff.

6. *The Fourfold Meaning of Reaction*

Ambiguity of "Reaction." The ambiguous use of the term "reaction" causes great confusion in the realm of the positive sciences. To illustrate it with a single example, according to Margaret F. Washburn, there can be question of "slow learning" in the inorganic world, for "a steel rail *reacts* differently to the pounding of the wheels after the process has been continued; it may snap under the train."[1] The same confusion of concepts seems to be the deciding factor in the case of those who want to unify many or all positive sciences under the title of "behavioristics."[2] Their reasoning appears to be that, since all material beings react, and whatever reacts behaves, all material beings behave, so that all positive sciences, which start from the experience of the material, are concerned with behavior.

To demonstrate the ambiguity which is at work in such assertions, we will rely again on a phenomenology of concrete scientific research. In this way it will be easy to prove that the various men of science, although they always speak of reactions, refer to quite different things. We propose to examine here four distinct cases.

First Meaning of "Reaction." "Zinc reacts with hydrochloric acid." The chemist means that the chemical process at time t_{n+1} results from the condition of the zinc and the acid at time t_n. If he knows accurately the quantity and quality of these two substances, as well as all other factors, such as temperature and pressure, at time t_n, he will be able to foresee what is going to happen at t_{n+1}. Whatever happened before t_n—more poetically expressed, the prehistory of the zinc and the acid—is wholly irrelevant with respect to his prediction. What he calls a chemical reaction is nothing but the chemical changes in structure which occur between t_n and t_{n+1}.

Second Meaning of "Reaction." "This plant reacts to the lack of nitrogen by slow growth." In saying this, the biologist, botanist, or agronomist mean the following: the condition of the plant at t_n reveals an important phase of its life, perhaps even its whole past; not only its undernourishment at t_{n-1}, but also that at t_{n-2} and t_{n-3} etc. must be taken into account in judging its physiological condition. Thus the "prehistory" of the plant with its various temporal wholes manifests itself at t_n. On the other hand, its weakened condition at t_n will influence not only its state at t_{n+1}, but also that at t_{n+2}, t_{n+3}, etc.;

---

[1] *The Animal Mind,* 4th impr., New York, 1936, p. 28. Italics of the author.
[2] Cf. above, p. 231.

briefly, the whole or at least an important phase of its future is affected by it. This also is taken into account by the physiologist and the botanist when they speak of the reaction of a vegetative organism. Thus we see that here "reaction" indicates the succession of two or more phases in accordance with biological laws.

Third Meaning of "Reaction." Let us think here of a very simple experiment. A rat has in its cage two little troughs *A* and *B*. Whenever it goes to *A*, it receives an electric shock. After a series of attempts to reach *A*—the number of which can be counted—the rat eats only from *B*. Now the psychologist asserts: "The rat *reacts* by eating only from *B*."

Let us examine this case very carefully. If there was question only of "nourishing itself," we would have to do here with a purely instinctive action,[3] and would not be faced with new problems. The instinctive action has its typical phases which are mutually ordered by means of primordial relationships of "earlier," "simultaneous," and "later." These phases run their course in a fixed and irrevocable order until the instinctive action has taken place.[4] Accordingly, the concepts described above under the second meaning of reaction would be sufficient to provide an explanation. However, in the above-mentioned experiment the situation is different. The present condition of the living being is not simply the terminal result of an orderly series of phases. It is not simply *the* past, but certain events of this past which play the decisive role. Definite moments of "now"—namely, the painful experiences of electric shocks—contrast clearly and sharply with the dim and obscure past. From the otherwise undifferentiated past duration certain significant "nows" are detached and made present. Thus the future life of the animal is co-determined, or at least conditioned, by these experiences that are past and nevertheless not past. This is what Maurice Pradines calls "to bring the experience of the past to bear upon the present."[5] In daily life we express the same matter more simply and say that the animal has learned something. In this way our analysis shows clearly that it is impossible to express in the language of physics and chemistry what "learning" is. For the physicist, a past cause which still acts and has effects is a contradictory

---

[3]We leave aside here the question whether all instinctive actions are purely instinctive.

[4]Cf. Study VII, Sect. 2, p. 195.

[5]Cf. p. 200.

concept. But the notion of time of which the psychologist makes use here differs from that of the physicist.

The Animal Mode of Being in Time. One could ask whether we want to suggest in our example that the animal is conscious of its experiences. We will take the liberty of declining to answer this question. For one thing, the term "consciousness," as it is used in the question, implies being conscious of something (according to Pfänder's analysis, it would correspond to the second meaning of consciousness[6]). To consciousness in this sense varying degrees of clearness and distinctness must be attributed. Hence it is conceivable, for instance, that someone would qualify as "semiconscious" a psychical phenomenon which another would call "subconscious." Moreover, we have no true insight into this matter. Whatever we would affirm or deny in this respect would lack phenomenological justification. On the other hand, the animal's behavior shows clearly that a definite experience of its past turns up in connection with a definite situation of the present. It is quite accurate to say that we are unable to explain a definite type of animal behavior without making this assumption. Consequently, we have to do here with an indirect self-evidence. But indirect self-evidences too may have a compelling character. We therefore rightfully infer the conclusion that the animal's past consists of temporal wholes which are not entirely fused together so as to constitute simply *the* past, but remain to a certain extent movable and detachable. Within certain limits, they are at the disposal of the subject, which, of course, does not mean that they are at its *free* disposal. Thanks to their temporal mobility, experiences made in the past can be actualized, i.e. they can be presentified so as to enable the animal to prepare its future life in a meaningful way.

This Mode of Being-in-Time is Typical of Animal Life in General. It allows the animal to react to the same object now positively and then negatively or not to react at all, even though its relation to the object, as described in terms of physics, chemistry, or physiology, has not changed. The reason is that the animal's past somehow interferes with its actual experiences. For instance, a feeding trough which first was apprehended as an attractive thing later exhibits the character of a dangerous being. Because of the fact that its past experiences can emerge again, the animal is capable of learning, determining its attitude, and correcting its way of reacting. A vegetative organism is

---

[6]Cf. Study VII, Sect. 5, p. 210 ff.

unable to do this. Thus we could perhaps characterize the animal's higher mode of being by means of this formula: the life of every organism is, in the temporal respect, an organized duration, but within certain limits the animal is able to organize its own duration.

Fourth Meaning of "Reaction." "I react to the sound of a car's horn by crossing the street faster." This case has something in common with the preceding one. Somehow I have learned that the sound of the horn means danger. It does not matter how I have learned this, whether it was by personal experiences or the warnings of others. In either case an event that occurred in the past is actually present to me. But this is not all. While reacting, I am aware of a future situation which to me is desirable—namely, to be on the other side of the street. Evidently, I presentify here a future state of affairs which has a certain value for me.[7] Therefore, while crossing the street at the moment t_n, I connect an experience made at t_{n-x} with an expectation concerning the state of affairs at t_{n+y}.

7. *Reaction and Behavior*

We think that only the reactions described above under the third and fourth meaning of the term may be considered as modes of behavior. Only these types of reaction can induce the psychologist to make specifically psychological judgments. In his laboratory the psychological experimenter will try to elicit reactions of these two kinds. Therefore, *we correctly speak of "behavior" whenever a subject prepares his future by actualizing one or more past experiences.* If we were to examine exclusively the reaction described under the fourth meaning, we would be forced to give a different definition. For in this case the subject does not prepare his future in general but a definite future situation. The future is to him a dimension of being which contains the possibility of certain promising situations and of others that are terrifying. Perhaps it would help to clarify the terminology of psychology if consistently a distinction were made between *purposive behavior* and *behavior in general*. We would like to propose that the term *purposive behavior* be used *whenever a subject prepares his future by relating a definite expectation to one or more experiences.*

----

[7] In this case only one could rightfully speak of a certain "foresight." Cf. W. and K. McDougall, "Insight and Foresight in Various Animals," *Journal of Comparative Psychology,* vol. 34 (1937), pp. 413 ff.

It should be noted that our definitions do not treat of the problems of empirical psychology as such. They simply indicate the minimum conditions under which psychological methods can be applied so as to lead to the discovery of specifically psychological truths. This is the reason why they say nothing concerning the mode of actualizing experiences. Nor do they characterize the subject's manner of anticipating his future. Questions as to the form under which this anticipation is realized, whether it be based on a drive, an association, an imaginative synthesis, or a clear insight into a goal, are typically psychological. They cannot be answered by the philosopher. Such problems can be solved only by systematic observation and experimentation.

8. *Psychology and Physiology*

From these considerations it appears that the term "reaction" is equivocal. To prevent misunderstandings, it would be advisable to speak of a reaction in the narrower sense whenever an inorganic factor (or constellation of factors) causes an inorganic effect. As to the reaction in the wider sense, described under the second meaning, we would like to compare it with a process of "development." "To develop" would mean: to pass from one stage of vital evolution to another in accordance with rigid laws of sequence. It is evident that this idea of development would be an artificial technical concept. The popular connotation, for instance, of slowness should be excluded from it. Nor should it be confined to evolutionary and growth processes. A mere reflex action, such as vomiting, would belong to the category of "development."[1] The physiologist is obviously interested in the influence of environment factors on "developments," in the large sense which we have assigned to this term. The psychologist, on the other hand, as we have shown, is not concerned with the laws of development. A simple sequence of stages following one another according to immutable rules does not offer him any opportunity to make specifically psychological statements.

---

[1] On the level of animal life mere reflexes are perhaps mere abstractions; but even then they could be *abstractions cum fundamento in re*, abstractions based on reality. Cf. A. Gelb and K. Goldstein, *Psychologische Analysen hirnpathologischer Falle*, Part I, Leipzig, 1920; K. Goldstein, *Der Aufbau des Organismus*, The Hague, 1934; Maurice Merleau-Ponty, *La structure du comportement*, Chaps. I and II; F. J. J. Buytendijk, *Traité de psychologie animale*, Paris, 1952, Chap. IX.

Sensation and Perception. In this context the difference between sensation and perception deserves special attention. Sensation conceived as a mechanical reaction of a sense organ to stimuli is a concept denoting "development." The same cannot be said of perception, for perception presupposes the subject's prepredicative understanding of a world, an environment, or at least of some of its structures. As a matter of fact, the distinction between sensation and perception is accepted not only by numerous phenomenologists, but also by aphenomenological and antiphenomenological psychologists. Guillaume, for example, frankly admits that it is impossible for the experimenter to show the existence of pure sensations by means of psychological methods:

> The same critique applies to the notion of *sensation.* According to the traditional views, sensations would be the elements of all mental life. But, paradoxically, nothing would be rarer and more difficult to observe than a pure sensation. A preparation would be necessary to apperceive it, so to speak, in its naked state.[2]

He then sketches some typical pseudo-observations of sensations and criticizes them severely:

> In reality, there is question here of theories. . . . The subjects who make these subtle observations know the *physiological conditions* of perception and are preoccupied with certain problems. They do not merely want to observe but to explain. They are led to make distinctions among the phenomena and to consider as primitive those whose distinguishing features seem to agree best with the properties of peripheral physiological stimulations, and as derivative those which deviate from them.[3]

Thus, according to Guillaume, the notion of sensation is a concept introduced to explain theoretically the physiological conditions of perception. Robert Woodworth expresses himself in a simpler and shorter way:

> Sensation points to the sense organs with their nerves and nerve centers as the object of study; *perception* points to the object of the world.[4]

As a matter of fact, sense organs and their nerves are objects of physiological studies, whereas the scientific description of the subject's

---

[2]*Introduction à la psychologie,* Paris, 1946, p. 27. Italics are mine.
[3]*Op. cit.,* p. 28. Italics are mine.
[4]*Experimental Psychology,* 2nd. ed., New York, 1944, p. 450.

turning towards his world is the proper task of the psychologist.[5] The difference existing between the concepts of sensation and perception therefore correspond exactly to the different typical approaches of the physiologist and the psychologist.

On the other hand, a conditioned reflex can undoubtedly be examined by means of psychological methods. However, conditioning flows from experience and learning. The first words, therefore, which the psychologist has no longer in common with the physiologist are "to perceive," "to experience" and "to learn."

---

[5]Cf. Study VII, Sect. 8, pp. 224 f.

GLOSSARY OF TERMS

Accumulation: any relative unity of similar elements which are reciprocally connected by one and the same accidental relationship. Cf. p. 113 f.

Adjuction: a structural union in which one or more members of one or both structures have the special function of securing the connection and collaboration of both structures. Cf. p. 132.

Anonymous Ego=Primordial Ontological Center: the subject which must necessarily be thought as facing the different objects and quasi-objects. It is called "anonymous" because it is prior to the social and personal ego. Cf. p. 105.

A Priori or *Aprioristic:* that which is prior to and a condition of a certain (lower) form of experience, because it is based upon an insight into more fundamental structures of being. This objective concept of "a priori" must not be confused with Kant's subjective "a priori."

Besoul, to=to Animate: insofar as man is concerned, to make material realities participate in the existence of a spiritual formative act. Cf. pp. 142 ff.

Body, My: the whole of my real and possible concrete quasi-objects. Cf. p. 100 f.

Commutation: the modifications of the total order caused in an ordered whole by the insertion of a new member or the elimination of an old member. Cf. p. 137.

Conjunction: a structural union in which each member of one structure is, in principle, capable of entering into a connection with every member of the other structure. Cf. p. 132.

Directedness: see *Intentionality.*

Disposal, at my: an object or quasi-object is at my disposal insofar as my primordial ego can dispose of it intentionally and even eliminate it. Cf. p. 49.

Egology: the science of the primordial self-evidences concerning the ego. Derivative: *egological.*

Ego Source: see Primordial Ego.

Eidos: essence. Derivative: *eidetic.*

Elimination: The processes by which an old member of an ordered whole ceases to function as a member. Cf. p. 137 f.

Embody, to: the activity by which my self-subsistent soul makes material realities participate in my being. Cf. pp. 148 ff.

Epoche=to place between brackets: the suspension of judgment with respect to something or leaving it out of consideration.

Existential Movement or *Existential Turning Towards:* the act by which every subject, in virtue of an essential necessity, turns towards the world, the vital or social surroundings. Cf. p. 147 f.

Experience: not only sense experience, but generally speaking, every pre-predicative familiarity with being and certain modes of being. Cf. p. 3 f.

Fluid Ordered Whole: a whole which can exist only by ceaselessly assimilating elements into members and dissimilating members into elements. Cf. p. 140.

Homogeneous Coupling: a relatively self-subsistent being in which the component parts are connected according as required by its formative principle. Cf. pp. 114 ff.

Idol of Self-Knowledge: According to Brentano and Husserl, the prejudice that the lived event is accessible to the knower in an absolute manner.

Immanence: see *Interiority.*

Insertion: the processes by which a new member is actively and passively adapted to, assimilated to, and integrated into an ordered whole. Cf. p. 137.

Intentionality=Directedness: being directed toward an object.

Interiority=Immanence: the presence with oneself.

Living Order: an order which keeps itself intact by its own ordinating activity. Cf. p. 138.

Material a Priori: the totality of aprioristic laws which characterize a certain section or level of being, such as being animated, being conscious, etc. This material *a priori* is opposed to the formal *a priori* of logic which is concerned with all beings. See *A Priori.*

Nihilate, to: to leave entirely out of consideration. Derivative: *nihilation.*

Object: any reality which *a priori* is capable of becoming the object of an existential orientation for a subject. Cf. p. 92.

Object Pole: that to which one is or can be intentionally directed.

Objectivation: the state of being objectivized.

Objectivizable: that which can become the object pole of my acts of knowing and willing.

Objectivize, to: to make something the object of an act of knowing or willing.

Ordered Whole: a whole ruled by an internal law which determines the way in which each part in particular is connected with all other parts, and this in function of the union of the parts in general. Cf. p. 119 f.

Order Theory: the systematic study of the relations by which in various ways parts can be organized into a whole.

Ordinabilitas: the capacity to be integrated into a definite order. Cf. p. 136.

Organized Duration: an ordered whole in the order of time. Cf. p. 201 f.

Originating Ego: see *Primordial Ego.*

Personal Ego: the sum total of the objective facts which make it possible for man to form a certain picture of his own person in the physical, psychical, and moral sense. Cf. p. 65.

Perspectives: the modes under which a material thing appears and which at the same time allow me to grasp it as a thing. German *"Abschattungen."*

Phenomenological Reduction: according to Husserl, a method which makes it possible to exclude any affirmation concerning real existence from the sphere of immanent phenomena. Cf. p. 3.

Phenomenology: see pp. 2 ff.

Phronesis: the inclination and ability to view the eternal and unchangeable ideas, or in modern terms, the capacity of grasping universal and necessary truths.

Place Between Brackets, to: see *Epoche.*

Presentify, to: the activity of the ego in virtue of which moments of time are made present-for-me and thus acquire a meaning and mutual relationship. Cf. p. 203. Derivative: *presentification.*

Primordial Ego=Originating Ego=Ego Source: the egological reality from which originates my whole concrete being myself with all its activities and passivities, its powers and dispositions, its properties and states. Cf. p. 65 f.

Primordial Ontological Center: see *Anonymous Ego.*

Psyche: the ordered whole of the temporal members of an organism. Cf. pp. 206 ff.

Psychical, the: the level of ordered duration of the organic body. Cf. p. 207.

Quasi-Object: any reality in me which can be the object of a retroverted act. Cf. p. 96 f. Derivatives: *quasi-objective, quasi-objectively.*

Reduction: abstaining by abstraction from making a judgment concerning this or that particular being or particular mode of being. Cf. p. 155 f.

Retro-Directed Act: see *Retroverted Act.*

Retroverted Act=Retro-Directed Act=Act Directed to the Ego: an act of which somehow I am the source and at the same time the recipient. Cf. pp. 83 ff.

Sedimentation: the process by which a content of consciousness is gradually more and more removed from actual consciousness till it is completely forgotten. Cf. p. 146.

Self-Evidence: 1. *Immediate:* an evidence that is based upon direct experience, i.e. not deduced from experience by means of abstract methods of thinking. 2. *Primordial:* an evidence which cannot be denied without being implicitly re-affirmed. For instance, anyone who argues with me that we are not free implicitly recognizes my freedom because he tries to make me agree with him.

Social Ego: the ego insofar as it is a center of social relations. Cf. p. 65.

Solipsism: the philosophic position that the ego is either the only possible starting point of philosophy or the only existing reality.

Structure: a whole composed of subordinated members which in connection with one or more superior members function as a single member, equal in rank to other members. Cf. p. 132. Derivative: *structural.*

Subject: a being which is naturally open to, and impressionable by certain goods. In consequence the subject is necessarily directed to certain beings considered as good. Cf. p. 141.

Subject Pole: the ego insofar as it is always and of necessity directed to something else.

Thetic: taking explicitly position with respect to being. Cf. p. 216.

Transcendental Ego: according to Husserl in his idealistic period, the source from which all objective phenomena derive their value, i.e. the ego to which phenomena appear as phenomena. Cf. p. 50.

Vital: biological, i.e. referring to life insofar as it is organic.

World, the: the universal horizon which comprehends all actual and possible objects of my directedness or intentionality. Derivative: *worldly.*

BIBLIOGRAPHY

Adler, A., *Praxis und Theorie der Individualpsychologie*, 4th ed., München, 1930.

Alexander, F. and French, Th. M., *Studies in Psychosomatic Medicine*, New York, 1948.

Andrews, T. G. (ed.), *Methods of Psychology*, New York-London, 1948.

Aristotle, *Opera Omnia*, Bekker edition, Berlin, 1831.

Barbado, M., *Introduction à la psychologie expérimentale*, translated by Ph. Mazoyer, Paris, 1931.

Berger, G., *Le Cogito dans la philosophie de Husserl*, Paris, 1941.

Bergson, H., *Essai sur les données immédiates de la conscience*, Paris, 1889.
   Matière et mémoire, 46th ed., Paris, 1946.
   L'évolution créatrice, 62nd ed., Paris, 1946.

Beysens, Tr., *Algemeene zieleleer*, 2nd ed., vol. I, Amsterdam, 1905; vol. II, Amsterdam, 1911; vol. III, Bussum, 1920.

Bigot, L. C. T., Kohnstamm, Ph., Palland, B. G., *Leerboek der psychologie*, Groningen-Batavia, 1946.

Binet, A., *L'ame et le corps*, Paris, 1920.

Binswanger, L., *Einführung in die Probleme der allgemeinen Psychologie*, Berlin, 1922.
   Grundformen und Erkenntnis menschlichen Daseins, Zürich, 1942.
   Ausgewählte Vorträge und Aufsätze, Vol. I, *Zur phänomenologischen Anthropologie*, Bern, 1947.
   "Die Bedeutung der Daseinsanalytik Martin Heideggers für die Psychologie und die philosophische Anthropologie," *Martin Heideggers Einfluss auf die Wissenschaften*, Bern, 1949.

Blondel, M., *La pensée*, 2 vols., Paris, 1934.

Bollnow, O. F., *Das Wesen der Stimmungen*, Frankfurt, a.M., 1941.

Boyer, C., *Cursus philosophiae ad usum seminariorum*, 2 vols., Paris, [1935].

Brederveld, J., *Het object der psychologie*, Groningen-Batavia, 1933.

Brennan, R. E., *General Psychology. An Interpretation of the Science of the Mind Based on Thomas Aquinas*, New York, 1937.
   History of Psychology from the Standpoint of a Thomist, New York, 1946.

255

Brentano, F., *Psychologie vom empirischen Standpunkt,* vol. I, Leipzig, 1874.

Brugmans, H. J. F. W., *Psychologische methoden en begrippen,* Haarlem, 1922.
　　"Een bijdrage tot begrip van het psychische," *Tijdschrift v. philosophie,* vol. 3 (1941), pp. 737 f.

Brunner, A., *La personne incarnée. Étude sur la phénomenologie et la philosophie existentialiste,* Paris, 1947.

Bühler, K., *Die Krise der Psychologie,* 2nd ed., Jena, 1929.

Burloud, A., *Principes d'une psychologie des tendances,* Paris, 1938.

Buytendijk, F. J. J., *Psychologie der dieren,* Haarlem, 1920.
　　Het spel van mens en dier als openbaring van levensdriften, Amsterdam, 1932.
　　Grondproblemen van het dierlijk leven, Antwerp-Brussels, Nymegen-Utrecht, 1938.
　　"De rangorde der organismen in de biologie," *Tijdschrift v. philosophie,* vol. 3 (1941), pp. 4 ff.
　　"Wezen en zin van de pijn," *Ibid.,* vol. 4 (1942), pp. 3 ff.
　　Het kennen van de innerlijkheid, Nymegen, 1947.
　　Algemene theorie der menselijke houding en beweging als verbinding en tegenstelling van de physiologische en psychologische beschouwing, Utrecht-Antwerp, 1948.

Calon, P. J. A., *Over de persoonlijkheidsontwikkeling by kinderen met aangeboren of vroeg verworven doofheid,* Nymegen, 1950.

Carrel, A., *L'homme, cet inconnu,* 2nd ed., Paris, 1946.

Cassirer, E., *"Psychologie und Philosophie," Bericht über den 12. Kongress der deutschen Ges. f. Psychologie in Hamburg 1931,* Jena, 1932, pp. 73 ff.

Conrad-Martius, H., "Schöpfung und Zeugung," *Tijdschrift v. Philosophie,* vol. 1 (1939), pp. 801 ff.

Couturier, W., *Compendium tractatus philosophici de homine sive anthropologia speculativa,* Nymegen, n. d. *Pro manuscripto.*
　　"Het menselijk lichaam in het thomistische denken," *Bijdragen,* vol. 11 (1950), pp. 111 ff.

De Bruyne, E., *Ethica,* vol. II, *De ontwikkeling van het zedelijke bewustzijn,* Antwerp-Brussels, Nymegen-Utrecht, 1935.

De Coninck, A., *L'unité de la connaissance humaine et le fondement de sa valeur,* Louvain, 1947.

De Greef, E., *Notre destinée et nos instincts,* Paris, 1945.
　　Les instincts de défense et de sympathie, Paris, 1947.

Delacroix, H., *Les grandes formes de la vie mentale,* 2nd ed., Paris, 1937.

De La Vaissière, J., *Éléments de psychologie expérimentale,* 6th ed., Paris, 1926.

De Montpellier, G., "La psychologie comme science empirique." *"Tijdschrift v. philosophie,"* vol. 2 (1940), pp. 152 ff.
    "Psychologie et dualisme," *Revue néoscolast. de Louvain,* vol. 41 (1938), pp. 542 ff.
    Conduites intelligentes et psychisme chez l'animal et chez l'homme. Étude de psychologie comparée, Louvain-Paris, 1946.

De Petter, D. M., "Impliciete intuitie," *Tijdschrift v. philosophie,* vol. 1 (1939), pp. 84 ff.
    "Intentionaliteit en identiteit," *Ibid.,* vol. 2 (1940), pp. 515 ff.

De Raeymaeker, L., *De philosophie van Scheler,* Mechelen, 1934.
    Grondbeginselen der algemene psychologie, Louvain, 1941. *Pro manuscripto.*
    The Philosophy of Being, St. Louis, 1955.

Derwordt, A., "Untersuchungen über den Zeitverlauf figurierter Bewegungen beim Menschen," *Pflügers Archiv f.d. ges. Physiol.,* vol. 240 (1938), pp. 661 ff.

Descartes, R., *Oeuvres,* edited by Adam and Tannery, Paris, 1904.

Dessoir, M., *Abriss einer Geschichte der Psychologie,* Heidelberg, 1911.

De Vries, J., *Denken und Sein,* Freiburg i.Br., 1937.

Dilthey, W., *Einleitung in die Geisteswissenschaften. Gesammelte Geschriften,* vol. I, Leipzig-Berlin, 1922 ff.
    Ideen über eine beschreibende und zergliedernde Psychologie, op. cit., vol. V, pp. 139 ff.
    Studien zur Grundlegung der Geisteswissenschaften, op. cit., vol. VII.

Donat, J., *Psychologia,* 8th ed., Barcelona, 1936.

Dondeyne, A., "Belang voor de metaphysica van een accurate bestaansbeschryving van de mens als kennend wezen," *Kenleer en Metaphysica,* Nymegen, 1947, pp. 35 ff.
    "Idealisme of realisme," *Tijdschrift v. philos.,* vol. 3 (1941), pp. 607 ff.

Driesch, H., *Philosophie des Organischen,* 2 vols., Leipzig, 1909.
    Ordnungslehre. Ein System des nicht-metaphysischen Teiles der Philosophie, Jena, 1912.

Wirklichkeitslehre. Ein metaphysischer Versuch, Leipzig, 1917.
"Der Begriff der organischen Form," *Abhandlungen der theoretischen Biologie,* vol. 3 (1919).
Grundprobleme der Psychologie. Ihre Krisis in der Gegenwart, 2nd ed., Leipzig, 1929.

Dumas, G., and 45 collaborators, *Nouveau traité de psychologie,* 9 vols., Paris, 1931 ff.

Dunbar, F., *Emotion and Bodily Changes. A Survey of Literature on Psychosomatic Interrelationships,* 1910-1945, 3rd ed., New York, 1946 f.

Eisler, R., *Wörterbuch der philosophischen Begriffe,* 4th ed., 3 vols., Berlin, 1927.

Elsenhans, Th., *Die Eigenart des Geistigen,* Leipzig, 1921.

Farber, M., *The Foundation of Phenomenology. Edmund Husserl and the Quest for a Rigorous Science of Philosophy,* Cambridge (Mass.), 1943.

Fink, E., "Die phänomenologische Philosophie Edmund Husserls in der gegenwärtigen Kritik," *Kantstudien,* vol. 38 (1933), pp. 319 ff.
"Das Problem der Phänomenologie Edmund Husserls," *Revue internationale de philosophie,* vol. 1 (1939), pp. 226 ff.

Fischel, W., "L'émotion et le souvenir chez les animaux," *Conduite, sentiments, pensées des animaux,* Paris, 1938, pp. 72 ff.

Flugel, J. C., *A Hundred Years of Psychology* 1833-1933, 5th ed., Duckworth, 1945.

Frankl, V. E., *Ärztliche Seelsorge,* 5th ed., Vienna, 1948.
Der unbewusste Gott, 2nd ed., Vienna, 1949.

Freud, S., *Gesammelte Werke,* edited by A. Freud, vols. I-XVII, London, 1940 ff.

Fröbes, J., *Psychologia sensitiva,* Valkenburg, 1911.
Psychologia speculativa, Freiburg i. Br., 1926.
Lehrbuch der experimentellen Psychologie, 3rd ed., 2 vols., Freiburg i. Br., 1929.

Gardeil, A., *La structure de l'ame,* 2nd ed., Paris, 1927.

Geiger, M., "Fragment über den Begriff des Unbewussten und die psychische Realitat," *Jahrbuch f. Philosophie u. phänom. Forschung,* Halle a. d. S., 1917, pp. 1 ff.

Gemelli, A., and Zumini, G., *Introduzione alla psicologia,* Milan, 1947.

Geyser, J., *Die Seele. Ihr Verhältnis zum Bewusstsein und zum Leibe,* Leipzig, 1914.

> *Lehrbuch der allgemeinen Psychologie,* 2 vols., 3rd ed., Münster i. W., 1920.

Goldstein, K., *Der Aufbau des Organismus. Einführung in die Biologie unter besonderer Berucksichtigung der Erfahrungen am kranken Menschen,* The Hague, 1934.

Gredt, J., *Die Aristotelisch-Thomistische Philosophie,* Freiburg i. Br., 1935.

Guillaume, P., *La psychologie animale,* Paris, 1940.

> *Introduction à la psychologie,* Paris, 1945.
> *Manuel de psychologie,* 2nd ed., Paris, 1948.

Gusdorf, G., *La découverte de soi,* Paris 1948.

Haas, W., *Die psychische Dingwelt,* Bonn, 1921.

Haberlin, P., *Der Gegenstand der Psychologie. Eine Einführung in das Wesen der empirischen Wissenschaft,* Berlin, 1921.

> *Der Leib und die Seele,* Basel, 1923.
> *Naturphilosophische Betrachtungen. Eine allgemeine Ontologie,* 2nd ed., Zürich, 1939. Vol. I, *Einheit und Vielheit.*
> *Der Mensch,* 2nd ed., Zürich, 1941.

Haldane, J. S., *The Philosophical Basis of Biology,* Dublin, 1930.

Heidegger, M., "Sein und Zeit," *Jahrbuch f. Philos. und Phänom. Forschung,* vol. VIII, Halle a. d. S., 1927.

Heimsoeth, H., "Kants Philosophie des Organischen in den letzten Systementwürfen," *Blätter f. deutsche Philosophie,* vol. 14 (1910), pp. 81 ff.

Heiss, R., "Psychologismus, Psychologie und Hermeneutik," *M. Heideggers Einfluss auf die Wissenschaften,* Bern, 1949, pp. 22 ff.

Hengstenberg, H. E., "Das Band zwischen Geist und Leib in der menschichen Person," *Christliche Philosophie in Deutschland 1920-1945,* edited by Paul Wolff, Regensburg, 1949, pp. 261 ff.

Hönigswald, R., *Die Grundlagen der Denkpsychologie. Studien und Analysen,* 2nd ed., Leipzig-Berlin, 1925.

Hugenholtz, P. Th., "Over het Ik en de psychismen," *Nederl. Tijdschrift v. Psychologie,* vol. 1 (1946), pp. 126 ff.

Hume, D., *Treatise of Human Nature,* Oxford, 1896.

Husserl, E., *Logische Untersuchungen,* bks. I and II, vols. I and II, 4th ed., Halle a. d. S., 1928.

Ideen zu einer reinen Phänomenologie und einer phänomenologischen Philosophie, edited by W. Biemel, vol. III of Edmund Husserl, *Gesammelte Werke,* The Hague, 1950.

"Formale und transcendentale Logik," *Jahrbuch f. Philos. und phänomen. Forschung,* vol. X, Halle a. d. S., 1929, pp. 1 ff.

"Nachwort zu meinen Ideen zu einer reinen Phänomenologie," *Ibid.,* vol. XI, 1930.

Cartesianische Meditationen und Pariser Vorträge, edited by S. Strasser, The Hague, 1950, vol. I of *Husserliana, Edmund Husserl Gesammelte Werke.*

Die Krisis der europaischen Wissenschaften und die transcendentale Phänomenologie. Versuch einer Kritik der logischen Vernunft. Typewritten manuscript of 1936. Partly published in *Philosophia,* vol. I (1936), pp. 77 ff.

Phänomenologie und Psychologie. Typewritten manuscript of 1917, "ausgearbeitet" by E. Stein.

Erfahrung und Urteil. Untersuchungen zur Genealogie der Logik, "ausgearbeitet" and edited by L. Landgrebe, Hamburg, 1948.

Studien zur Struktur des Bewusstsein. Typewritten manuscript "composed" by L. Landgrebe, around 1925.

"Vorlesungen zur Phänomenologie der inneren Zeitbewusstsein," edited by Martin Heidegger, *Jahrbuch f. Philos. u. phänomen. Forschung,* vol. IX (1928), Halle a. d. S., pp. 367 ff.

Fungierende Subjektivität und objektive. Stenographed manuscript. Husserl Archives designation, K III 6.

Zur apodiktischen Evidenz der Präsumption der Welt. Stenographed manuscript. Designation B I 13/II.

James, W., *The Principles of Psychology,* 2 vols., London, 1890.

Jaspers, K., *Philosophie,* 3 vols., Berlin, 1932.

Jodl, F., *Lehrbuch der Psychologie,* 2nd ed., Stuttgart-Berlin, 1903.

Jolivet, R., *Psychologie,* vol. II of *Traité de philosophie,* 2nd ed., Paris, 1947.

Jung, C. G., *Seelenprobleme der Gegenwart,* Zürich, 1946.

Die Beziehungen zwischen dem Ich und dem Unbewussten, Darmstadt, 1928.

Wirklichkeit der Seele, Zürich, 1947.

Psychologische Betrachtungen, edited by J. Jacobi, Zürich, 1945.

Kant, I., *Werke,* edited by A. Buchenau and E. Cassirer, Berlin, 1922.

Katz, D., *Gestaltpsychologie,* Basel, 1944.

Klages, L., *Der Geist als Widersacher der Seele*, 3 vols., Leipzig, 1932 ff.

Klemm, O., *Geschichte der Psychologie*, Leipzig, 1911.

Koffka, K., "Psychologie," in *Die Philosophie in ihren Einzelgebieten*, Berlin, 1925, pp. 493 ff.

Köhler, W., "Physical Gestalten," 3rd selection in *A Sourcebook of Gestaltpsychology*, London, n. d.

Kohnstamm, Ph., *Vrije wil of determinisme*, Haarlem, 1947.

Konczewski, C., *La pensée préconsciente. Essai d'une psychologie dynamiste*, Paris, 1939.

Külpe, O., *Vorlesungen über Psychologie*, edited by K. Bühler, 2nd ed., Leipzig, 1922.

Kunz, H., *Die anthropologische Bedeutung der Phantasie*, 2 vols., Basel, 1946.
    "Die Bedeutung der Daseinsanalytik Martin Heideggers für die Psychologie und die philosophische Anthropologie," *M. Heideggers Einfluss auf die Wissenschaften*, Bern, 1949, pp. 37 ff.

Lachelier, J., "Psychologie et métaphysique," *Du fondement de l'induction*, 4th ed., Paris, 1902.

Lalande, A., *Vocabulaire technique et critique de la philosophie*, 5th ed., Paris, 1947.

Landgrebe, L., *Phänomenologie und Metaphysik*, Hamburg 1949.

Langeveld, M. J., "De psychologie en de physiologie van de mens," *Tijdschrift v. philosophie*, vol. 7 (1945), pp. 223 ff.

Lavelle, L., *De l'acte*, Paris, n. d.
    Du temps et de l'éternité, Paris, 1945.
    Les puissance du moi, Paris, 1948.

Lehner, M., *Das Substanzproblem im Personalismus Max Schelers*, Weida i. Th., 1926.

Le Roy, F., *Le problème de Dieu*, Paris, 1930.

Lersch, Ph., *Seele und Welt*, 2nd ed., Leipzig, 1943.

Le Senne, R., *Traité de caractérologie*, Paris, 1945.
    Obstacle et valeur, Paris, n. d.

Levinas, E., *La théorie de l'intuition dans la phénoménologie de Husserl*, Paris, 1930.

Lewin, K., "Undtersuchungen zur Handlungs- und Affektpsychologie. I. Vorbemerkungen über die psychischen Kräfte und Energien und über die Struktur der Seele," *Psycholog. Forschung*, vol. 7 (1926), pp. 294 ff.

Lindworsky, J., *Experimentelle Psychologie,* 5th ed., München, 1931.

Lipps, Th., *Leitfaden der Psychologie,* 3rd ed., Leipzig, 1909.

Litt, Th., *Denken und Sein,* Zürich, 1948.

Locke, J., *An Essay Concerning Human Understanding,* edited by A. C. Fraser, Oxford, 1894.

Lotze, R. H., *Mikrokosm. Ideem zur Naturgeschichte und Geschichte der Menschkeit. Versuch einer Anthropologie,* 5th ed., Leipzig, 1896.

Maher, M., *Psychology: Empirical and Rational,* 9th ed., London, 1919.

Marc, A., *Psychologie réflexive,* 2 vols., Paris-Brussels, 1949.

Marcel, G., *Être et avoir,* Paris, 1935.

Maréchal, J., *Le point de départ en métaphysique,* vol. 5, Louvain-Paris, 1926.

Mennicke, C. A., *Moderne psychologie. Een poging tot synthese.* 2nd ed., Amsterdam, 1946.

Mercier, D., *Psychologie.* Book III of *Cours de philosophie,* 2 vols., Louvain-Paris, 1923.

Merleau-Ponty, M., *La structure du comportement,* Paris, 1942.
    La phénoménologie de la perception, 2nd ed., Paris, 1945.

Messer, A., *Psychologie,* 4th ed., Leipzig, 1928.
    Empfindung und Denken, 3rd ed., Leipzig, 1928.
    Einführung in die Psychologie und die psychologischen Richtungen der Gegenwart, 2nd ed., Leipzig, 1931.

Michotte, A. Van Den Berk, *Vergelijkend onderzoek naar voorwerp en methoden der psychologische en physische wetenschappen,* Louvain, 1945. *Pro manuscripto.*
    La perception de la causalité, Louvain-Paris, 1946.

Miller, J. G., *Unconsciousness,* New York-London, 1942.

Minkowski, E., *Vers une cosmologie. Fragments Philosophiques,* Paris, 1946.

Moreau, J., "Le temps selon Aristote," *Revue philosophique de Louvain,* vol. 46 (1948), pp. 57 ff. and 245 ff.

Müller-Freienfels, R., *Die Haupströmungen der gegenwärtigen Psychologie,* 2nd ed., Leipzig, 1930.

Münsterberg, H., *Grundzüge einer Psychologie.* Vol. II, *Die Principien der Psychologie,* Leipzig, 1900.

Natorp, P., *Allgemeine Psychologie nach critischer Methode.* Book I, *Objekt und Methode der Psychologie,* Tübingen, 1912.

Needham, J., *Time: the Refreshing River,* London, 1943.

Nogué, J., *L'activité primitive du moi,* Paris 1936.

Nota, J., *Max Scheler. Een worsteling om het wezen van de mens,* Utrecht-Brussels, 1947.

Nuttin, J., *Psychoanalyse en spiritualistische opvatting van de mens,* Utrecht, 1943.

Oesterreich, E., *Die Phänomenologie des Ich,* Part I, Leipzig, 1910.

Petermann, B., *Das Gestaltproblem in der Psychologie im Lichte analytischer Besinnung. Ein versuch zu grundsätzlicher Orientierung,* Leipzig, 1931.
   Wesensfragen seelischen Seins. Eine Einführung in das moderne seelische Denken, Leipzig, 1938.

Peters, J. A. J. and Snijders, J. Th., *Praeadviezen over de verhouding van philosophie en psychologie,* The Hague, 1946.
   Gabriel Marcel, ein Zeuge des Geistes, Regensburg, 1949.

Pfänder, A., *Einführung in die Psychologie,* Leipzig, 1904.
   Die Seele, Halle a. d. S., 1933.

Phillips, R. P., *Modern Thomistic Philosophy,* 2 vols., London, 1948.

Plessner, H., *Die Einheit der Sinne. Grundlinien einer Ästhesiologie des Geistes,* Bonn, 1923.
   Die Stufen des Organischen und der Mensch. Einleitung in die philosophische Anthropologie, Berlin-Leipzig, 1928.
   Lachen und Weinen, Arnhem, 1941.

Pos, H. J., "Descartes en Husserl," *Alg. Nederl. Tijdschrift v. Wijsbegeerte,* vol. 31 (1938), pp. 23 ff.

Rahner, K., *Geist in Weit. Zur Metaphysik der endlichen Erkenntniss bei Thomas von Aquin,* Innsbruck, 1939.
   Hörer des Wortes. Zur Grundlegung einer Religionsphilosophie, München, n. d.

Reinstadler, S., *Elementa philosophiae scholasticae.* Vol. II *Anthropologia, Theologia naturalis, Ethica,* 15th ed., Freiburg i. Br., 1934.

Révész, B., *Geschichte des Seelenbegriffes und der Seelenlokalisation,* Stuttgart, 1917.

Révész, G., *Die Formenwelt des Tastsinnes,* 2 vols., The Hague, 1938.

Rickert, H., *Allgemeine Grundlegung der Philosophie.* First part of *System der Philosophie,* Tübingen, 1921.
   Der Gegenstand der Erkenntniss, 2nd ed., Tübingen-Leipzig, 1904.

Roback, A. A., *Selfconsciousness Self-Treated,* Cambridge (Mass.), 1936.

Robbers, H., *Wijsbegeerte en Openbaring,* Utrecht-Brussels, 1948.

Roels, F., *Handboek der psychologie.* Vols. I and II, *Algemene psychologie,* Utrecht-Nymegen, Antwerp-Brussels-Ghent-Louvain, 1934.

Rohracher, H., *Einführung in die Psychologie,* Vienna, 1946.

Ronx, W., "Das Wesen des Lebens," *Kultur der Gegenwart,* Part III, 4th Division, vol. I, Leipzig-Berlin, 1915, pp. 173 ff.

Rosenmöller, B., *Metaphysik der Seele,* Münster i. W., 1947.

Rutten, Th., "Kan de empirische psychologie geven wat haar naam schijnt te beloven?" *Tijdschrift v. philos.,* vol. 2 (1939), pp. 340 ff.

Ruyer, R., *Éléments de psycho-biologie,* Paris, 1946.

Ryle, G., *The Concept of Mind,* 2nd ed., London, 1949.

Sartre, J. P., *Esquisse d'une théorie des émotions,* Paris, 1939.
   L'être et le néant. Essai d'ontologie phénoménologique, 8th ed., Paris, 1943.

Scheler, M., *Die transcendentale und die psychologische Methode,* 2nd ed., Leipzig, 1922.
   Der Formalismus in der Ethik und die materielle Wertethik. 3rd ed., *Jahrbuch f. Philos. u. phänomen. Forschung,* vol. VIII, Halle a. d. S., 1930.
   Vom Umsturz der Werte, 2nd ed., Leipzig, 1919.
   Vom Ewigen im Menschen, Vol. I, 2nd ed., Leipzig, 1923.
   Wesen und Formen der Sympathie, Bonn, 1923.
   Schriften zur Soziologie und Weltanschauungslehre, vol. I, *Moralia,* Leipzig, 1923.
   Die Stellung des Menschen im Kosmos, Darmstadt, 1928.

Schrödinger, E., *What is Life?,* Cambridge, 1943.

Siewerth, G., "Die Aprioriotät der menschlichen Erkenntniss nach Thomas von Aquin," *Symposion,* vol. I (1948), pp. 89 ff.

Sigmund, G., *Auf der Spur des Lebensgeheimnisses,* Fulda, 1947.

Sigwart, C., *Kleine Schriften,* Freiburg i. Br., 1881.

Siwek, P., *Psychologia metaphysica. ad usum auditorum universitatis gregorianae,* Rome, 1932.

Spranger, E., *Psychologie des Jugendalters,* 11th ed., Leipzig, 1929.

Stein, E., "Beiträge zur philosophischen Begründung der Psychologie und der Geisteswissenschaften," *Jahrbuch f. Philos. u. phänomen. Forschung,* vol. V, 1922.

Stern, W., "Psychische Präsenzzeit," *Zeitschrift f. Psychologie,* vol. 13 (1897), pp. 325 ff.

    Allgemeine Psychologie auf personalistischer Grundlage, 2nd ed., The Hague, 1950.

Strasser, S., "Het vraagstuk van het solipsisme by Edmund Husserl," *Tijdschrift v. philosophie,* vol. 7 (1945), pp. 3 ff.

    "Beschouwingen over het vraagstuk der apodicticiteit," *Ibid.,* vol. 8 (1946), pp. 226 ff.

    Objectiviteit en objectivisme, Nymegen-Utrecht, 1947.

    "Personne et Sentiment," *Proceedings of the 10th International Congress of Philosophy, Amsterdam August 11-18, 1948,* Amsterdam, 1949, pp. 645 ff.

    "Het gedrag als metaphysisch problem," *Alg. Nederl. Tijdschrift v. Wijsbegeerte en Psychologie,* vol. 42 (1949) pp. 1 ff.

    "Het Ik-bewustzijn," *Annalen v.h. Thijmgenootschap,* vol. 38, pp. 1 ff.

    "Le point de départ en psychologie métaphysique, *Revue philosophique de Louvain,* vol. 48 (1950), pp. 220 ff.

    "Psychosomatisch onderzoek en traditionele mensbeschouwing," *Annalen v.h. Thijmgenootschap,* vol. 38 (1950), pp. 148 ff.

    Das Gemüt. Grundgedanken zu einer phänomenologischen philosophie und theorie des menschlichen Gefühlslebens, Utrecht-Freiburg i. Br., 1956.

Straus, E., *Vom Sinn der Sinne,* Berlin, 1935.

Thielemans, H., "Kant en de scholastiek," *Bijdragen,* vol. 15 (1938), pp. 319 ff.

Thomas Acquinas, *Opera Omnia,* New York, 1948.

Van Breda, H. L., *De transcendenteel-phaenomenologische reductie in Husserl's laatste periode (1920-1938).* Typewritten manuscript of doctoral dissertation, with two appendixes, Louvain, 1941.

Van Der Horst, L., "Tijd onder psychologisch aspect," *Nederl. Tijdschrift v. Psychologie,* vol. 3 (1948).

Van Der Veldt, P. J., *Prolegomena in psychologiam,* Rome, 1938.

Van Haecht, L. J. M. G., *Het lichaam in de hedendaagse wijsbegeerte. Edmund Husserl—Raymond Ruyer—Gabriel Madinier.* Typewritten manuscript of doctoral dissertation, Louvain, n.d. (1944).

Van Steenberghen, F., *Epistemologie,* Louvain, 1945.

Verbeke, G., *Noten bij de cursus van metaphysica,* Louvain, 145-46.
"De wezensbepaling van het spirituele," *Tijdschrift v. philosophie,* 1946, pp. 435 ff.

Von Bertalanffy, L., *Theoretische Biologie,* vol. I, Berlin, 1932.

Von Weizsäcker, V., *Der Gestaltkreis. Theorie einer Einheit von Wahrnehmen und Bewegen,* 3rd ed., Stuttgart, 1947.
Falle und Probleme. Anthropologische Vorlesungen in der medizinischen Klinik, Stuttgart, 1947.

Walgrave, P. H. J., "Zelfkennis en innerlijke ervaring bij St. Thomas," *Tijdschrift v. philosophie,* vol. 9 (1947), pp. 1 ff.

Wertheimer, M., *"Gestalttheory."* First selection in *A Sourcebook of Gestalt-psychology,* London, n.d.

Willwoll, A., *Seele und Geist. Ein Aufbau der Psychologie,* Freiburg, i. Br., 1938.

Wolff, Chr., *Psychologia empirica,* 2nd ed., Frankfurt-Leipzig, 1738.
Psychologia rationalis, 2nd ed., Frankfurt-Leipzig, 1740.

Wolff, G., "Leben und Seele," in *Das Lebensproblem,* Leipzig, 1931, pp. 317 ff.

Woodger, J. H., *Biological Principles,* London, 1919.

Woodworth, R. S., *Experimental Psychology,* New York, 1944.

Wundt, W., *Vorlesungen über die Menschen-und Tierseele,* 3rd ed., Hamburg-Leipzig, 1897.

INDEX OF NAMES

INDEX OF SUBJECT MATTER

Date Due

AP 8			
AP 2T			
JA 4'			
MR 5			
AP 14 '66			

Demco 293-5